Constructing Mexico City

Constructing Mexico City

Colonial Conflicts over Culture, Space, and Authority

Sharon Bailey Glasco

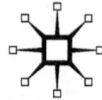

CONSTRUCTING MEXICO CITY
Copyright © Sharon Bailey Glasco, 2010.
All rights reserved.
First published in 2010 by
PALGRAVE MACMILLAN®
in the United States—a division of St. Martin's Press LLC,
175 Fifth Avenue, New York, NY 10010.

Where this book is distributed in the UK, Europe and the rest of the world, this is by Palgrave Macmillan, a division of Macmillan Publishers Limited, registered in England, company number 785998, of Houndmills, Basingstoke, Hampshire RG21 6XS.

Palgrave Macmillan is the global academic imprint of the above companies and has companies and representatives throughout the world.

Palgrave® and Macmillan® are registered trademarks in the United States, the United Kingdom, Europe and other countries.

ISBN: 978–0–230–61957–9

Library of Congress Cataloging-in-Publication Data is available from the Library of Congress.

A catalogue record of the book is available from the British Library.

Design by Newgen Imaging Systems (P) Ltd., Chennai, India.

First edition: July 2010

10 9 8 7 6 5 4 3 2 1

Printed in the United States of America.

*To Jeff, for sharing with me a historian's fascination with the past
And to James and Sophie, for keeping me firmly grounded in the present*

CONTENTS

List of Maps		ix
List of Tables		xi
Acknowledgments		xiii
One	Shaping the Colonial City	1
Two	Splendor and Misery in the Viceregal Capital: The Physical, Material, and Political Environment of Bourbon Mexico City	17
Three	In Sickness and Health: Disease, Healing, and the Urban Population	49
Four	A Basic Necessity: Water and the Urban Environment	77
Five	Restoring Order Out of Chaos: Garbage Collection in Theory and Practice	97
Six	Mastery over the Streets: Drainage, Street Paving, and Renovation of Urban Space	127
Seven	Concluding Thoughts	155
Notes		163
Glossary		189
Bibliography		191
Index		199

MAPS

2.1 *Traza* boundaries and predominantly
     Indian neighborhoods   27
2.2 Neighborhood divisions in eighteenth-century
     Mexico City   29
2.3 Major streets and landmarks in eighteenth-century
     Mexico City   31
4.1 Location of *Cañerías* and *Fuentes Públicas* built by
     Viceroy Revillagigedo   88
5.1 Location of city dumps, 1790s   114
6.1 Location of drainage projects during tenure of
     Viceroy Revillagigedo, 1790–1794   136
6.2 Major paving projects in Mexico City, 1767–1796   146

TABLES

2.1	Mexico City's population, 1772–1820	20
3.1	Epidemic outbreaks for Mexico City, 1711–1810	51
4.1	List of *Fuentes Públicas* built in Mexico City, 1740–1805	80
4.2	List of public buildings with private access to public water supply in Mexico City	80
4.3	Source and location of *Fuentes Particulares* in Mexico City, 1806	81
4.4	List of *Cañería* construction in Mexico City, 1792–1795	86
4.5	Construction of *Fuentes Públicas* in Mexico City, 1793–1796	87
6.1	Listing of drainage projects during the tenure of Viceroy Revillagigedo, 1790–1794	135
6.2	Major paving projects in Mexico City, 1767–1796	145
6.3	Organization of goods sold in the Volador market	150

ACKNOWLEDGMENTS

My first introduction to Mexico City was in 1987, as I was returning stateside after a semester abroad studying in Costa Rica, Guatemala, and Nicaragua. I distinctly remember flying into the capital on a remarkably clear and sunny day, where it seemed like the vista of the city went on forever, and was astonished by both the size and the scope of the modern metropolitan area. I had the good fortune to spend a week exploring and learning about the city's history, architecture, culture, and people, and from there a fascination was born. From that first encounter, I went on to graduate school, where I fed my passion and love for all things *chilango*, and from which this study emerged. I feel truly fortunate to be able to spend my days teaching and researching the history, past and present, of this remarkable city.

I have many people to thank for the completion of this project, none more important than my graduate school advisor and mentor, Kevin Gosner. His experience has been invaluable, in both orienting me in the literature of the profession, as well as pushing me to expand my conceptual frameworks and theoretical understandings. He offered valuable insight as I worked to transform my dissertation into this book, and I have appreciated his friendship and guidance as I moved from the role of graduate student to teacher and scholar. Most notably, he has helped me understand the importance of balancing the career of a professional historian with the roles of spouse and parent, for which I can never fully express my appreciation. Laura Tabili and Bert Barickman have also been inspirational mentors and teachers, challenging me to expand my ideas and arguments beyond the confines of Mexican history. Laura especially worked tirelessly helping me improve and clarify my writing. I would also like to thank the late Michael Meyer, who started me on the path of Mexican history back in 1991, and instilled in me the value of rigorous and thorough research.

Acknowledgments

I learned much from my peers in the history graduate program at the University of Arizona, who provided an intellectually challenging environment, while offering unconditional support and friendship. Special thanks go to Phyllis Smith, Michael Brescia, Vicki Weinberg Black, Osvaldo Barreneche, Marie Francois, Bianca Premo, Laura Shelton, and Jeff Shumway. As we have moved on to various careers in academia, they continue to provide me with wonderful models of intellectual curiosity and creative scholarship. I would also like to thank my dissertation support group (otherwise known in my house as the Monday Night Party Group), Jodie Kreider, H. Michael Gelfand, Meghan Winchell, and Jerry Pierce, for getting me through the difficult phases of writing with an ample supply of beer, chocolate, and good conversation, as well as reading and offering comments on early drafts of chapters. Their continued support as I worked to transform this study has been invaluable. Department chairs past and present in the department of History at the University of Arizona, Helen Nader and Richard Cosgrove, and the office staff, especially Donna Watson, greatly facilitated my work, and their assistance and support is much appreciated.

While completing this project, I benefitted greatly from the generous help and support from numerous people. Elements of this study were presented and discussed at academic conferences hosted by the following—The American Historical Association, The Conference on Latin American History, The Rocky Mountain Conference of Latin American Studies, and the Urban History Association—and I am indebted to the valuable critique and feedback that I received from commentators, fellow panelists, and the audience. Friends, colleagues, and students at Linfield College created a supportive environment in which I could thrive. I wish to thank Amy Orr, Kay Livesay, Dawn Nowacki, Reshmi Dutt-Ballerstadt, Sonia Ticas, and Barbara Seidman for their continued friendship and intellectual camaraderie. Many thanks to Vice President for Academic Affairs and Dean of Faculty Victoria McGillin, for her interest in my project and her help in paving the way for its publication I would also like to recognize the many students who have taken my Latin American history classes, especially those in my Culture of Cities in Latin American history course. Many of the arguments in this book are integrated into that class, and student's questions about the themes of urban reform, colonial class relations, and modernity helped me to refine my ideas, and to look at the material in new and different ways.

Acknowledgments

Various sources of financial support were instrumental in conducting the research for this project: a mini-grant from the Social and Behavioral Sciences Research Institute at University of Arizona, a New World and Comparative History Fellowship at the John Carter Brown Library at Brown University, and a Faculty Development Grant from Linfield College. The staffs of the Archivo General de la Nácion, the Archivo Histórico de la Ciudad de México, and the Centro de Estudios de Historia de México in Mexico City, and the John Carter Brown Library at Brown University in Providence, Rhode Island were always helpful. I would like to especially thank especially the staff of the colonial research room at the AGN for going out of their way to access material for me as well as photocopying documents, and Jorge Rodríguez y Rodríguez of the Archivo del Tribunal Superior de Justicia del Distrito Federal for allowing me special access to materials therein. As I conducted a good portion of the research for this project, Don Alfonso Díaz Infante Capdevielle made my stay in Mexico City an enjoyable one, and helped me negotiate the challenges of living in one of the world's largest cities.

I have come to greatly appreciate the many people whose time and energy has been devoted to moving this study from a general proposal and manuscript to a finished book. The editors at Palgrave Macmillan have always been a pleasure to work with, and I thank them for their patience and guidance, especially when work and family demands pushed deadlines to and beyond their limits—Julia Cohen, Samantha Hasey, Robyn Curtis, and Matt Robison. Lindsey Hunt provided valuable research assistance in Mexico City, and Ben Willis and Morgan Christensen aided during the final editing stages and with compiling the index. Finally, I would like to thank my family, who in many ways has made this book possible. My sister, Susan Brown, helped me tremendously in creating the many maps in this study, important additions that add visual dimensions to my arguments. And to my husband (and fellow historian), Jeff Glasco, and my children, James and Sophie, for their unconditional love, patience, and support through this very long and sometimes difficult endeavor. This book is dedicated to them.

CHAPTER ONE

Shaping the Colonial City

This book examines the spatial, material, and cultural dimensions of life in Mexico City during the late colonial period. It focuses specifically on how and why the colonial state sought to renovate and reshape urban space in the viceregal capital at the end of the eighteenth century, and in doing so, it reveals numerous points of conflict and discord over how various urban groups defined and shared the public spaces in the city and understood their place within a wider colonial system. I examine these relationships within the specific contexts of sanitation reform, the renovation of city streets through new paving and drainage projects, new potable water projects, and the rebuilding of key urban structures, such as public plazas, canals, markets, and bathhouses. On the surface, city leaders organized and justified these renovations within the framework of improving public health and welfare for all city residents. Disease was an endemic problem (epidemics notwithstanding), and the health benefits of containing garbage, limiting standing water, and guaranteeing clean water for city residents were clearly understood. My study, however, goes beyond the surface justifications to engage deeper meanings regarding what these urban renovations meant, both for colonial elites (political, economic, and religious) trying to hold onto power and for segments of colonial urban society seeking to retain autonomy and control within their daily lives and activities.

The broader justifications for these projects, I argue, can be found within two contexts. First, the design and implementation of urban renewal served as a proxy for elite anxieties about the socioeconomic realities of the city they lived in and the desire to quell these anxieties through a reshaping of plebeian culture. City and colonial political officials, representatives of the church, and members of prominent colonial families all argued that the various ills and blights on daily life were due in part to the unruly and polluting activities of the lower classes; activities such as public drunkenness, defecating in the streets and public markets, congregating in public places for illicit reasons, public nudity, and a lack of personal hygiene. They argued that the nature of lower-class culture was debased and uncivilized, and that part of the solution to creating a more orderly and efficient city was to reeducate the masses on proper personal habits and appropriate use of public spaces. Urban planners, under the guidance of local and imperial politicians, structured and designed urban reform projects to help acculturate the masses to what elite society viewed as proper, civilized public behavior. However, this process was highly contested, as the subjects of these reforms resisted what they perceived as intrusion by the state into their daily lives and activities. The ultimate success of these projects depended on the amount of cooperation or resistance that the urban population extended. The response to these city- and state-sponsored urban planning projects brings into question the nature of colonial authority and legitimacy toward the end of the colonial period.

Second, I believe that urban planning projects illustrate new debates in late colonial Mexico about the theme of modernity, and it underscore the beginnings of a shift from colonial control to modern, independent nation states, which would be fully vetted with the Wars for Independence and the ensuing struggle between liberals and conservatives in the nineteenth century. This study engages incipient discussions about modernity that grew out of Enlightenment ideas of order and progress but examines them under the lens of urban planning—architecture, urban design, organization and construction of public space, access to and control of public services, and so on. There existed a fundamental struggle toward the end of the eighteenth century, as colonial institutions and agents sought to hold on to power, while calls for independence and a break from the colonial system were on the rise. An examination of the changing structure and image of Mexico City, I argue, helps to bring into focus this struggle in new and unique ways. What was the centerpiece of the Spanish Empire to look like? How was it to reflect the power of the empire, and more importantly, the power of the state? How did colonial leaders try to maintain relevance in the lives of its subjects as it increasingly faced opposition and a growing loss of legitimacy?

In the late eighteenth century, Mexico City suffered from a host of urban physical maladies: endemic disease and serious, periodic epidemics; a lack of clean drinking water; indiscriminately dumped garbage and waste; streets made impassable by flooding and poor paving; crowded, dirty markets; and buildings in various states of disrepair. Rising population levels in the city exacerbated these problems. Rural peoples, especially Indians, had fled areas hard hit by environmental crises. Periods of misted rain and lack of rain caused drought and corresponding shortages of corn, especially in 1770–1773, 1778–1780, and 1785. The problems were so severe in 1785 that colonial officials termed it *el año de hambre*, or year of hunger.[1] Changes in tribute payments from kind to cash, as well as attempts to avoid these payments, also enticed Indians to migrate to the city.[2] Rising populations in the countryside, especially among indigenous groups, increased pressure within and between communities, particularly regarding access to land and water. With not enough resources to go around, many people looked to the city as a place of economic opportunity.

Yet poverty and environmental crisis alone cannot explain the steady rise in population levels in Mexico City throughout the eighteenth century. Historically, Mexico City was a popular place of residence for both the rich and the poor. Poverty was not the only reason to migrate. The capital provided colonial elites with various social and cultural opportunities, and economic opportunities abounded, including specialized training in artisan professions, as well as access to higher education.[3] For lower-class groups, especially Indians, population pressures in the countryside encouraged people to move to the city. Families also often sent daughters to the city to work as domestics, or sons to the construction trade, creating some economic security through the wages sent home, while lessening material pressures on the family by having one less person to provide for.[4] In the end, however, the demand for work far exceeded the supply. Although elites found many opportunities, life for most of the people in the city was precarious at best, and the presence of disease and other urban ills only added to the uncertainty and misery of daily life.[5]

Extremely poor sanitation practices were one of the most visible examples of the problems connected with increased urbanization and rising populations in the viceregal capital.[6] Apart from the constant dumping of garbage in the streets, dead animals and rubbish from the city's butchers floated in and blocked canals generally used for drainage of water and sewage. Public fountains, when functioning, served not only as important sources of clean drinking water for the urban population, but were also used to wash clothes and bathe both people and animals. The public sewage system was inadequate to handle the increasing needs of a growing population, and in certain areas of the city, it was indistinguishable from the public water supply. There were also no sanitary controls over food vendors in the markets. This kind of urban environment only helped the proliferation and spread of disease during the eighteenth century.

Besides the ever-present filth, parts of the city were literally falling apart. Streets were often impassable due to a combination of flooding, poor to nonexistent paving, and the common practice of using the streets as public toilets. Abandoned and decrepit buildings served as gathering places for those deemed a menace by elite standards. The disorganization of building codes and the lack of labeling of city streets and homes made it difficult for the police and fire squads to do their jobs. In addition, the city's many alleyways and lack of street lighting added to the disarray by providing a perfect context conducive to crime and disorderly conduct.[7] For example, in 1793, Don Ignacio Oreyana, a resident and businessperson of the city, wrote to the municipal government, the *cabildo*, urging that they close an alleyway adjacent to his home. He stated, "I have a beautiful home on one side, and the other is ugly due to the vagrants."[8] In 1794, Don Ignacio Lucero, also in a letter to the cabildo, expressed his concern over immodest behavior, stating that the alleyway outside his house had become a place for rendezvous between married women and single men.[9]

The irony of this squalor is that Mexico City was the wealthiest and most important city in the empire. State and ecclesiastical power, at the highest levels, resided there. The viceroy and archbishop were perhaps two of the richest men in the city, if not the empire, and their material wealth was on full display in their dress, residences, and celebrations in their honor. The city was the preferred locale for many elite families who could be seen flaunting their wealth as well, riding in their carriages throughout the streets, attending the theater bedecked in jewels and their finest frocks imported from Europe, and spending Sunday afternoons leisurely strolling through the Alameda, the largest public park in the capital. Power and wealth were concentrated here, and it was near impossible not to encounter the trappings of this wealth daily.

At the same time, immense poverty and physical squalor existed alongside the incredible opulence of the city. On the streets of some of the most important addresses lived the homeless, passed out in the gutters drunk from *pulque*.[10] Calle de San Francisco, one of the main thoroughfares and home many of the wealthiest families and finest shops, constantly endured problems with both the paving of the street and a continually clogged sewage ditch that ran alongside it. Elites, on their way to mass, would encounter those so poor that they literally had nothing and ran around in little more than a few shreds of clothing. Opulent wealth and debilitating poverty lived side by side in Mexico City; there was no way to escape it.

In many ways I argue, this daily and intimate contact between the disheveled and dangerous lower classes with the most powerful of colonial society created a considerable amount of anxiety within upper-class groups. The constant negotiation between the private and orderly spaces of home and the chaotic and messy spaces of the public realm continually reminded urban elites that there were many aspects about the wider contexts of their lifestyles, which they themselves could not control. This anxiety manifested itself in overt concerns over the debased nature of plebeian culture, instigated a broad attack on popular customs, and emphasized the need to create norms of civilized and rational (read elite) behavior for the masses to emulate.

At the same time, Mexico City represented the political heart of the empire, so city leaders, including members of the municipal government, and state sponsored architects, had the power to deal with these urban problems not only on an administrative level, but also in concrete and immediate ways that affected people in their daily lives. In confronting issues of the city's living environment and public health, city leaders, by the eighteenth century, became increasingly concerned with projecting the image of Mexico City as orderly and organized. The image of the capital had to be one that reflected Bourbon ideals of Mexico City as the heart of a dynamic and changing empire. Population levels were on the rise, the economy was growing, and the state was trying to reestablish its influence and power after a period of decline. At the same time, more people questioned the nature of Spanish rule, native-born *criollos* challenged *peninsular* preferences imported from Spain in politics and the economy, and rural groups protested through violent action attempts to reimpose state control over the political economy. During the late colonial period, and especially during the administration of Viceroy Revillagigedo (1789–1794), the colonial government in Mexico City became increasingly concerned with reshaping the city's image and structure to reflect a more modern environment, in keeping with the Bourbon's policy of a streamlined and efficient colonial system.

By examining the spatial and public health dimensions of class relationships, social control, and state power in Mexico City specifically, this project follows in the steps of earlier scholars who have examined social control and class relations within the context of the Bourbon Reforms and the Enlightenment. By this time, the state increasingly tried to control certain sectors of the urban population through legislation aimed at changing their perceived disorderly, immoral, and ultimately dangerous activities, such as popular religious celebrations, overconsumption of alcohol, undisciplined work habits, criminal activity, and public urination. Historians such as Linda Curcio-Nagy, Susan Deans-Smith, Cheryl English Martin, Gabriel Haslip-Viera, Michael Scardaville, Juan Pedro Viquera Albán, Silvia Arrom, and Pamela Voekel, point to the ways in which various groups in colonial society challenged and resisted control measures developed by the Bourbon state.[11] Ordinary people did not accept state policy passively; they were active participants within the colonial system, and often interpreted in their own terms, the measures aimed at changing their behavior and activities.[12]

In her work on the Mexico City poorhouse, historian Silvia Arrom argues that by the end of the eighteenth century, political institutions in Mexico City had very little control or influence over the urban population. If the goal of the Bourbon Reforms was to provide greater control and influence in the lives of its citizens and to strengthen the state, in the realm of day-to-day life it was failing miserably. If anything, states Arrom, Mexico City was experiencing a profound urban crisis by the latter decades of the eighteenth century, as an overwhelming number of poor residents seeking relief crushed the city's existing welfare system.[13] This in turn heightened elite concerns about the prevalence of the poor, and the corrupting nature of their behaviors and popular customs. Arrom argues that these concerns on the part of elite groups reflected a much more significant shift in the ways in which the upper classes viewed the poor and what she terms the "culture" of poverty.[14] As material wealth increasingly gained importance as a marker of status for elites in colonial society, they came to understand poverty as an individual failure, rather than a concept that supported religious notions of charity previously so important to elite identity.

In a broader sense, Arrom's arguments about Mexico City's crisis of the poor toward the end of the colonial period are applicable to an understanding of how urban renewal and reform functioned. I argue that the failure of the state to realize many of the sanitation reforms they enacted reflected a level of autonomy on the part of colonial residents. On the one hand, it does seem puzzling that a wide variety of urban groups rejected many of the reforms enacted to make the city more livable and its residents healthier. Certainly insufficient funding was part of the problem. However, a lack of legitimacy on the part of imperial representatives, city officials, and urban planners also explains the reluctance on the part of the people of Mexico City to support these endeavors. I pose many of the same questions as Arrom: How did the poor function in the spatial organization of the city? What was the relationship between poor and elites in negotiating this space? How were debates over urban sanitation and public services framed in broader clashes over culture and emerging concepts of modernity?

This study also engages questions around the processes of urbanization, the human impact on the environment, the development of public health and disease, and relations between the state and society. Pedro Fraile has argued that ideas surrounding urban planning as a form of social control that were present in Spain and other parts of Europe during the colonial period were transferred to the New World, and particularly New Spain, as Enlightenment ideals of rationality, efficiency, and order influenced the types of public works and urban planning projects that developed.[15] Urban policy was designed to impose norms upon the city's population for the purpose of organization and control; cleanliness, sanitation, and order were imposed upon the entire body of city dwellers. Elites understood urban spaces, and the city as a whole, as areas to be divided and reorganized in order to be controlled. Their plans to divide the city into *quarteles,* or districts, in 1782, and construct new markets, hospitals, prisons, and cemeteries, for example, would lead, they hoped, to an ordered urban space, inhabited by a disciplined population. The regulation of city streets and squares, along with building codes, would bring symmetry and austerity to public spaces and help to delineate the blurring of public and private space, which so hampered elite desires for spatial, and thus societal, order in the viceregal capital.

This desire for order can be traced back before the Enlightenment, in the writings and ideas of thinkers such as Descartes, who argued for a relationship between political and spatial order. Harmoniously constructed districts would call to mind the power of government, for city building of this kind was visible evidence of good government in action that would induce and inspire good behavior in people. From the Italian Renaissance of the sixteenth century to the end of the French Enlightenment, philosophical and psychological explanations for how the environment functioned inspired and rationalized imaginative plans for scores of ideal new cities and hundreds of projects to rebuild parts of existing ones.[16] In the case of colonial Mexico City, the state initiated new public works projects aimed at reordering the physical layout of the city, while linking these projects to their desire to eradicate troublesome behaviors. City leaders, the viceroy, members of the church, and prominent citizens all argued that these behaviors, such as public urination and defecation, public drunkenness, and vagrancy, led to more dangerous activities, such as property crimes and physical violence.

In many ways, the increasing focus on urban planning and order that manifested itself toward the end of the colonial period reflects a long tradition of urban planning in the colonial Americas. Indeed, in the case of Latin America from the earliest stages of conquest, city planning was highly organized. Based on the grid system, which predominated in Spain at the time, streets ran on a north-south and east-west axis, with a main plaza (Plaza Mayor) at the center, housing the main church or cathedral, government offices, and the addresses of some of the most prestigious families.[17] City planners, following the lead of the Crown, also adopted the practice of reserving the center parts of town, or the *traza*, exclusively for Spanish residents, the *república de los españoles*, while relegating Indians, the *república de los indios*, to neighborhoods surrounding the city center. Ideally, this practice was to protect Indians from the bad examples set by the Spanish, while at the same time insulating the Spanish from the inferior Indian population.

In reality, however, this system of separation broke down quickly. In Santiago de Guatemala, for example, the initial division between Spaniards and Indians fell apart as casta populations began to take over predominantly Indian *barrios* (neighborhoods), and Spaniards encroached upon Indian space by buying up lots in their neighborhoods.[18] Unlike Manila, another Spanish city where the laws supporting divisions between Spaniards and Chinese were stringently upheld, in Santiago de Guatemala, cabildo officials were "largely indifferent" to the collapse of separate spaces for Indians and Spaniards.[19] A similar chain of events took place in Mexico City. Initial city organization prohibited Indians from living in the center district, pushing them out instead to areas north and west of the traza. This spatial division broke down quickly, as Indians, Spaniards, and casta groups began to move freely between the two areas. By the eighteenth century, elites perceived the blurring of the division of these spaces as a threat to stability and order in the city.

Enlightenment commitment to order and reason manifested in projects such as street building emerged in Europe as early as the seventeenth century, as urban planners applied scientific principles to city layouts and structures. Surveying and engineering methods advanced rapidly, as did map making. Graphic artists learned to depict topographical and spatial features in map or plan form with greater control and accuracy.[20] Geometrical principles of order, harmony, and proportion gave Europeans the feeling that they had gained mastery over urban space.

I argue that colonial administrators in Mexico City attempted to do the same through their projects in the late eighteenth century. Planners devised new ideas regarding waste disposal, drainage, street design, renovation of urban space, and access to potable water to create an element of organization, symmetry, and tranquility within the viceregal capital. These projects also developed, in part, because of growing public pressures and concerns over the consequences of popular practices deemed damaging and dangerous to the daily order of urban colonial society, most notably the lack of propriety connected to public hygiene. There were indeed structural motivations that pushed urban renewal during this time, but culturally based motivations had their place as well. However, rather than entrusting these programs to engineers, whose technical backgrounds were more suited to developing functional urban systems, colonial leaders in New Spain relied on architects, who prioritized form. Ultimately, this focus on the design of urban space and services, rather than their ability to solve urban problems in real and tangible ways, compromised their success.

Mexico City during the late colonial period provides an excellent opportunity to explore the connections between public health, urban planning, and the social conflicts that came with these processes. First, it was the center of the Spanish Empire in the New World, as well as its largest city. As the administrative and economic heart of New Spain, it became the focus of the Bourbons' policy to reassert state control over the political system and the economy. It was also the social and cultural heart of the empire and in many ways reflected the status of colonial society.[21] Due to its rapidly rising population throughout the colonial period, as well as its geographical location, built on a former lake, the city suffered intensely from the many urban ills mentioned earlier, as well as other environmental problems, such as flooding, poor drainage, and lack of potable water in various neighborhoods.[22] These difficulties made many of the residents' daily activities cumbersome, but the urban poor were particularly hard hit. For example, residents of the largest, and poorest, indigenous neighborhood in the city, Santiago Tlatelolco, did not have access to potable water via public fountains, and they had to spend an increasingly large amount of their time and income buying water from the city's vendors.[23] In his letter to the viceroy in April, 1797, Balthasar Ladrones de Guevara argued that if bread and meat, two important necessities in the lives of the citizens of Mexico City, received so much attention from the government, then access to water should be just as, if not more, important. He noticed that there were many days when the city's public fountains, especially those serving the poor, lacked water, thus forcing the poor to purchase it elsewhere. This reality posed an extraordinary hardship framed within an already precarious economic situation of the poor.[24]

Second, the Bourbons mission, the "reconquest" of the colonies, focused on making the colonial project more organized and efficient in the realm of not only politics and economics but socially and culturally as well. The multiracial, multiclass reality of eighteenth-century Mexico City provides a unique look at the cultural and social conflicts, which arose in colonial society, and the demographic reality of the city brings issues of conflict and control into sharp relief. Basing their ideas on Enlightenment thought, Bourbon era leaders wanted to reform society, ridding it of the chaos that resulted from the vice-filled lives they perceived the lower classes to be living. They advocated legislation controlling the consumption of alcohol, sumptuary laws, and attempts to alter or eradicate lower-class popular pastimes as ways to bring productivity, discipline, and order into the lives of the *gente de bajo*.[25] A new dimension to understanding these processes can be found in the ways in which the Bourbon state attempted to control its urban population by controlling urban space. By the late eighteenth century, Enlightenment ideas of rationality and organization began to influence what urban spaces should look like and represent. In Mexico City in particular, there were serious attempts to control the use of public space, from new ordinances mandating more orderly waste disposal and use of public resources, to attempted controls on taverns and other drinking establishments, as well as public dress codes and rules for behavior during public festivals and in public areas, such as the Plaza Mayor and the Alameda.[26] This desire for a more orderly urban environment also extended to public works projects involving drainage, paving, the establishment of new markets, and the expansion of potable water to various sectors of the city. The constant, overwhelming presence of disease in the city influenced the types of projects undertaken, as well as perceptions as to how to use public space. The state desired to reshape and control public space in an attempt to make the city more "healthy"; this inherently involved trying to change the ways in which people both perceived and utilized public space. Some believed that the proliferation of disease was due not only to the laziness of the urban poor, who brought illness upon themselves, but also to the inappropriate use of public space. If the state could only get control of it and clean it up, the city's population would be more ordered and disciplined, as well as healthier.

Complicating this process were the cultural differences in which Mexico City found itself situated, which reflected an urban society with competing understandings about the uses of public and private space. One of the inherent problems that urban planners faced was contested views between different social sectors over the definitions and uses of public and private space. On the one hand, the preindustrial economy of Mexico City often combined work and residence in a single site. People viewed the street as an extension of their homes, and used it as such, for the disposal of garbage, of human and animal waste, and as a site to wash horses and carriages.[27] Butchers and other vendors used the streets and canals as their personal dumpsites. On the other side, you had residents who, by virtue of their wealth, constructed oasis of privacy within this urban chaos. When forced out of their protected worlds, they came face to face with this disorder. They complained that vagrants used abandoned buildings and disabled public fountains as places to partake in vulgar and sinful behavior. These complaints, I argue, reflect deeper anxieties on the part of urban elites regarding the social and physical world in which they lived, and the perceived threats to their identity and power that plebeian cultural practices entailed.

An excellent example of this tension can be seen in property owner and tenant disputes, and often hinged on attempts by the property owner to control the behavior of the tenant using the threat of eviction. For example, Don Leandro Manuel de Goxenechca y Cazeaga brought a case before the Justice Tribunal in Mexico City on January 14, 1755, against his tenant, Matheana Gonsales, regarding a dispute over her occupancy in one of his buildings. Apparently, Don Leandro, who considered himself one of the leading citizens in his neighborhood of Santa Ana, because he had given money in support of a new water system for the Plaza de Santo Domingo, wanted to evict Matheana. According to Don Leandro, Matheana spent too much time drinking at the local *pulquería* (tavern), *El Mezon de la Gilas*, and consequently did not have enough money left over to pay her rent. Matheana, on the other hand, argued that she had nowhere to go. She was a widow with children, and that her extended family would not take her in. She promised not to frequent the pulquería in the future.[28] The case record ends here, so we do not know how this dispute was ultimately resolved, but it was one typical of renter/tenant relationships. From Don Leandro's concern over Matheana's drinking, coupled with his self-perceived status in the community, it is probably safe to assume that at issue for him was not only her inability to pay the rent, but also any negative reflection her public activities at the pulquería might have on him.[29] Matheana's lack of support from her extended family could be a sign of her continuing dependence on alcohol, or it might simply be a reflection of their state of poverty and lack of material resources to pass on to her. Regardless, one of the challenges that faced local government in its attempts to reorder the city was that their idea of the "proper" use of public space often contradicted popular perceptions of that space. Embedded in these conflicts were cultural differences over behavior, cultural activities, and moral assumptions that those things carried. At street level, the colonial process remained highly contested.

While I argue that urban reform and renewal is understood within the framework of political, social, and cultural conflict, it is important to emphasize that there were significant, and immediate, material reasons behind these projects as well. Both the environmental as well as physical impact of disease in the urban context provide yet another valuable framework in which larger debates surrounding questions of modernity arose during the late colonial period. Medical professionals at this time still connected the spread of disease to the presence of foul and putrid air. They put their focus on programs that would "cleanse" the air. New engineering approaches to epidemic disease emphasized preventative action, including improved ventilation, drainage of stagnant water, street cleaning and paving, reinterment of cadavers, cleaner sources of water, fumigation of infected sites, and burial of garbage.[30] This was especially true in Mexico City. While there is strong evidence that the precolonial Mexica kept the streets and plazas of Tenochtitlan clean through regular refuse collection and canal sanitation measures, the geography of disease shifted under Spanish rule. Spanish leaders, in their attempts to establish their control over the city, turned Lake Texcoco into a giant cesspool through poorly conceived drainage projects, frequent flooding, and inadequate sewage disposal. While the Mexica managed to coexist with their surrounding environment, the Spaniards tried to master it through massive drainage projects and the construction of canals.

Important in examining Mexico City elites' desire for urban organization and aesthetic beauty is the understanding of the role that endemic disease and periodic epidemics played in the articulation of and justification for urban renewal projects. Mexico City throughout the colonial period, but especially in the eighteenth century, was plagued by disease, and in many ways, sickness was another physical manifestation of the ills that the city suffered. Just as the "body" of Mexico City suffered under the "illnesses" of urban disorder and decay, so too did the "bodies" of the city's inhabitants suffer a number of different maladies, from epidemics of smallpox and measles to more common ailments such as a variety of fevers, respiratory illnesses, and a host of gastrointestinal problems. Elites viewed the constant reality of disease as illustrative of plebeian choices regarding their bodily actions, vices, and filthy living environments; choices that had the potential to cause significant social disorder. Many public proclamations during epidemic periods implied or openly stated that the poor were only to blame for their general state of poor health. The imagery of infectious disease and sanitation problems became the metaphor for the social changes produced by the process of urbanization and the rise of the urban poor. Elites used the discourse of disease and public health, which inherently included the use of urban beautification and renovation, to attempt to restrict urban groups, especially the lower class. In the name of the public good and safety, the state used the discourse of disease and public health to reshape Mexico City physically.

In the end, there were significant physical reasons for pushing urban renewal projects that committed to public sanitation, systems of potable water, passable streets, open and well regulated public spaces, and so on. The debilitating effects of endemic and epidemic diseases were a constant reminder of some of the physical challenges of living in the city; challenges that could compromise the very functioning of the colonial capital if left unchecked. However, focusing on just the material overly simplifies the complex realities of urban society during the colonial period. Elites were anxious over the possibilities of physical disorder bleeding into social and cultural disorder and constantly were reminded of this reality as they negotiated the public spaces of the city. Cleaning the city realized both aesthetic and health benefits, but its goal of reforming city residents was paramount. Through sanitation programs, as well as plans to reorganize city space (both work and leisure), city officials worked to "reeducate" the urban poor into a more Bourbon representation of citizen and society: hardworking, tidy, moral, and able to contribute to colonial society in a positive and productive way. It was an image of a self-contained individual, someone who was not a public embarrassment or hindrance to the orderly functioning of colonial society. One of the emphases of the urban reforms that colonial officials chose was to educate and enlighten urban residents, changing their "traditional," or backward, behavior into "modern" behavior, both productive and nonthreatening.

A brief word on scope. This study is grounded in an examination of urban planning and reform projects during the administration of Juan Vicente de Güemes Pacheco y Padilla, second Count Revillagigedo, viceroy from 1789 to 1794. Considered one of the most outstanding rulers of New Spain, he devoted more time, energy, and resources to city planning and the renovation of public services and urban space than any other official did during the colonial period. Personally fastidious to a fault, the filthy and repugnant people who coursed through the streets and public spaces of Mexico City repulsed him. The very idea that a single representative of the Crown could yield so much influence in the day-to-day workings of Mexico City, so late into the colonial period, helps us to understand the nature of imperial politics in the years leading up to the Wars of Independence. Even as the colonial system came under increasing stress, still there were contexts where the viceroy could demonstrate real power and legitimacy. Or could he? Although his changes provided the means to turn the viceregal capital into a spatial representation of Bourbon order, security, and productivity, clearly the responses to these projects belie the reality that the changes he advocated were not necessarily welcome, and that in some corners of colonial society he lacked legitimacy and relevance.

The chapters that follow examine the relationship between public health and urban planning in colonial Mexico City and examine more closely the discourse of disease and sanitation that elite groups and the state used to justify their projects, especially in terms that these issues were framed within contexts of social control and state power. They will also focus more closely on the projects themselves, how they were organized, implemented, and their success.

Chapters two and three set up many of the material, cultural, and political contexts of eighteenth-century Mexico City. Chapter two examines the physical organization, with special attention to the social, material, and political culture of the people who live there. It explores the important place of the city within the context of the colonial project, as well as the unique political circumstances and structures that made the creation, justification, and implementation of urban renewal projects a tricky business. One of the greatest consequences of these conditions was the presence of endemic and epidemic disease in the city, which is the focus of chapter three. Disease and the larger issues of urban organization and social control were intertwined. In many ways, sickness was another physical manifestation of the ills that the city suffered. Just as the "body" of the viceregal capital suffered under the "illnesses" of urban disorder and decay, so too did the bodies of the city's inhabitants suffer in the web of disease. This significant presence of disease bothered elites, especially health professionals, immensely. They tended to view it as a problem caused by the lower classes, a reflection of plebeian lifestyles filled with vice, poverty and unsanitary living conditions. The connections they made between the activities and habits of the poor and the presence of disease reflected larger anxieties on the part of elites, politicians, doctors, and the church regarding the stability of urban society, and their place within it. More importantly, as with their critiques of other aspects of lower-class life, such as drinking, work habits, and popular diversions, elites used the rhetoric of disease and public health, as they used the themes of urban planning and beautification to justify their attempts to physically reshape the city and reshape the activities of the urban lower classes.

Chapter four discusses prevailing attitudes about both the use of water as well as public rights to access to this resource and considers major renovations made to the public water system as well as new rules and regulations applied to bathhouses. Within the context of water as a public resource, I consider the social and economic dimensions of urban planning as well as emphasize the reinforcement of race and class inequalities in the conceptualization of public services. On the one hand, the expansion of these city services as well as the participation of the urban poor in the construction of public works projects were intended to help mold colonial citizens into the Bourbon ideal of order, tranquility, and self-control. However, because city planners tended to focus more on the form of these projects rather than their function, it meant that the environmental problems, including lack of access, expense, and diseases which resulted from polluted sources, that many city residents faced with their water sources did not significantly change.

Chapter five discusses garbage collection as a key component of larger sanitation reforms, both in theory and in practice, by examining the contested images and perceptions of cleanliness, order, and space between the elite and popular classes. While ordinances mandating the collection and containment of waste were well-organized, especially under the tenure of Viceroy Revillagigedo, enforcement of these rules proved to be difficult. There existed tremendous conflict in how different urban groups wished to use public space, and in general city residents viewed state systems as inefficient and an intrusion into their daily lives. City leaders walked a fine line in terms of maintaining social order and could not push change too rapidly or too far. Nevertheless, some of these reforms did achieve a certain level of success. Despite the fact that the colonial state was increasingly under fire, and the authority of the state in constant question, at times colonial leaders could prevail.

Chapter six considers the design and implementation of drainage and paving projects, as well as the major renovation of the Plaza Mayor and establishment of the Volador Market. Here I examine the social and economic dimension of urban planning, as well as emphasize the reenforcement of race and class inequalities in the conceptualization of public services. The fact that the city planners tended to focus more on the form of these projects rather than their function meant that the environmentally based struggles most city residents faced did not significantly change. At the same time, city leaders intended to use the expansion of city services, as well as the participation of the urban poor in public works projects, to mold colonial citizens into the Bourbon ideal of order, tranquility, and control.

CHAPTER TWO

Splendor and Misery in the Viceregal Capital: The Physical, Material, and Political Environment of Bourbon Mexico City

In 1785, Hipólito Villarroel, one of Mexico City's chief prosecutors, wrote an extensive and scathing critique of the problems that Mexico City faced, saving his harshest words to describing the urban poor and the physical environment they lived in:

> An effort has already been made to make known the deplorable state of this unhappy city.... it is an impenetrable forest filled with evil and dissolution, which makes it uninhabitable for cultured people. It is filled with innumerable lairs and other hiding places, where vile persons shelter themselves and which one may properly call pig-sties rather than houses for rational beings. Each one swarms with a multitude of filthy and repugnant men and women, who are the abomination of the rest of us because of their disordered lives and customs. They are brothels of infamy and a shelter that should not be permitted, for all kinds of unimaginable vices are committed there; an ugly and disgusting blot on culture and civilization. Finally, they are the storehouses of the lazy, daring, insolent, shameless, and untamed multitude who strike fear in the rest of the inhabitants.[1]

Clearly, Villarroel's assessment and emphasis on excessive filth and the dirty, contemptible habits of the urban masses represented views, which argued that Mexico City was on the verge of a moral and environmental crisis. On the other hand, some descriptions at the time paint a positive portrait of the urban milieu. Throughout the colonial period, Mexico City proved a popular destination with travelers, who wrote glowing reviews about this jewel of the empire. In 1648, Englishman Thomas Gage noted how clean the city streets were, stating, "There is a common proverb that says there are four beautiful things in this country; its women, the clothes, the horses, and the streets." He went on to observe that never had he seen such beautiful carriages, and that the prevalence of gold, silver, precious stones, and fine woven textiles bordered in gold rivaled anything he had seen in China.[2] Approximately 175 years later, British traveler G.F. Lyons, even though critical of the state of the city's markets, agreed with Gage's sentiments about the general beauty of the city:

> From an eminence we came suddenly in sight of the great Valley of Mexico, with its beautiful city appearing in the center, surrounded by diverging paseos, bright fields, and picturesque haciendas... it's lively whiteness and freedom from smoke, the magnitude of churches, and the extreme regularity of its structure, gave it an appearance which can never be seen in a European city, and declare it is unique, perhaps unequaled, of its kind.[3]

Some visitors, however, did echo Villarroel's contempt. Frenchman Jean de Monsegue, visiting in 1714, was appalled at the number of vagabonds in the city, people he considered lazy, dishonest, and in some cases murderous. These people, in his opinion, made it unsafe for most residents to go about their daily activities. Another Frenchman, Villiet d'Arignon, repeated these sentiments. During his visit in 1785, he was shocked at the number of robbers present in the city and the daring nature of their acts. Shopkeepers suffered constant robberies, especially at night.[4]

These facts highlight the complex position in which Mexico City found itself during the last years of colonial rule. On the one hand, its opulence and wealth was dazzling. Magnificent homes of the elite, impressive public buildings, and open public spaces adorned the city landscape. On the other hand, the horrific poverty of both the city's residents and its environment offered a shocking contrast to its great wealth. The clear majority of urban residents lived in poverty, ranging from the working poor, to the underemployed, to the destitute.[5] Inadequate housing, a substandard diet, and a lack of clothing and other material goods reflected their misery, as did the physical environment, pervaded by pollution and chaos, in which they lived.

Although Villarroel and others wrote in such hopeless terms about the state of the viceregal capital and its residents, the reality was that it housed both the splendor and misery common to most major cities in the world at this time.[6] The establishment of Mexico City in 1521, on the site of the ruined Mexica capital of Tenochtitlan, was conqueror Hernan Cortes' idea, although it went against popular opinion at the time. More importantly, it set up a series of long-term problems for city leaders and residents alike. First, the marshy base, which served as the foundation for the city, meant that environmental problems, especially flooding, hampered the physical development of the city. Second, the swamp-like surroundings made access to clean water difficult; along with drainage issues, the city's sanitation problems constantly challenged colonial leaders. Finally, the fact that the Mexica built Tenochtitlan on a relatively small island meant very close physical proximity to the surviving Indians.[7] Consequently, urban planning, by creating from its inception physical divisions that helped support emerging hierarchies and cultural divisions based on race, focused on separating Spaniards and the non-European population. While the Spanish minority was heavily dependent on the labor of the indigenous majority for the functioning of the colonial economy, the fear of an urban indigenous uprising and inevitable toppling of the colonial system strongly influenced the relationship between Spaniards and Indians in Mexico City. The establishment of a European only zone (traza) was one of the Spaniards' first attempts to enforce separation and physical control. The development of a highly structured racial hierarchy, which placed Spaniards at the top and Indians at the bottom, functioned to justify Spanish superiority, Indian inferiority, and formed the basis of the colonial regime. It also served as a system of social control that in theory was to provide security and stability in the city.[8] Urban planning and sanitation projects, in particular refuse collection, drainage projects, street paving, and potable water systems reinforced this racial hierarchy. These projects favored the historical traza area, which by the late eighteenth century was still significantly European and wealthy, over the poorer, outlying Indian and *casta* (mixed race) neighborhoods.

Clearly, the specific physical environment in and around Mexico City created unique problems and challenges. To understand fully how the environment affected the daily activities of the city's residents, as well as how it influenced elite perceptions and concerns, we must first examine the physical and material context in Mexico City during the late colonial period.

Demographics and the Role of Migration in Mexico City's Population

As the administrative, economic, and cultural center of New Spain, the population of Mexico City grew continuously throughout the colonial period, with a more dramatic jump between 1770 and 1820. It was, however, something of a Europeanized and class-stratified urban island in a rural Indian and mestizo sea, thus a cultural and racial anomaly. Table 2.1 shows population numbers for the late colonial period.[9]

According to estimates, by the late colonial period, half of the city's population was substantially European, culturally or by descent. Two groups divided the Spanish population: criollos, or American born Spaniards (65,000) and peninsulares, or European born Spaniards (2,500). Approximately 24 percent were listed as Indian. Close to 20 percent were classified as mestizo (those of mixed Spanish and Indian ancestry) and approximately 10 percent as mulato (those of Spanish and African ancestry). These percentages were far different from New Spain as a whole, where Indians predominated (60 percent), followed by mixed castes (22 percent), and finally Europeans (18 percent).[10] For political, economic, and sociocultural reasons, the city, and urban life in general, was highly preferred among criollos and peninsulares, and the high concentration of Europeans in the city guaranteed the presence of an elite class that would be a material reflection of the city's wealth. On the other hand, Indians attached to communal lands and

Table 2.1 Mexico City's population, 1772–1820

Year	Population
1772	112,462
1790	112,926
1792	120,602
1804	137,000
1811	168,846
1813	123,907
1820	179,830

Source: Anna, *The Fall*, 4.

agrarian economies resisted migration to the cities unless circumstances proved it necessary or advantageous.

Rising population numbers in Mexico City during the late eighteenth and early nineteenth centuries were due to a number of factors. First, population levels in general throughout New Spain were growing at this time. After suffering dramatic demographic collapse due to disease and consequences of the *encomienda* (grants of Indian labor given to Spaniards), Indians began to recover their numbers beginning in the mid-seventeenth century.[11] The severe epidemics of smallpox, measles, and typhus, which had decimated the Indian population in the sixteenth and early seventeenth centuries, were far fewer in number by the eighteenth century. While Indians still succumbed to these diseases, generations had built up immunities so that epidemic outbreaks, when they did occur, did not wreak the same kind of demographic havoc as in earlier centuries.[12]

A variety of different demographic studies of the eighteenth century emphasizes one general trend for the central valley of Mexico: rapid growth. For example, Charles Gibson found the population doubled from approximately 120,000 Indians in 1742 to approximately 275,000 by 1800, a growth rate of roughly 3 percent per year.[13] Even an examination of colonial Mexico as a whole, not just the Central Valley, suggests a population explosion. David Brading emphasizes a more moderate growth rate of approximately 1.2 percent per year, from 3,336,000 inhabitants in 1742 to 6,122,000 in 1810 and attributes much of this growth to the resurgence of the Indian population.[14] In addition, by the eighteenth century, Indian population numbers had recovered to such an extent that the establishment of *pueblos de indios*, land set aside exclusively for Indian settlement and production, rose dramatically.[15] In his study of this institution, Bernardo García Martínez argues that population minima for the establishment of this corporate body were easily met by the early eighteenth century, as more and more Indians attempted to organize together to meet common interests, such as legitimating and defending land claims, or the need to articulate a system of hierarchy or authority.[16]

Of course, not all areas experienced growth. Some, most notably the city of Puebla and its surrounding environs, actually saw their population stagnate or decline.[17] This was due not only to factors such as lower birth rates and higher death rates, but migration as well.[18] In his study of the central valley during the eighteenth century, Arij Ouweneel argues that younger generations of Indians tended to migrate, seeking their fortunes elsewhere.[19] Of course, epidemic disease and natural disasters, such as drought and famine, often pushed individuals out of their communities. Certainly, growing population numbers also encouraged people to migrate, as competition for land increased, not only among Indians, but also among mestizos, mulatos, and casta populations.[20] Many non-Indians found that registering themselves as Indian offered them not only attractive legal protections and benefits, but most importantly, access to village plots. In turn, conflict resulted between Indians and non-Indians over land rights and usage, and many villages in the central valley were losing their economic viability in the eighteenth century, especially after 1770, and outmigration resulted.[21]

So, where did these people go? The most common destinations were larger regional towns and cities, including Mexico City. Mexico City was particularly popular because it was the largest city not only in the region, but also in the empire, including Spain itself. After the Spanish conquest, it quickly became the pre-eminent city in the New World, far outpacing any other city in size. Toward the end of the colonial period, while Mexico City's population stood at 168, 846, New York had a population of only 96,000 (1810), Lima and Philadelphia both had 53,000 (1810), and Boston 33,000.[22] In Europe, only London, Paris, Naples, Istanbul, Moscow, St. Petersburg, and Vienna outpaced Mexico City in size.[23] For people of all classes, the imperial capital represented economic and social opportunity. Its place on the continent, between Europe and Asia, placed it at the crossroads of trade routes that linked the New World to both of these regions. It was also the center of domestic production and exchange of goods in New Spain. The second half of the eighteenth century saw a dramatic increase in the population of the city, with one-half to two-thirds of this increase due to migration.[24] Other major cities, such as Puebla, might have been attractive for some, but it was undergoing economic as well as population stagnation at this time and offered far fewer opportunities than Mexico City.[25]

For Indians, leaving one's village for the city was a big step. It involved numerous lifestyle changes, such as diet and language, but more importantly, labor opportunities. Industrial-oriented jobs, such as small-scale manufacturing and production, replaced the agrarian economy that rural Indians were accustomed to.[26] Families would send their daughters to the city to work as domestics, or sons to the construction or transportation trades.[27] Other types of employment common for unskilled migrants included: *plateros* (silversmiths), *cargadores* (carriers), *sombreros* (hatters), *pintores* (painters), *carboneros* (coal merchants), *aguadores* (water carriers), *porteros* (porters), *cocheros* (drivers), *herreros* (blacksmiths), *alfareros* (potters), and *bordadores* (embroiderers) among the men, and *costureras* (seamstresses), *lavanderas* (laundresses), *tortilleras* (tortilla makers), *fruteras* (fruit sellers), *molenderas* (corn grinders), and *atoleras* (*atole* sellers) among the women.[28] Clearly, jobs were gender specific, with men focused on transportation and production of material goods, which demanded harder physical labor. Women dominated the production and selling of food, as well as other domestic and gender appropriate tasks.

Just as migrants the world over, those relocating to Mexico City were often helped by family and community connections. While some migrated without any connections, many found that they could rely on the previous movement of family members or neighbors to make the transition less traumatic.[29] In many respects, it was more often the opportunity of the city, and not necessarily grinding rural poverty, that encouraged Indians to move. Yet, migration by poor Indians from rural areas was not the only reason for population increases in Mexico City. The migration of ethnically diverse middle groups to the city was also a factor. Merchants, artisans, educated professionals, actors, musicians, and architects also viewed the city as a place of opportunity, where they could take advantage of specialized training, expanded career opportunities, and the social and cultural possibilities that the city offered. Most of the wealthiest families in colonial Mexico also had a residence in Mexico City, which helped them organize and run family businesses, as well as keep up on the latest business trends and activities. The city was also one of the primary centers of consumption, which further encouraged business opportunities.[30]

For educated professionals, such as lawyers, doctors, and clerics, Mexico City was a logical choice for several reasons. First, more schools for boys were located in the capital than any other city in New Spain: seven *colegios* and one seminary, as well as the only university in the New World.[31] Second, the city also housed the headquarters for both the government and ecclesiastical hierarchies, so that the most prestigious jobs were in these sectors. It was also home to a large number of monasteries and convents, as well as the institutions that the church used to minister to the poor and sick, such as hospitals, insane asylums, hospices for the poor, and orphanages. However, economic opportunity and development were not the only reasons that elites favored Mexico City. It was also an arena for the display of wealth and achievement and the consumption of cultural activities. Elites viewed large cities as the centers of civilized and cultured life, and to become a resident of one of the major cities in the empire afforded a family prestige.

Wealth was on display every day in the city, and the ostentatious nature of Mexico City elites came in part from a society that measured status in the possession and display of material goods. Opulent carriages traversed the city streets, keeping elites well above the filth that hampered travel on foot. Women, dressed in their finest outfits imported from Europe, took in the latest theatrical release. The massive homes of elite families, such as the Conde de Santiago de Calimaya, the Marqués de Jaral, the Conde del Valle de Orizaba, and the Conde de Regla dominated the neighborhoods directly off the *Plaza Mayor* (main plaza).[32] A French cleric traveling through Mexico City in 1768 described what he considered the most sumptuous buildings in the city: its churches, chapels, and convents:

> There are a great many in this city, which are very richly ornamented, among others the cathedral. The rail around the high altar is solid silver, and what is still more costly, there is a silver lamp, so capacious that three men get in to clean it: this lamp is enriched with figures of lions' heads, and other ornaments of pure gold. The inside pillars are hung with rich crimson velvet, enriched with a broad gold fringe. This profusion of riches in the churches at Mexico is not very surprising to whoever has seen the cathedral of Cadiz, and the immense treasures contained in it.[33]

Through the patronage of elite families such as the Conde de Regla and the Conde de Santiago, Mexico City was also able to support a large arts community, providing jobs for architects, sculptors, painters, musicians, dancers, singers, and actors. These individuals, in turn, provided elites with "cultured and civilized" diversions.[34] The arts, especially the theater, were also viewed by elites as an "efficient medium for the refinement and edification of the common people," by imposing class specific norms of behavior.[35] By supporting the high arts, such as the theater, over street culture, such as popular music and dance, the arts became an arena in which elites tried to impose their view of proper behavior and morality on the rest of colonial society.

Physical Organization of the City

Cities played an important role from the inception of colonialism in the New World. From the founding of ill-fated Navidad on the island of Hispañola by Christopher Columbus, to the establishment of Veracruz on the eastern coast of New Spain by Hernan Cortes, cities represented Spanish presence and control in the New World. This was especially true when the Spanish tore down Indian cities and replaced them with Spanish urban centers, as in the case of Mexico City.[36] As mentioned earlier, Spanish elites also preferred the creature comforts of urban lifestyles, considering life in the city as more refined, cultured, and civilized than its rural counterpart dominated by indigenous communities.[37] This is especially ironic given the fact that the economy of colonial Mexico focused on primarily rural enterprises: agriculture, stock raising, and mining. Despite the fact that most people in colonial Mexico lived in rural areas, Mexico City dominated the colonial landscape.[38]

To understand how the structure and physical organization of Mexico City influenced discourse regarding sanitation and public space in the late colonial period, it is important to examine the development of urban planning from the city's inception. In the early postconquest period, Spaniards established cities based on a series of laws in the *Ordenanzas de Descubriemiento y Población*.[39] These codes provided guidelines for a number of issues surrounding town planning and growth: selection of sites, the size and location of the central plaza, the alignment of streets, and the positioning of major buildings, such as the viceregal palace, municipal hall, churches, and markets. The *Ordenanzas* also gave advice regarding sanitation, such as drainage and garbage disposal.[40] The difficulty of these guidelines, as we will see in subsequent chapters, is that while colonial cities structurally were quite organized and followed the statutes set up in the *Ordenanzas*, trying to keep cities clean turned out to be a constant struggle for residents. The inherent order imposed on urban spaces during their construction did not translate down to orderliness on a day-to-day basis. On the one hand, outsiders admired places such as Mexico City for their wide streets, imposing structures, and public spaces. Spanish author Salvador de Madariaga compares the cleanliness of Mexico City in the late seventeenth century to that of London, arguing that the viceregal capital was both elegant and noble. London's St. James Square, he notes, was "A receptacle for all the offal and cinders, for all the dead cats and dogs of Westminster." He goes on further to describe a city where drainage was bad; streets abounded in potholes; and residents used windows opening on to London streets to rid households of excrement, garbage, and refuse with little or no regard for the passerby below. By contrast, Mexico City was a virtual paradise, "clean and well policed."[41] However, by the eighteenth century, elites such as Hipólito Villaroel, and visitors such as Jean de Monsegue and Villet d'Arignon deplored the city for its filth, in both its material waste and its large number of impoverished residents. Certainly, the dramatic rise in population during the latter half of the eighteenth century had a major impact on the cleanliness and orderliness of the capital. As the population grew, the city administration proved less able to deal with the consequences of this growth and did not adequately plan with new housing, infrastructures, and public services.

The planning and establishment of Mexico City, beginning in 1521, followed the classical grid pattern that was popular in Spain at the time. Streets ran on north-south and east-west axes, with the main plaza, the Plaza Mayor, at the center. City planners, following the lead of the Crown, also adopted the practice of reserving the center part of the city, or the traza, exclusively for Spanish residents. This "European/Spanish only" zone extended approximately thirteen blocks in each direction from the Plaza Mayor.[42] Meanwhile, new plans for urban organization relegated Indians, the city's original inhabitants, to neighborhoods surrounding the city center. The region immediately surrounding the traza became the Indian community of San Juan Tenochtitlan, while the other predominantly Indian neighborhood was Santiago Tlateloco, located on the northern fringes of the city (see map 2.1).[43] Unlike the symmetry of the city center, the Indian barrios, especially to the north, reflected a chaotic mix of jagged streets and poorly defined public spaces. Ideally, colonial leaders created these physical divisions to protect Indians from the bad examples and influences of the Spanish, while insulating the Spanish from the inferior Indian population. Physical separation also equated social separation. The physical distance the Spanish imposed between themselves and the indigenous population echoed the social and racial divisions they were quickly establishing. They intended this separation to both justify and legitimize Spanish superiority over the vast Indian population they conquered, and to help support their process of colonization.[44]

However, this spatial division between Spaniards and Indians broke down very quickly. As different Spanish factions, both civil and religious, began to fight over access to Indian labor and tribute, they reconfigured the boundaries meant to limit Indian movement. This was especially the case with Indian parish boundaries, which as early as 1560s and 1570s began to overlap into the traza.[45] Indian labor was necessary for different economic activities in the city center, allowing for constant movement of Indians in and out of the traza. This inevitably developed into permanent Indian settlement there.

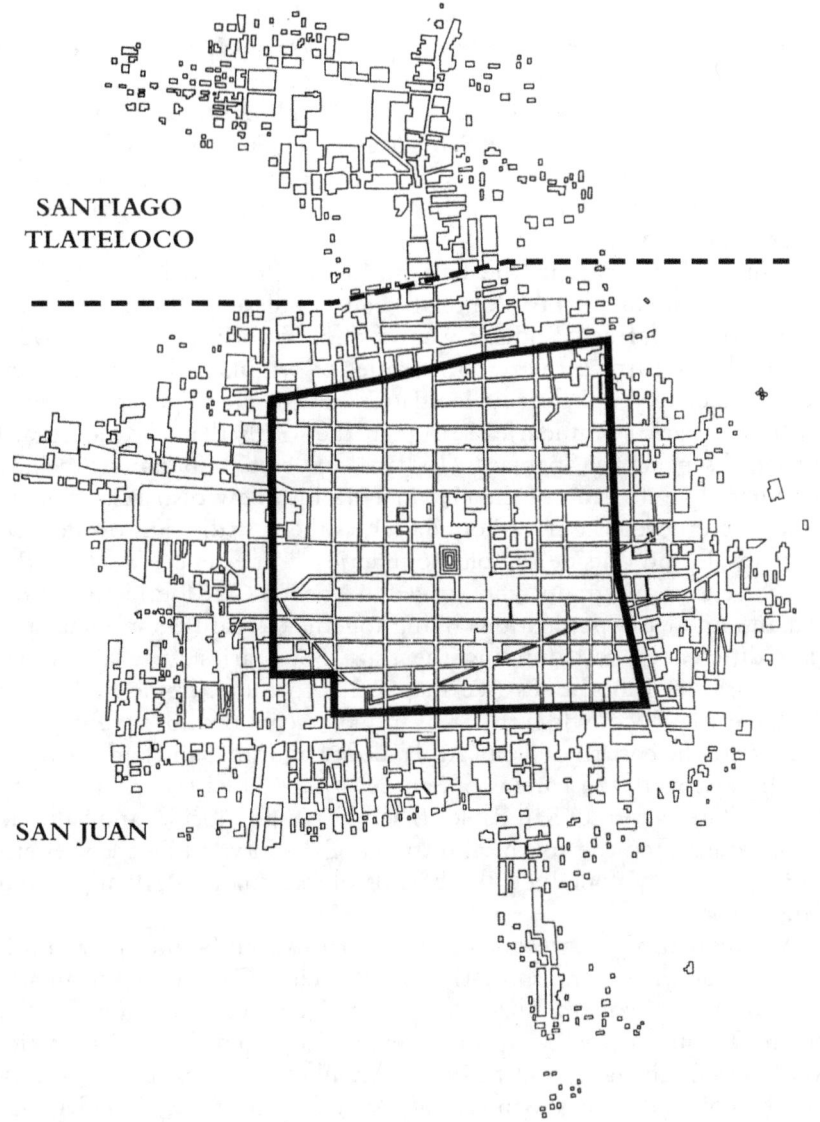

Map 2.1 *Traza* boundaries and predominantly Indian neighborhoods.

Indians, however, were not the only ones blurring the boundaries. Spaniards also began moving outside the center, encroaching upon Indian space. By the 1560s, the Spanish cabildo, or city council, in Mexico City began to authorize Spanish ownership of property in Indian neighborhoods, revoking earlier legislation that had forbade their residence in Indian communities.[46] Neighborhoods in the northern part of the city, especially Santa María, San Sebastián, and Santiago Tlatelolco steadily became more interspersed between Spaniards and Indians.[47] This breakdown of urban space continued throughout the seventeenth century.

After a major riot in the city in 1692, efforts focused again on separating Indians from the non-Indian population.[48] The traza was once again redefined: Indians were forbidden to live there and were required to return to their communities of origin.[49] The city council never effectively upheld this legislation. Further complications came with new parish boundaries set up in the 1770s that had no regard for racial separation. Spaniards, Indians, and casta populations melded together. The division of the city in 1782 into new districts, or quarteles, also ignored the traza boundaries, as the new districts overlapped areas inside and outside the old boundaries.[50] In essence, by the eighteenth century, migrants who arrived in Mexico City found Spaniards, Indians, and casta populations living together, regardless of racial and class differences. Surrounding the traza boundaries were a number of specific neighborhoods (see map 2.2). To the extreme north was Santiago Tlatelolco, while the areas immediately north of the historical traza were the barrios of Santa Anna, de la Lagunilla, and San Carmen. To the east were the barrios of San Sebastían, Santa Cruz, and Santo Tomas. The barrios of San Pablo, Belén y Campo Florida, and Salto de Agua constituted the southern districts of the city, while the western edge of the city contained the barrios of San Juan, la Alameda, and Santa María.[51]

A combination of streets and canals that existed before the Spanish arrived dominated transportation in the city. Causeways originally built by the Mexica connected the island city to Guadalupe in the north, Tacuba in the west, and Mexicalzingo and Coyoacan in the south, although they went through a number of reconstructions during the colonial period. San Cosme, which connected to Tacuba, was the widest of these, at 14 *varas* across, while San Antonio Abad, which ran southward, was the longest, at 7,000 varas.[52] Through the sixteenth century, major efforts by Spanish colonizers transformed many of the canals within the city into streets, although this was a project that

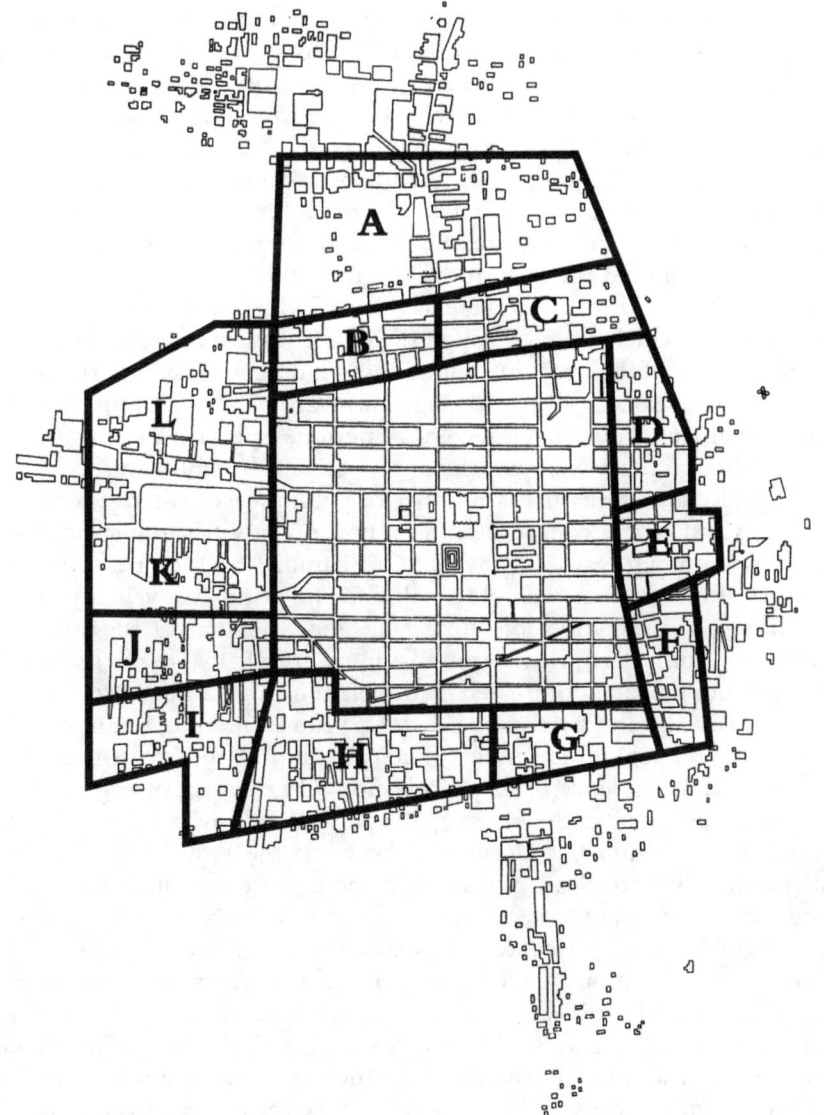

Map 2.2 Neighborhood divisions in eighteenth-century Mexico City.

Key to barrio divisions: A. Santa Anna; B. La Lagunilla; C. San Carmen; D. San Sebastían; E. Santa Cruz; F. Santo Tomas; G. San Pablo; H. Salto de Agua; I. Belén y Campo Florida; J. San Juan; K. Alameda; L. Santa María.

continued throughout the colonial period. By the end of the eighteenth century, Mexico City contained 355 streets and 146 alleys.[53] Major streets included Plateros, San Francisco, Tacuba, Santa Clara, and San Andrés, west of the Plaza Mayor, Cadena, Capuchinas, and San Bernardo just south of the city center, Santo Domingo north of the cathedral, and Corpus Christi, which ran along the southern side of the Alameda (see map 2.3).[54] A few major canals remained intact, primarily because of their importance as arteries for transporting goods to city markets from outlying areas. The two most important of these was one which entered the city from the north and ran along the eastern side of the traza directly to the Plaza del Volador and the Plaza Mayor; and another which passed through the city from east to west, along the northern side of the traza, just south of the indigenous neighborhood of Santiago Tlateloco, before curving southward.[55] Several minor canals also remained throughout the colonial period, especially in Indian barrios, although these were not the focus of Spanish improvements.

The city also contained a number of public spaces where people of all races and classes congregated for a host of activities: domestic tasks such as shopping, gathering water, and laundry, and leisure activities such as attending mass and other religious functions, as well as eating, drinking, and spending idle time. The most popular of these spaces were the numerous plazas, around ninety in all, that were scattered throughout the city, dominated by the Plaza Mayor.[56] The Plaza Mayor was historically the heart of the city and the scene of constant social, political, and economic activity. The cathedral bound it to the north, as well as the residence of the Archbishop. On the eastern edge sat the viceregal palace and the municipal hall, where government activity took place. Behind the viceregal palace was the Royal Mint, where silver on its way to Spain was minted and certified.[57] On festival days and other important occasions, such as the arrival of a new viceroy, the Plaza became the center of great celebration and processions. It also served as one of the city's main markets. Indians from surrounding areas would travel daily to the Plaza, to sell their goods, such as fruits, vegetables, grains, flowers, textiles, and the like. The Plaza Mayor was also home to the Parián, which catered to customers looking for a wide variety of items, such as Talavera pottery from Puebla, linens and fabrics imported from Europe and Asia, fine jewelry, and a host of other manufactured goods.[58] Other plazas lent structure to the city by serving as public spaces. The Plaza de Santo Domingo, three blocks north of the Plaza Mayor, housed the Royal Customhouses and the Inquisition. The Plaza de Volador, directly southeast of the Plaza

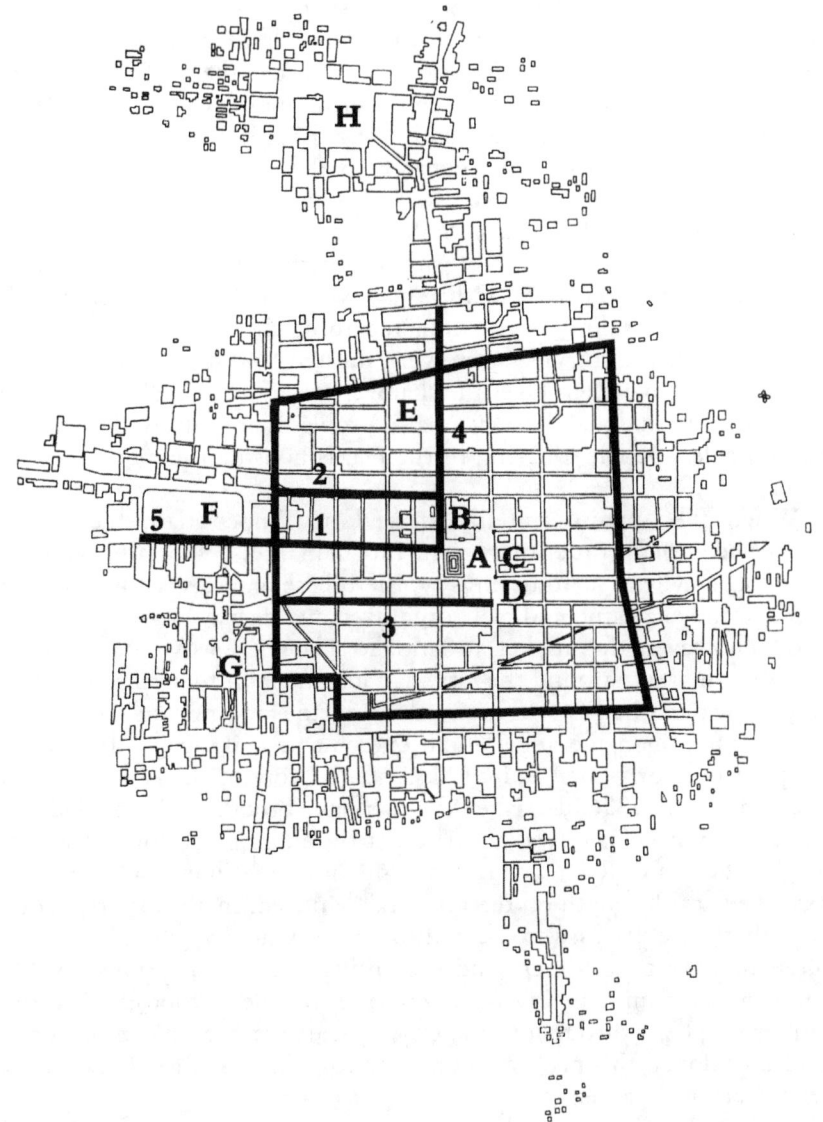

Map 2.3 Major streets and landmarks in eighteenth-century Mexico City.

Key to major streets and landmarks above: 1. Calles Plateros and San Francisco; 2. Calles Tacuba, Santa Clara, and San Andrés; 3. Calles Cadena, Capuchinas, and San Bernardo; 4. Calle Santo Domingo; 5. Calle Corpus Christi; A. Plaza Mayor and the Parían; B. Cathedral; C. Viceregal Palace; D. Plaza de Volador; E. Plaza de Santo Domingo; F. Alameda; G. Plaza de San Juan; H. Plaza de Santiago Tlateloco.

Mayor, was a key market for foodstuffs such as vegetables and grains. In the late eighteenth century, it underwent dramatic changes, as the main market in the Plaza Mayor was relocated there. The Plaza de Santiago Tlatelolco on the city's northern fringes continued to serve the predominantly Indian neighborhood, just as it had during the time of the Mexica, providing residents with the necessities of daily life. The greatest problem associated with these markets was their irregular organization and lack of space. Stalls were temporary structures rather than permanent and sat tightly packed together. Wealthy citizens and poor alike jostled for space within narrow aisles. No quality standards governed goods sold or regulations regarding the preparation and sale of food. Sanitation services were very limited, and it was common for patrons to relieve themselves in whatever space was available. Garbage and waste abounded. There were also problems at night with vagrants and homeless people loitering in the plazas housing these commercial enterprises.

When the Spanish initially arrived in Tenochtitlan, they were impressed with the orderliness of the Indian markets, especially Santiago Tlateloco.[59] Clean surroundings typified these markets, with plenty of space to move around and well-organized and displayed goods. By the 1560s, however, the market at Santiago Tlateloco, as well as most of the other markets around the city, had lost much of their charm. They were now described as poorly paved, prone to flooding, and filled with mountains of garbage and human excrement, making it difficult for people to perform their daily tasks.[60] G.F. Lyons, a British traveler to Mexico City in 1826, described the markets as good, but "crowded and lamentably dirty." He was surprised at the number of "little cookeries" present, as well as "a drunken man, and sometimes a woman also, extended at full-length on the ground."[61] Indeed, there was great concern that these plazas were becoming spaces where vagrants gathered, often molesting customers and disrupting daily transactions. While authorities attempted early on to confine the sale of foodstuffs to the numerous plazas throughout the city, by the seventeenth century officials abandoned this plan, as Indians continued to sell food and drink wherever they wanted.[62]

Besides the various markets, certain streets in the city dominated the sale of particular items. For example, silver shops and jewelry stores dominated Calle Plateros, running directly off the Plaza Mayor toward the west. One block south, on Calle de Tlapaleros, were copper, plaster of paris, glue, chalk, dyes, and sponges for sale. Merchants along Calle de Meleros, near the University, sold sugar and honey. Calles de

Mecateros, Empedradillo, and San Jose de Real, blocks running south out of the Plaza, sold fabrics, maguey ropes, sacks and bags, leather straps used for transporting goods, and jute.[63]

To the west of the Plaza Mayor was the Alameda, a beautiful, tree-lined park that was popular with residents, rich and poor, as an area to meet up with friends, stroll at leisure, and pass idle time. For elites especially, it was a context in which they could flaunt their material wealth. Most arrived at the park attended by their servants in their horse-drawn carriages, and proceeding to promenade in the latest fashions from Europe, gossiping with friends about the news of the day. The Alameda was the place to be seen on a Sunday afternoon. The park was also a popular spot with poorer residents of the city, much to the dismay of elites. Villarroel complained that the presence of poor people, often dirty and dressed in next to nothing, was a disgrace, and that their odors were offensive.[64] He was also annoyed by the smells that emanated from the variety of little cookeries that were allowed to provide food and drink to the plebeian population who frequented the park.[65] Nevertheless, next to the Plaza Mayor, the Alameda was one of the most important public spaces in the city.

There were of course other places elites could promenade and meet besides the Alameda. Two popular boulevards that were built in the late eighteenth century included the Paseo de Bucareli, named after Viceroy Antonio María de Bucareli, and the Paseo de Revillagigedo, named after Viceroy Revillagigedo, Juan Vicente de Güemes Pacheco de Padilla, the second Count Revillagigedo.[66] The Paseo de Bucareli ran south from the Alameda, while the Paseo de Revillagigedo ran south out of the southeast quadrant of the city. Both again provided space where elites could stroll and enjoy each other's company. The church, both through its properties and its members, was a constant fixture of everyday life in Mexico City. The urban skyline was dominated by the towers of numerous churches, and one could not pass a day without encountering elements of this institution.[67] First, since the church was one of the wealthiest institutions in colonial Mexico, ecclesiastical buildings were among the most opulent in the city. The cathedral, of course, was the most dominant of all of these, taking up the full northern side of the Plaza Mayor. The tolling of the cathedral bells often served as a marker of time for colonial residents.[68] By the end of the colonial period, the city was home to twenty churches, twenty-one convents, fifteen monasteries, and eighteen schools, hospitals, and asylums.[69] These structures were scattered throughout the city, but its western fringes in and around the Alameda were particularly popular with the church. This included the neighborhood of San Cosme, which was considered one of the loveliest parts of the city, with tree-lined streets and gardens dominating the landscape.[70] Many members of the elite made their residence here, away from the filth that marked other parts of the city, so it is no surprise that the church would favor this area as well. It was home to more than half of the city's convents, the Hospicio de Pobres, one of the few institutions to serve the city's poor, and the Hospital Real de los Naturales, one of the six hospitals that served the city, devoted exclusively to caring for Indians.[71] Nevertheless, church buildings, ever-present symbols monitoring the moral health and piety of colonial residents, dominated most plazas and main thoroughfares throughout the city.

Although church buildings were one symbol of the institutional power of the Catholic Church in colonial Spanish America, they also reflected the poverty that existed within urban society. According to prominent residents of the city, many of the dark recesses of church buildings were used by the poorer residents of the city as sheltered space to sleep, urinate, defecate, and commit other "vile and immoral" acts. Large, cavernous, and generally not very well lit on the inside, churches provided an element of privacy that eluded most vagrants. The physical layout of churches also made it difficult for the police to catch people "in the act," so to speak.

Priests and nuns, easily recognizable by their distinctive dress, participated in daily activities just like anyone else. Apart from their ecclesiastical duties, both groups were heavily involved in the colonial urban economy, from the production and marketing of a variety of goods, to their vast property holdings and could be found interspersed among the different groups in the various plazas and markets in the city. Their roles as educators and providers of social services also allowed them to interact with people from a variety of classes and races, from tutoring the children of elites, to maintaining a number of hospitals for the care of the sick, as mentioned earlier.

To the south of San Cosme and the Alameda, beyond the neighborhoods dominated by the elite, stood the Royal Tobacco Factory, which produced tobacco products for both domestic consumption and export. It was one of the largest employers in the city, providing jobs primarily for lower-class workers. The city government viewed the factory as a "refuge for Mexico City's poor," where they could make a decent living off the streets.[72]

In general, Mexico City was a fairly well-designed city, dominated by the homes of the rich, government offices, and ecclesiastical structures. It provided city resident's space to enjoy during their leisure time, as well as plenty of markets and shops to procure daily goods. Large differences in material well-being, however, separated the rich from the poor.

Material Contrasts between the Rich and the Poor

Mexico City during the eighteenth century reflected a city experiencing rapid growth without developing the corresponding economic and infrastructure to manage this growth. Extreme contrasts and obvious inequalities resulted: the wealthiest and poorest in colonial society lived side by side; ostentatious mansions and miserable one room shacks; wide, paved avenues and muddy, garbage infested streets; Spanish women in imported silk dresses and Indians in cotton rags. Daily activities clearly represented one's standing in colonial society: what they did, where they lived, where they shopped, the things they bought, the clothes they wore; how they spent their leisure time. On the top of the social structure, of course, were elites, made up of Spaniards, but dominated by criollos. They were the ones who lived the lavish lifestyles reflected in their palatial homes, expensive carriages, and imported material goods. This group, which included the titled nobility, typically had made their fortunes through mining, trade, and commerce, and as large landholders. The Conde de Regla, for example, had a personal wealth estimated at 2.5 million pesos, most of it derived from his mining ventures.[73] Owning and administering urban properties was also an avenue to wealth for some elites, and many families accumulated substantial income as urban proprietors. Nobles such as the Conde de Santiago Calimaya, who owned 31 urban properties, and the Conde de Rabago, who had 108,000 pesos invested in numerous structures, viewed these holdings as important sources of income, which supported their sumptuous lifestyles.[74] In their roles as landlords (and sometimes slumlords), they influenced the type of living arrangements available to urban residents. Finally, elites formed the highest levels of city government, the church, and the royal bureaucracy, which in turn influenced how much relief from urban squalor they afforded the poor.

Below the elites was a loosely organized middle class, consisting of not only Spaniards and criollos, but also mestizos, mulatos, and even well connected Indians. This group dominated economic activities such as retail merchants, shopkeepers, artisans, and textile manufacturers, as well as more educated professions such as managers, lawyers, doctors, and teachers. Lower levels of the clergy and the colonial bureaucracy were also part of this group.[75] For the most part, these were people of more modest means, with few liquid assets. Unlike the very rich, who diversified their wealth into many different economic activities, the middle class generally did not have this luxury, and thus were more susceptible to economic downturns. Materially, their lifestyles were comfortable, but much more modest than their elite counterparts were.

The largest segment of Mexico City's population, however, rested in its large, and mostly poor, urban lower class, which was dominated by Indians, mestizos, mulatos, and other casta populations, along with poor Spaniards and criollos. The economic situation of this group varied tremendously. At the top were small vendors who operated stalls in one of the city's markets, as well as street vendors, lower-level artisans, and unskilled laborers. These people generally had a steady income, albeit very limited and sometimes precarious. Unskilled labor was particularly attractive to rural peasants who had migrated looking for a better life but lacked the skills necessary for urban employment.[76] Below them were domestics and day laborers, positions dominated by rural migrants. This was a fluid group, moving in and out of the city to meet labor needs, constructing and occupying temporary structures. They were very poor, with few, if any material possessions, basically living on a day-to-day basis.

Finally, there were the *léperos* (beggars, vagrants), mostly mestizo, mulato, and Indian individuals who had no permanent residence or job. Generally, if they gained any income, it was through begging or very sporadic employment. They lived in the streets, alleyways, plazas, and other public spaces. They had few, if any, material possessions, and the most basic of clothing. They often spent much of their time and the small amounts of money they might procure on drinking. As a social group, they were the most identifiable of the poor, not only because they occupied public space, but also because of the extreme nature of their physical situation. Visitors to the city, as well as social critics such as Villarroel, wrote about how they dominated the city's public landscape. American Edward Thorton Tayloe, who traveled through Mexico City in 1825, also said nothing positive about the prevalence of vagrants in the streets of the capital:

> The city is...thronged with the dirtiest, the most diseased, deformed and half naked wretches you can imagine. Disgusting sights every moment present themselves—at the corners of every street (each square has a street), at the doors of the churches which

you must constantly pass by in your walks—and sometimes in the area of a private residence, you are importuned by miserable beggars, some of whom, not satisfied with a modest refusal, chase you into charity, which you are satisfied, is misplaced. We meet very few well dressed people in the streets—and the ladies never walk them, except to their mass, before breakfast, the only time I see any pretty faces. Such is the character of the *street population* [in original] of Mexico. So much filth, so much vice and so much ignorance are nowhere else—not among the lazzaroni of Italy, whom you have seen, and who can give you some idea of the *léperos* here—and yet, I am told, numerous as they now are, they have diminished amazingly within two years past, leaving some hope of greater improvement in the stability of the government. The police of the city are even now committed occasionally, tho' it is not considered unsafe to walk the streets at night without a sword. They are the greatest thieves in the world—never omitting an opportunity to rob.[77]

Joel Pointsett, the first U.S. minister to Mexico, estimated that in 1822 at least 20,000 of the city population of 150,000 belonged to this group.[78] Léperos placed a huge strain on social services provided by both the state and the church and were for much of the social disorder and crime that was an ever-present part of urban life.

Material conditions most easily distinguished the rich from the poor, whites from people of color. The city provided numerous opportunities for elites to display their wealth. First, the residences of the elite were the most sumptuous of the city, with perhaps the exception of ecclesiastical structures. Most elite homes were located on Calle San Francisco, which ran westward off of the Plaza Mayor, and Calles Capuchinas and Cadena, two blocks south of Calle San Francisco.[79] Families built these residences at an outrageous cost. For example, the Marqués de Jaral gave his daughter, as a wedding gift, a mansion worth 100,000 pesos; the house of the great silver miner José de Borda cost 300,000 pesos; the house of the Conde de Jala cost 107,000 pesos. In an economy where the average yearly income was approximately 300 pesos, these structures were a material reflection of the massive wealth that had been gained by some colonial families.[80] They were often multistoried, well-ventilated, and spacious, with grand staircases, numerous balconies, and exterior details in the opulent Churrigueresque style.[81] Large courtyards, lush gardens, aviaries, and fountains provided opulent living spaces inside. These homes also contained a variety of rooms, most importantly those used for entertaining family and guests. Rooms were often decorated with the finest imports from Europe and Asia, such as French style furniture, and porcelain and rugs from Asia.[82] Just as the convents and monasteries dominating the city, elites were also able to construct their own private sewer and water systems, so that they always had access to clean water, unlike most other residents. One of the most spectacular of these homes was that of the Marqués del Apartado, designed by one of the premier architects of the late colonial period, Manuel Tolsa. It was a three-storied structure, dominated by grand windows and rectangular pillars in front. Situated near the Plaza Mayor, it faced on to an open space that afforded the family views of the ruins of the *Templo Mayor* (Main Temple) of the former Mexica capital, Tenochtitlan.[83] These homes, while expensive to build, were also equally expensive to keep up, and elites devoted much of their monetary wealth to perpetuating their comfortable lifestyles. Many families had an extensive cadre of servants: cooks, laundresses, drivers, personal attendants, and so on to cater to their every need.

Elites also had significant leisure time to fill and did so with numerous activities. Besides providing leisure activity, elites structured their culture in such a way as to separate themselves from the rest of society, in that their cultural preferences were much different from popular, or plebeian, culture. Plebeian culture was public in nature, focusing on the streets. Drinking, gambling, dancing, gossiping, as well as participation in church celebrations and saint's days, all marked popular culture. It was Baroque in its design and form: uninhibited, expressive, and reckless. While popular culture embraced the insecurity of life for the lower classes, it represented to elites the presence of social disorder and chaos. During the eighteenth century, elites began to adopt the Bourbon style of austerity, grandeur, simplicity, and order, when it came to cultural expression. Popular pastimes for the elite were marked by restraint and composure, and through official legislation and unofficial pressure, elites would try to force this Bourbon style and aesthetic onto the plebeian classes.

As mentioned earlier, strolling through the Alameda, as well as the paseos de Revillagigedo and Bucareli, was popular. Going to mass and participating in other church activities were especially desirable among elite residents, partially to demonstrate their piety and commitment to good works to the rest of society. Perhaps one of the most popular activities for elites, as well as all classes in colonial society, was taking in the latest performance at the theater. By the late eighteenth century, most theatrical performances took place at the Coliseo, located on Calle

Colegio de las Niñas, slightly northwest of the Plaza Mayor. It was an imposing structure, dominated by three huge arches in the front, but getting there was a challenge in itself. The major street leading up to the Coliseo, Calle Acequia, often flooded, and otherwise was constantly under repair, so traversing it by foot was difficult. Elites, however, would never imagine "hoofing it." Respectable people arrived in their carriages, attended by their drivers. In fact, traffic around the Coliseo on performance nights was so bad that Viceroy Bernardo de Gálvez instated one-way streets and no parking zones to try to alleviate the problem. Once inside, the wealthy occupied the best seats, directly to the right of the stage, away from the masses of unruly plebeians who often had to view the performances standing.[84]

The elite fondness for carriages caused numerous problems, and urban commentators often criticized their overuse. Villarroel, of course, spoke plainly when it came to this subject. He estimated that 637 coaches were in use in the city daily, and that they caused numerous inconveniences: traffic, excrement left behind by the horses, and the destruction of street paving. He was also concerned with the message of excess that the use of carriages portrayed. While the use of coaches seemed most appropriate on festival days and during special occasions, Villarroel argued that they had become too commonplace and were used instead by the elite to vulgarly flaunt their wealth and status to the rest of colonial society.[85] Indeed, in a culture where the opulence of one's material possessions equated social power and status, it should not be surprising that people wanted to show off their wealth to others around them. It was part of the process of both defining and maintaining elite identity and status within the colonial world.

The rest of the population of Mexico City did not live such materially comfortable lifestyles. One of the most dramatic differences between elites and plebeians was in living conditions. While the upper echelons of the elite class built and owned massive homes, most people in Mexico City rented property in the city proper, built rudimentary structures on the city outskirts, or had no residence at all, simply living in the streets. The most common type of living arrangement for those who could afford it was the *casa de vecindad*, or block of flats. These buildings were located throughout the city, among the church structures, state offices, elite homes, and various markets and plazas that dominated the city streets. They were multistoried structures that offered, depending on one's means, a somewhat private and safe place to live.[86] The upper floors generally were preferred, because they offered more light and ventilation, and often the property owner himself would live there, along with his family and other dependents. Casas de vecindades typically consisted of multiroomed apartments, which distinguished them from the lower floors, which owners rented out by the room. Servants and employees of the proprietor lived in the street-level rooms, along poorer residents of the city, such as lower-level artisans, and unskilled and day laborers. These rooms were often dark, dank, and very crowded. The ground floor was also commonly used for a business, either the landlord's or another tenant's.[87] The spatial arrangements in these buildings also reflected class differences: higher-class status afforded the luxury of physical separation from the noise, filth, and disorder that typified many colonial streets. Residents of modest means were not so fortunate.

Poorer members of the plebeian class who could not afford the rents of a casa de vecindad had a few other options. Some managed to construct tiny adobe structures or shacks on the outskirts of the city. Others appropriated space wherever they could find it.[88] Quite often, they had to share their environment with the worst filth the city produced: garbage, human and animal waste, and stagnant pools of water. The very worst off had no other option than to live in the streets.

Unlike their elite counterparts, most urban residents did not have private access to city services, such as sewage and water. Most threw out garbage and waste into common sewers that ran along side city streets, or into the canals, intended for drainage and transportation. For those who lived in the bottom floors of multifamily dwellings, the stench at times was unbearable. Water came from a variety of public fountains throughout the city, but they were often in a state of disrepair, or more commonly in use as laundry and bathing facilities. In addition, most of these fountains were located in the city center. People living in outlying barrios (e.g., Santiago Tlateloco) were often forced to spend large portions of their day getting water themselves, or pay a water carrier.

The places where people shopped also marked differences between elites and poorer classes. Markets were a common place where elites and the poor often came together, and virtually every street in the city had some type of business that provided material goods for urban residents. By the beginning of the nineteenth century, it was estimated that the city supported 2,000 stores of various sizes, including 98 clothing stores, 410 wine shops, 40 stores that sold sugar, 40 candle shops, 90 bakeries, 50 butchers, 40 pharmacies, 55 silvershops, 120 tailors, 221 taverns, and 55 small grocery stores.[89] Elites tended to shop in the more fashionable markets downtown, in and around the Plaza Mayor. Particularly popular was the Parián, a permanent market where they could purchase a host of imported goods. Poorer residents also bought goods from a variety of open-air markets throughout the city, but also tended to frequent small neighborhood establishments, or *pulperías* (small store selling basic foodstuffs and household items).

What people bought also emphasized differences. Elites, of course, had lots of disposable income to spend, and they did spend. Their basic necessities of food, clothing, and shelter often bordered on the luxurious and extravagant. The Parián supplied many of the imported silk and crepe fabrics that were fashionable at that time. Other merchants were devoted to the import-export trade that brought in furniture, food, and other domestic goods from Europe. The many fine jewelry stores in and around Calle Plateros supplied elite residents with bracelets, necklaces, watches, and other expensive baubles.[90] As mentioned earlier, elites also spent large amounts in building and outfitting their homes, maintaining fine carriages, and supporting a staff of servants.

The poorer classes, however, lived a precarious life. Those fortunate enough to have a job brought in anywhere from 60 to 300 pesos a year, and most, if not all of this income would be spent on necessities.[91] By far the largest percentage went to food, which could consume more than half of one's earnings. The poor often were not only forced to buy inferior-quality food, but also often purchased on a "day-to-day basis and in the minutest quantities."[92] When agricultural crises hit, and the cost of corn went up, the poor were the hardest hit; their wages never made up for the differences in cost. Perhaps the worst year for the urban poor was in 1786, when a disastrous period of drought nearly destroyed the corn harvest of that year. Prices between June and September of that year reached a sky-high forty-eight *reales* per fanega; prices in an abundant year usually averaged between nine to eleven reales per fanega.[93] Many of the urban poor faced periods of intense hunger and in some cases starvation before conditions slowly began to improve the following year.[94] In general, the quantity and quality of food for the majority of urban residents was deficient.

Housing was the other item that generally took up much of the urban poor's wages. As mentioned earlier, most residents of the city lived in cramped and crowded rooms within larger rooming houses, small adobe structures, and a variety of shacks and other temporary structures. Only the wealthiest actually owned their homes. Those who could afford rented space from either the church or wealthy property owners, the two prominent property owners in Mexico City at that time. Even that option, however, was out of reach for many. The problem in Mexico City was not a shortage of housing. There was plenty of property available. What was lacking was affordable housing. Most rents were simply out of reach for the working poor. For example, in 1785 the rents for homes along Calle San Bernardo, one of the main thoroughfares in the city center, ranged anywhere from 120 to 300 pesos per year. A lot on Callejón de las Viscaínas, on the outer edge of the traza, rented for 275 pesos per year, although a structure was included in the price.[95] While this might have been affordable for some, given the fact that the yearly average salary was 60–300 pesos, it was unattainable for most city residents. Priced out of the market, many set up temporary shelter wherever they could or crowded together into one very small room. The very worst off in colonial society called the streets their home.

The precarious nature of urban employment sometimes led to numerous disagreements between landlords and tenants. It was common for tenants to skip out on their rent payments.[96] Others often found that they had to make new arrangements with their landlords during hard times. For example, in 1755 Don Juan Ignacio de Acosta sued his tenant, Don Juan Cavallero for backrent of thirty-six pesos. Cavallero explained that he had become delinquent in his rent because he was experiencing a period of "bad luck." He stated, however, that he intended to pay off the debt by pawning some of his possessions.[97] Pawning was, in fact, a common practice among both the rich and the poor in Mexico City. For the poor, it often provided the necessary cash to survive. It might often make the difference between sleeping on the streets, or in a shared room; between having some food to eat, or going without for another day; between having a drink or two to help forget about a desperate situation, or being unable to escape reality, if only for a moment.[98]

After food and housing, not much remained to spend on other material goods. Personal possessions were very few, consisting of some domestic goods such as pots for cooking, a *metate* for grinding corn, a few straw mats for sleeping, and perhaps a blanket or two.[99] Multiple changes of clothing was often considered a luxury for the poor. While most could cover the bare minimum, such as pants or a skirt, a shirt, and perhaps a shawl, many could not afford shoes.[100] A French cleric visiting the city described some of the better dressed of the working poor:

> the women go half-naked, and show a most frightful neck. The usual dress of the Indian women consist of two pieces of stuff, one that is fixed about their waist, and hangs half way down their legs in the shape of a petticoat; and the other, like a tablecloth, wraps

over their shoulders, and covers them down to their waist. This kind of cloak, which they call a *pagnorobos*, they seldom wear but when they go abroad; at home they commonly pull it off, and so remain half-naked. As to the men, they wear linen trousers, much like those of the sailors, and over these another pair made with skin. Their body is covered with a waistcoat without sleeves, or else they throw a woolen thing over their shoulders.[101]

Those who could not afford to buy clothes often dressed in rags or in many cases nothing. Indeed, public nudity was a constant problem in the city, where it was common to encounter the unclothed poor while going about one's daily activities. By 1777, perhaps as much as 75 percent of the population lacked proper clothing.[102] Despite the precarious nature of life for most residents in Mexico City, the poor still enjoyed their leisure time, limited as it was, and partook in a number of different activities. Church activities provided some diversion for elites and poor alike. The most popular were festival days, such as Corpus Christi and *Semana Santa* (Holy Week), where people were given time off to gather together with friends and celebrate. A party atmosphere often accompanied these celebrations with food for sale and drinking to excess. The pious foundations of these events were often lost on many of the participants, who generally viewed them as a time to forget their troubles and have a good time. Elites, on the other hand, and the church hierarchy in particular, were dismayed at the excesses taking place during what was supposed to be a religious celebration.[103] Rather than representing the new Bourbon ideals of austerity and control, religious celebrations continued to be excessive, closer to their Baroque roots of the sixteenth and seventeenth centuries. However, Bourbon-inspired leaders of the eighteenth century sought to create limits on activities surrounding these celebrations, such as the sale of food, alcohol consumption, and the imposition of public dress codes.

Other plebeian leisure activities were focused on the streets. In many ways, the streets were the privileged space of the urban poor. Unlike their elite counterparts, whose homes afforded privacy, most urban residents lived in cramped quarters with no privacy, or out in the streets themselves. The streets were the scene of many occupations, such as construction, porters, painters, and merchants. Stores dominated just about every street in the city. Travelling vendors and water carriers sold their goods. People traversed the streets to go shopping, to get to mass, to go to the theater, and to visit friends. Isolation from the streets was reserved only for those who could afford it, and even so, daily activities forced even the very wealthy out into public space with the rest of urban society. City leaders also preferred that the activities of the poor take place in the streets. It was much easier for them to monitor the lower classes this way and to control their activities.[104]

One of the popular activities was drinking, and much socializing focused on the local pulquería. Pulque was the favored beverage of the poor in Mexico City, affordable, and widely consumed by both men and women. Pulquerías filled with people, either stopping by for a quick drink or lingering to pass the time with friends. These taverns, however, were the sites of many problems in the eyes of city officials. Many of the city's poor drank to excess, probably in an attempt to escape the misery of their daily lives. People unconscious in the gutters around the city were a common sight, and the over-consumption of alcohol became the scapegoat for both the increase in criminal activity in the city and the moral decay of its inhabitants. While the state tried to pass legislation in the late eighteenth century to limit consumption by increasing the price of pulque, ultimately these attempts failed. On the one hand, the social problems associated with pulque were serious, especially in the eyes of the church, yet the taxes on pulque brought in a large amount of revenue for the Crown. The viceregal government was loath to pass any major legislation limiting this important source of income.[105] So drinking continued to be an important pastime in the lives of the poor.

Other street diversions, such as acrobats, puppeteers, exotic animals, people with deformities, and games, such as *pelota*, a popular ballgame, and gambling filled the free time of the urban poor.[106] They occupied urban recreational space, such as the Alameda, as frequently as the rich did. Elites, however, viewed the masses as bringing disorder to an otherwise peaceful and orderly space. As mentioned earlier, Villarroel reserved some of his harshest criticisms of the urban poor to their activities in the Alameda. He argued that the naked and barely clothed were throughout the park, their bad odors offensive to those around them. He also complained that vendors overran the park with the foul smells of the numerous stalls that were set up to sell food and drink to the lower classes. It was a travesty, he wrote, that the police allowed such disorder and barbarity to continue unopposed.[107] Nevertheless, in an urban milieu where economic opportunity was limited, where affordable housing was in short supply, and where city leaders actually considered privacy an obstacle to the control of the masses, the streets and other public spaces unavoidably became the arenas where the urban poor spent the majority of their time. In short, the authorities complained about the unsightly poor, but reluctantly accepted them as an unavoidable part of urban life.

The Political World of Revillagigedo

Besides the material, social, and cultural complexity Mexico City represented, the viceregal capital also reflected a unique political world in which urban reform was situated. The milieu created by the Bourbon Reforms, along with the status of Mexico City as both the capital of the viceroyalty of New Spain as well as a city proper, meant that this city was a place where imperial and local politics intersected. At the top of imperial politics was the viceroy. As the king's representative in the New World, the viceroy sat at the top of the imperial political hierarchy. Responsible for the overall administration of the colonies, these men held significant power, in part because the monarchs in Spain willingly entrusted them with such power. Communication between the Old and New World was cumbersome and slow, which meant that it was impossible for the Crown to micromanage their colonial holdings. However, this did not mean that viceroy's acted absolutely. The colonial system put checks and balances in place to moderate and limit how viceroys could rule. Most important of these checks and balances was the Audiencia. As the highest judicial body within the colonies, the Audiencia reported not to the viceroy, but to the king himself. Often times at odds with the workings of individual men, the Audiencia provided a valuable limit to viceregal power. Mexico City was not only an important place of imperial politics, however. It was also a city, with local inhabitants reflecting local needs and dynamics. Therefore, another layer of politics existed with the city government, structured around the cabildo, or city council. Just as the name implies, this municipal level of government was responsible for purely local matters, such as defending the city, keeping order and public safety, controlling prices in the markets, allocating lots for construction, urban sanitation and controls, drainage, water supplies; the regulation of the multitude of activities associated with the day-to-day running of a city.

The dual identity of politics within Mexico City meant that there were times when these two levels of politics became intertwined, and the story of urban renewal during the late eighteenth-century exemplifies this intersection. The power of the viceroy, as seen in Revillagigedo, illustrates how imperial politics could intercede in daily affairs. Indeed, the tension between Revillagigedo's plans and ideas and the interests of city officials often clashed over issues such as implementation, enforcement of penalties, allocation of labor, and most importantly, funding. On the one hand, the example of Revillagigedo enforces the idea that even as colonial power was in decline, the viceroy could still demonstrate significant personal power and legitimacy. Yet at the same time, local officials pushed back, claiming political space and control that they understood as rightfully theirs. This tension underscores many of the challenges that urban reform and renewal programs faced, both in their implementation, and ultimately in their success.

The other significant political context that pushed urban reform programs during the eighteenth century was the Bourbon Reforms. Initially developed in response to the decline of the power and efficacy of the Hapsburg monarchy, the Bourbon Reforms instituted a series of administrative, economic, and ecclesiastical reforms meant to strengthen Spanish monarchical control over its imperial holdings. Key to these reforms was the creation of more efficient and rational economic structures, more organized and streamlined political institutions, greater emphasis on defending the northern borders of New Spain, and limits on the expanding power of the Catholic Church vis-à-vis the Crown. In essence, the goal of the Bourbon Reforms was to "recolonize" the New World and to bring it back firmly under the wing of the Spanish Crown, for the benefit of the Crown. The implementation of these reforms began in the 1760s, and by the 1780s they were firmly in place.

Beyond the political and economic themes of the Bourbon Reforms, however, lay important implications for social and cultural institutions and structures. As much as the reforms sought to bring order and efficiency into the realm of colonial politics and the economy, these reforms also extended their reach into the daily lives of colonial residents. In the latter decades of the colonial period, the Bourbon state increasingly tried to control certain sectors of the urban population through legislation aimed at changing their perceived disorderly, immoral, and ultimately dangerous activities, such as popular religious celebrations, over-consumption of alcohol, undisciplined work habits, criminal activity, and public urination.[108] In a sense, the order and efficiency achieved within the political and economic sphere extended into, and onto, the bodies and actions of the colonial populace. Larger plans for urban renewal in Mexico City reflect an application of Bourbon ideas about order, containment, and self-control.

Concluding Thoughts

Although Mexico City housed some of the richest men and women in the Americas, if not the world, the material lives of most people who lived there were constrained by insecurity and instability. The lack of meaningful employment, poor housing, and little to no material wealth, as well as the physical environment in which most residents lived, reflected this dire situation. Mexico City, while spatially fairly well ordered, was a filthy city. It suffered from numerous problems: flooding resulting from a poor drainage infrastructure, indiscriminate dumping of garbage and sewage into city streets and canals, the abuse and misuse of public fountains, poorly paved and lit city streets, and chaotic public spaces. The lower classes lived in the midst of this physical chaos. People who occupied the lower floors of rooming houses could not escape the stench emanating from the streets. The destitute, who slept in alleyways, abandoned buildings, and city markets at night, did so in the midst of the filth. Even elites, who had the privilege of living space away from this disorder, had to negotiate it while going about their daily activities. Perhaps this is one reason why carriages were in such abundance by the end of the colonial period. Not only did they serve to display the wealth and power of the rich, but also they physically kept them above the stench and filth dominating the city streets. This physical disorder, of course, was a concern for city leaders, who could not help but connect the "dirt" of the streets with the "dirt" of the poor. They both represented a city lacking order and control, of both its environment and its population.

One of the greatest consequences of these conditions was the presence of endemic and epidemic disease in the city. If life for most residents was a daily struggle, this struggle was complicated by diseases such as smallpox, measles, typhus, and influenza, as well as more common everyday ailments such as a variety of fevers, respiratory illnesses, and gastrointestinal problems. Of course, the horrific living conditions of most residents not only made them more susceptible to getting sick, but also made the spread of disease easier. Even the rich, whose wealth afforded those excellent living conditions and an ample diet, did not escape the effects of disease. This issue colored the way city leaders viewed both public works projects designed to reorder the city, and the ways in which they perceived and understood the urban poor, their lifestyle, and activities. The place of disease in the urban context, and its connections to disorder, is where we will now turn.

CHAPTER THREE

In Sickness and Health: Disease, Healing, and the Urban Population

One of the most significant challenges that colonial leaders in Mexico City faced, in terms of managing the city, was the presence of disease. From the time the Spanish set foot on the mainland of New Spain, epidemics of smallpox, measles, and typhus decimated indigenous populations. Epidemic outbreaks of smallpox, measles, and typhus, along with endemic diseases, such as fevers, respiratory illnesses, gastrointestinal ailments, and skin and eye disorders plagued colonial residents. Unlike other aspects of material life in the colonies, disease did not differentiate between rich and poor, young and old. Everyone was susceptible, and illness touched all individuals at some point in his or her lives. However, while disease knew no class boundaries, the poor generally had much higher mortality rates than their wealthy counterparts. Elite groups had the tools and material resources to avoid many of the everyday aliments that the poor suffered from, especially those connected with deficient diets (in terms of both quantity and quality of food), lack of access to potable water, and unsanitary living conditions. These same material resources often allowed them to survive epidemic outbreaks as well, often through their ability to "self-quarantine" within their homes or to leave the city altogether until the crisis passed.

Intertwined were disease and the larger issues of urban organization and social control. In many ways, sickness was another physical manifestation of the ills that the city suffered. Just as the "body" of the viceregal capital suffered under the "illnesses" of urban disorder and decay, so too did the "bodies" of the city's inhabitants suffer under the web of disease. Urban planners, health officials, agents of the church and state, and prominent colonial elites all linked disease to the choices that the lower classes made regarding their material conditions and living environments. The connections they made between the activities and habits of the poor and the presence of disease reflected larger anxieties on the part of elites, politicians, doctors, and the church regarding the stability of urban society, and their place within it. More importantly, as with their critiques of other aspects of lower-class life, such as drinking, work habits, and popular diversions, elites used the rhetoric of disease and public health, as they connected to the themes of urban planning and beautification, as justifications in their attempts to physically reshape the city, thus restricting the urban lower classes.

Despite the commonality of disease, the healthcare system in colonial Spanish America, and Mexico City in particular, was limited in its ability to provide effective treatment, and in many ways represented tensions between the world of traditional, indigenous-based health care and that of a more modern, Western-oriented system. Residents had two choices. Formal care was dominated by state-licensed physicians and hospitals controlled by the church. Both of these groups focused more on caring for the infirmed rather than curing the illness. In the case of the church, the spiritual well-being of patients was an important component of the healing process, and the job of caregivers in this context was not only to use prayer and penance as healing tools, but also to prepare patients for life after death when appropriate. The high fees physicians demanded priced many out of the market. Most people turned to a second major source of health care, the informal care of traditional healers, or *curanderos*, whose treatments were often much more successful. However, the Protomedicato, the medical regulatory body in colonial New Spain, saw this group as both a dangerous threat to the formal medical community as well as an obstacle to creating more "modern" healthcare systems, based on European training and ideology.

Clearly, the context of disease, and its intersections with urban resources and systems such as water, sanitation, and urban space, illuminates the contentious relationship that existed between elite and plebeian society in the viceregal capital toward the end of the colonial period. To understand fully the importance of disease to the debates surrounding how urban systems and space were to be reformed and redesigned to modernize the city, we must first consider the place of disease and health care in the capital.

Sickness and Health

Epidemic and Endemic Disease in an Urban Context

Smallpox, measles, and typhus, along with an occasional period of pneumonia and chicken pox, constituted the major epidemics in Mexico City during the eighteenth century.[1] Table 3.1 shows epidemic outbreaks for the Valley of Mexico from 1711 to 1813.[2] The epidemics that proved most serious in Mexico City were typhus out breaks in 1736–1739 and 1813; smallpox in 1779–1780 and 1797; measles in 1768–1769; and pneumonia in 1784–1787.[3] On two of these occasions—1768–1769 and 1784–1787—food shortages severely complicated the outbreaks. In 1768–1769, all grains were in limited supply. From 1784 to 1787, consecutive years of drought and mistimed rain virtually wiped out the corn harvest, causing widespread malnutrition and death.[4] Certainly, in these examples, diets lacking in calories and essential nutrients contributed to the spread of the epidemics, as victims were unable to fend off the disease due to an already weakened physical state.

Historians have well documented the important role that smallpox played in aiding the Spanish in their conquest of the New World.[5] Since Indians, unlike Europeans, had no natural immunities to smallpox, the disease ravaged indigenous populations, in some cases destroying entire communities.[6] Because the high mortality rates connected

Table 3.1 Epidemic outbreaks for Mexico City, 1711–1810

Year	Type of Outbreak
1711	Smallpox; Pneumonia
1714	Typhus
1727–28	Measles
1731	Typhus
1734	Smallpox
1736–39	Typhus
1748	Smallpox
1761–64	Smallpox; Typhus
1768–69	Measles
1772–73	Typhus
1779–80	Smallpox
1784–87	Pneumonia
1793	Chicken Pox
1797	Smallpox
1806–10	Typhus

Source: Gibson, *The Aztec*, 450–451.

with smallpox had the potential to destabilize social, economic, and political structures, residents of the viceregal capital, as well as city leaders, particularly feared outbreaks of smallpox. It also proved to be very difficult to contain, with thirteen major outbreaks in and around Mexico City between 1521 and 1821.[7]

Smallpox comes in two forms: *variola major*, with a 30 to 50 percent mortality rate, and *variola minor*, with significantly fewer deaths. The variola major form can be broken down into five subcategories: benign semiconfluent, with a 10 percent mortality rate; benign confluent, with a 20 percent mortality rate; malignant semiconfluent, with a 25 percent mortality rate; malignant confluent, with a 70 percent mortality rate; and fulminating smallpox, which is always deadly. As these are twentieth-century categories, it is unclear what type of smallpox most victims in Mexico City suffered from during the eighteenth century, but the outbreaks in 1779 and 1797 killed approximately 16 percent and 6 percent of the population, respectively.[8] The virus spreads through secretions of the mouth and nose, as well as exposure to open lesions. It generally enters the body through the respiratory tract and has an incubation period of eight to ten days. Those in Mexico City who were exposed to the disease reported symptoms that started with a fever and malaise, while the pox themselves erupted on the third day after initial exposure. Starting out as small pimples, they would eventually turn into larger pustules and erupt, scarring the skin.[9] This particular characteristic of the disease was particularly troubling to victims, for those who survived were left permanently disfigured from their ordeal.[10] In that sense, smallpox was a very public disease, and it was difficult, if not impossible, for sufferers to hide their condition from friends and neighbors. Most importantly, however, those infected with smallpox could not escape medical and municipal authorities, who often advocated forced quarantine to slow the spread of the disease. Most residents in Mexico City, rich and poor alike, were completely opposed to the use of quarantine, due to the general fear of the *lazarettos* (buildings on the city outskirts that held the sick *en masse*). This attitude was not unique to Mexico City; some believed that the lazarettos used during in an earlier outbreak in Oaxaca, south of the capital, had been places of horror and death.[11]

Measles, on the other hand, is a short-term and acute virus, passed via respiratory secretions. The onset of fever, appearance of a spotted rash, and development of a cough marks the disease. Unlike smallpox, it does not leave permanent scarring. While it is highly communicable, especially in a population such as Mexico City where residents during the colonial period lived together in close quarters, the level of mortality was much lower than that of smallpox.[12] For that reason, although it was a dangerous disease, residents did not fear it nearly as much as smallpox. Complications included infections of the middle ear, pneumonia, and encephalitis.[13] The most serious outbreak of measles for the eighteenth century in the viceregal capital took place in 1768–1769.

Epidemic outbreaks of typhus in Mexico City also marked the late colonial period, including major infections in 1736–1739 and 1813. Typhus spreads through the feces of the body louse and generally enters the human body through a cut or abrasion, such as a scratched insect bite. Incubation generally lasts approximately ten to fourteen days. Symptoms include headache, loss of appetite, fever, general malaise, and a rash, which appears as red or dark red spots all over the body. Mortality rates range from 5 to 25 percent, with fatal episodes marked by delirium, coma, and cardiac arrest. There are three forms of typhus. The first is endemic, or murine typhus, spread by the flea. The second is tsutsugamushi disease, carried by mites and most common in parts of Asia. Finally, there is epidemic, or classical typhus, transmitted by the body louse and results in heavy mortality. This type is the most dangerous, not only because of the high mortality rates, but also because it thrives in urban areas where poor sanitation systems and densely settled communities provide an ideal environment for contagion and spread of the disease.[14] This form of typhus wreaked havoc on the viceregal capital. With its growing population, closely settled and prone to the worst of sanitation habits, typhus found an environment in which it could thrive.

While urban residents generally feared epidemics more, the presence of endemic disease provided a constant undercurrent of illnesses in the capital, which were much more pervasive in the daily lives of its residents. A variety of fevers, respiratory ailments, such as bronchitis, asthma, and sore throats, and gastrointestinal problems (including diarrhea, constipation, and digestive disorders) were the most prevalent, along with ailments of both the skin and eyes, especially glaucoma. Venereal diseases were commonplace, particularly syphilis. Rabies was also a major problem in the capital, where it was customary for residents to let their dogs run wild and unattended. In an effort to curb these dangers, city officials passed a series of laws in the late eighteenth century to deal with the increasing problem of vagrant dogs and the spread of rabies. In all cases, the laws advocated extermination, to protect the safety and public health of city residents.[15] Not surprisingly, children were particularly susceptible to illness; medical professionals considered whooping cough one of the primary threats to children's health, and home remedies explaining how to deal with the illness were sometimes published for public consumption.[16]

A number of factors contributed to the overwhelming presence of disease in the viceregal capital during the late eighteenth century. High population densities, poor sanitation and hygiene practices, a weakening economy, and lack of economic opportunities all affected one's experience with illness and disease. Rising population levels during the eighteenth century, along with high population densities within the city itself, provided an excellent environment for the spread of disease. Most residents of the city lived in confined, crowded spaces, which encouraged increased contact between infected individuals, heightening the spread of disease. Seasonal factors also influenced the nature of disease. Seasonal variables in both temperature and humidity affected not only the types of diseases that developed, but also the living conditions of a population. For example, measles and smallpox epidemics seemed to develop in the late summer, as regional trade was at its height, and continued into the fall and winter months, as residents moved indoors and spent more time in confined quarters. Typhus also thrived when people were pushed indoors during the winter months.[17] Close quarters, combined with fewer opportunities to bathe, gave the body louse ideal conditions in which to propagate and spread the disease.

Despite the continual presence of epidemic outbreaks of smallpox, measles, and typhus, as well as chronic endemic disease, the overall decline of the economy in the waning years of colonial rule meant that city leaders allocated less money to hospitals for the purposes of health care and maintenance. The sources of funding that hospitals in the capital relied on were precarious and never adequately covered even minimal expenses. Consequently, administrators were constantly petitioning the Crown for more capital. As Spain increasingly dealt with internal concerns toward the end of the eighteenth century, the corresponding shift away from colonial fiscal issues only exacerbated the problems in a healthcare system continually strapped for cash. Part of this tension was alleviated through cultural understandings regarding the role of the church vis-à-vis medicine and health care. The responsibility of caring for the sick and infirm did not fall to the state but rather to the church. Christian piety demanded that care of the sick and destitute be incorporated into elite identity; not only as a means to demonstrate wealth, but also as a means to demonstrate religious faith and conformity. It also helped to justify and reify differences between the rich and the poor and illustrated the important role that the presence of the poor filled in the maintenance and continuation of elite status and prestige.

Examining city resident's living conditions also reveals the connections between sanitary conditions and material wealth and thus to the susceptibility to infection. While all groups in colonial urban society faced illness daily, both endemic disease and epidemic outbreaks disproportionately affected the city's poorer populations. First, their socioeconomic condition made them more prone to disease. Shortages of clean water, diets deficient in both calories and essential nutrients, and housing that lacked space, light, and ventilation, or offered little protection from the elements, all contributed to the weakened physical state of the urban poor. A lack of key nutrients, as well as clean water, led to problems such as diarrhea and other intestinal ailments. These illnesses were especially dangerous for infants and small children, whose immature systems could not easily fight off water- and food-borne parasites. Lack of important vitamins and minerals in the diet, as well as adequate amounts of protein and fats, also contributed to health problems and made it difficult for individuals to fight off infections of a more serious nature.

Second, the dirty urban environment of Mexico City encouraged the constant presence of disease. Standing garbage and human excrement, flooding, sewage infesting the clean water supply, and inadequate burial practices all became the breeding ground for bacteria and parasites, aiding both the flourishing and spread of disease. Since the most inexpensive forms of housing existed on the ground floor of buildings, the city's poor generally lived intimately among the filthy conditions of the street. Wealthy residents could escape, to an extent, the elements that threatened the stability of their health. Spacious homes, solidly constructed and well-ventilated, provided a daily refuge from urban dirt and decay. Their diets were varied and plentiful, and many constructed their own private sewage and water systems. For example, many of the wealthiest families in the viceregal capital, including the Conde de Regla, the Conde de Santiago de Calimaya, the Marqués del Valle de Orizaba, the Marqués de Jaral, and the Conde de San Mateo de Valparaíso were able to build separate water and sewage lines that connected directly to public lines, thus guaranteeing a fresh supply of drinking water as well as a readily available system that disposed of bodily waste cleanly and efficiently. These practices provided elites with an element of containment and order when it came to disposing of personal waste, as opposed to the popular custom of simply tossing waste water out a second story window on to the unfortunate pedestrians in the street below.[18] During epidemic periods, the rich also had the resources to flee from the city altogether, biding their time on rural properties until the crisis was over. Even the viceroy, who ideally should have stayed behind to coordinate epidemic relief, sometimes left the city during outbreaks. This was true of Viceroy Branciforte, who fled to his mountain retreat in Orizaba, during the smallpox epidemic of 1797, leaving residents in the city behind to fend for themselves.[19]

The Struggle between Mexica and Spanish Medical Practices

While the constant presence of disease in the lives of colonial residents affected day-to-day activities, the medical profession's understanding of the origins and spread of disease, as well as the systems they developed to combat illness, proved less exact. Complicating this was the fact that in colonial Mexico, both Mexica and European beliefs and practices influenced the world of disease, medicine, and health care. Specific beliefs on both sides shaped the development of colonial medical practices, providing yet another context in which supposed European superiority and indigenous inferiority clashed. While Spanish practitioners rejected many elements of Mexica medical knowledge, in reality, colonial residents accepted and regularly relied on indigenous medicine, especially the role of curanderos, local healers who combined traditional indigenous remedies, magic, and elements of Catholicism in their treatments. What resulted was a syncretic mix of European methods and Mexica treatments.

As with many other aspects of Mexica civilization, the practice of medicine, especially in terms of diagnosis and treatment, was sophisticated for the time, especially when compared to practices in Europe. Much of what we know about Mexica medicine, especially the use of medicinal herbs and other concoctions, comes from three important sources. First is the *Badianus Manuscript,* or *An Aztec Herbal of 1552.* Commissioned by Francisco de Mendoza, the son of the first viceroy of New Spain, the work was originally written in the Aztec's language, Náhuatl, by Martín de la Cruz, an Indian physician who was a teacher at the Imperial College of Santa Cruz de Tlateloco. Another Indian teacher at the college, Juan Badiano, later translated it into Latin.

It includes 118 pages of drawings of medicinal herbs as well as text describing their usage. Second is *A Brief Treatise on Medicine*, written by Fray Agustín Farfán, an Augustinian friar who received his doctorate in medicine from the University of Mexico in 1567. First published in 1567, and reprinted with revisions in 1592, 1604, and 1610, it describes the "Anatomy, Medicine, Pharmacology, and Surgery" as practiced by the Mexica. Finally, the *History of the Plants of New Spain*, by Spanish physician Dr. Francisco Hernández, offers us a detailed description of the wide variety of plants used by the Mexica for medicinal purposes. Spain's King Philip II sent Hernández to New Spain in 1570 to try to recover more of the valuable Mexica medical knowledge, which had been lost or destroyed during the Spanish conquest. He spent five years working with Indian practitioners and returned to Spain with drawings and descriptions—in Náhuatl, Spanish, and Latin—of 3,000 plants. He edited down this number to 1,000 before the publication of his work in 1649.[20]

Religion and mythology played major roles in preconquest interpretations of health and disease. As in other facets of Mexica civilization, the gods had the power to influence all aspects of daily life; in the case of medicine, they had the ability both to inflict disease as well as to provide the cure. The practice of medicine and surgery, as well as medical research, which included empirical study of the body, effects of plants on different ailments, and the development of medicine and theories of treatment, were considered so important by both the Mexica emperor as well as the priesthood, that specific deities were associated with them. For example, Tláloc, the god of rain, was not surprisingly also the god of respiratory diseases—pneumonia, tuberculosis, asthma, and the common cold—all ailments associated with cold, wet, and stormy weather. The earth goddess, Tonantzin, also revered as the goddess of medicine, provided the Mexica with a rich source of medicinal herbs. Tzapotlatena, the goddess of pharmacy, gained that recognition through the popular belief that she led Mexica practitioners to the use of *uxtli*, a wood-tar preparation for treating skin disorders.[21] Xipetótec, the patron of doctors, was also associated with skin disorders and was generally depicted wearing the skin of a sacrificial victim. Specific physical representations also marked Nanáhuatl, the god of what the Mexica deemed "loathsome diseases"—leprosy, syphilis, and elephantitis. He was often portrayed in a grotesque and repulsive manner.[22] Other important gods associated with the medical profession included the following: Amímitl, the god of dysentery; Xoatlecuhtli, who presided over sleep and dreams and was associated with psychiatry;

Tlazoltéotl, the goddess of carnal pleasure, as well as gynecology and obstetrics, pediatrics, and venereal diseases; and Coatlicue, the goddess of death.[23] The variety of diseases attached to specific deities points to an element of sophistication and understanding on the part of Mexica practitioners.

Mexica healers believed a variety of sources for the cause of illness and disease supernatural, magical, natural, or a combination thereof. One's interaction with the gods could bring on illness, especially if the gods were punishing with the actions of an individual or a group.[24] Consequently, treatments for various diseases corresponded with their causes. Mexica physicians treated diseases attributed to deities with rituals, offerings, confession, and prayers. For example, people afflicted with skin disorders would participate in rituals and celebrations dedicated to Xipetotec, the aforementioned god of skin diseases, to aid in their recovery.[25] The uses of placebos, as well as symbolic remedies such as sympathetic magic, were important in healing magically inspired afflictions. In the case of illnesses deemed natural in their cause, the Mexica had a whole host of empirical remedies, based on, and developed from the natural world at hand.

Much of precolonial medical practices, however, did not survive conquest and the emergence of colonial rule. The Spanish, in the capture of Tenochtitlan, destroyed the imperial botanical gardens, a key source of Mexica medical study and experimentation. The collapse of the Mexica imperial structure meant the end of the state-supported medical system. Many Mexica physicians, as with the Indian population as a whole, died during the conquest and their medical knowledge was lost with them in the early years of Spanish control. The destructive presence of smallpox, and the inability to explain the disease or offer concrete remedies, resulted in a loss of legitimacy for those Mexica healers who survived.

What did survive, and perhaps the most important Mexica legacy to the development of medicine in colonial Mexico, was the introduction and widespread use of indigenous herbs, plants, and flowers in their empirical remedies. As noted earlier, the manuscripts of Martín de la Cruz, Agustín Farfán, and Dr. Francisco Hernández detailed the wide variety of plants, roots, flowers, and minerals that Indian healers employed. In the most comprehensive of the three sources, de la Cruz identified thirteen different groupings of herbal remedies, ranging from the traditional (curing fevers, gastrointestinal problems, the common cold, and other respiratory problems) to the cosmetic (dandruff, balding, and body odor), and the gender specific (there is ample discussion of herbal aids for the pains of childbirth and menstruation, encouraging the flow of milk postpartum, as well as the care of breast tumors). While some of these remedies bordered on the bizarre, and potentially unhealthy, such as the common practice of using animal excrement and body parts, quite a few recognized and utilized the natural healing properties of plants, flowers, and minerals at the Mexica's disposal.[26] Spanish physicians, while critical of many aspects of Mexica medicine, adopted some of the more conventional herbal remedies, in part because they saw the results. Empirical proof of the effectiveness of Mexica medicines gained approval among the more "rationally" trained Spanish practitioners. One of the problems that colonial doctors faced in using indigenous herbs was that they often adopted them in the context of European medical theories rather than using them in their Native American context. This often either led to their misuse or affected the efficiency of the remedies.[27]

Because so many imperial physicians died in the course of conquest and colonization, curanderos replaced Mexica physicians as the primary conduit of indigenous medical practices in colonial Mexico City. Through a combination of familiarity with local plants and herbs, along with a belief in the supernatural and magical component of disease and healing, curanderos grew increasingly popular among the city's plebeian classes.[28] Even though Cortes and many of his followers admired the medical abilities of the Mexica, others found their magico-religious cosmology incompatible with Christian beliefs and European rationality. Spanish doctors, classically trained in the theories of Galen and Hippocrates, and who focused their diagnosis and treatment on humoral theory, feared curanderos who implicitly contradicted and perhaps threatened their positions of authority within colonial society. Dr. Francisco Hernández, who as previously mentioned spent five years cataloguing Mexica medicine, was extremely critical of traditional healers, primarily because they did not follow classic humoral theory. The fact that they did not utilize bleeding as widely as European physicians delegitimized their medical knowledge. Curanderos, in his mind, did not follow nature, but instead applied their remedies in direct conflict with natural developments and ignored the important prognostic clues about the progress of disease. For example, Mexica healers treated fevers with heat remedies and rubs, which were in direct conflict with humoral theory, which would have called for bleeding or some sort of cooling remedy to release the heat.[29] As with so many other aspects of Mexica culture and traditions, the Spanish deemed the different medical philosophies and practices of the Mexica as uncivilized, irrational, and a threat to the practice of European based medicine in the New World.

The supernatural and magico-religious influences within indigenous healing practices were deeply troubling to the Spanish, whose worldview rested in the Catholic faith and who, in part, viewed the conquest as an opportunity to save a pagan culture from its spiritual defects. Diagnosing disease and treating the sick helped to perpetuate supernatural power and authority in Mexica daily life, and the Spanish saw the rituals connected to healing as another example of erroneous non-Christian beliefs. It was necessary to destroy these practices to solidify Spanish power and hegemony.

Even though the Spanish criticized the influence of superstition and magic utilized by curanderos, they themselves turned to their own Catholic beliefs when shaping medical discourse and treatment. Historically, the institutional church not only connected outbreaks of epidemic disease in a society with a prevalence of morality and sin, but also used these categories as a way to explain the presence of more common ailments. In trying to account for the damaging consequences of disease, church leaders blamed societies' sin and failure to live in accordance with God's laws. Disease and death were God's vengeful punishment on a disobedient human race.[30] The church's conceptualization of disease makes sense, to an extent, since church leaders were, for the most part, as uneducated about medical matters as were the people they ministered. Placing moral judgments and justifications upon the presence of disease in colonial society gave the church a voice of legitimacy and power in attempting to explain why such a destabilizing and destructive force found its way into everyday life.

Doctors, on the other hand, had more knowledge on which to base their understanding of disease, and attempted, at least, to approach disease containment in more rational and material ways. Even then, it was often sketchy and incomplete, and remedies used to treat illness were quite ineffective. Until the eighteenth century, most physicians, including those in Mexico City, based their understanding of disease on the theories of Hippocrates and Galen. They believed an imbalance of the four humors (bodily fluids) that corresponded to the four elements from which all matter was formed: fire, earth, air, and water, and to the four qualities, hot, cold, dry, and moist, caused disease. Treatment of illness, therefore, was undertaken in an attempt to reestablish balance of the bodily humors.[31] Since doctors were unable to observe and evaluate disease organisms in detail, they relied on deductive methods to explain disease. Connecting signs of illness, such as inflammation, and symptoms, such as nausea or headaches, to each other, while placing them within the context of humoral imbalance, allowed them to establish methods of treatment. Doctors in colonial Spanish America, taking cues from their counterparts in Europe, used methods such as bleeding, purging, sweating, and dietary regimens to realign the body's systems, thus rendering it healthy once again.[32]

By the beginning of the eighteenth century, increased focus on rationality, science, experimentation, and observation, began to alter European medical training and ideas about disease and its treatment. While educated elites still considered Edinburgh, Scotland the renowned center of medical education in the world at this time,[33] Spain's medical schools, at the University of Salamanca, Seville, and Valencia, respectively, proved to be just as progressive by the mid-eighteenth century.[34] Medical training at the University of Mexico, however, still lagged behind its Spanish and European counterparts, while training into the early part of the nineteenth century strongly depended on the classical theories of Hippocrates and Galen, and identification and treatment of illness still focused heavily on humoral theory. Public debates among students and teachers at the University, however, point to the fact that more progressive medical textbooks were making their way into New Spain. Some Mexican physicians were up to date with modern developments, especially the movement away from humoral theory to defining illness and treatment through observation.[35]

The physical environment also played an important role in the propagation of disease and its treatment. Doctors throughout the Spanish colonial period held that the connecting link between the macrocosm (earth and the celestial spheres) and the microcosm (individual human beings) was air. As every respectable physician knew, it was bad air that caused disease.[36] On the one hand, this focus on air reveals that despite how well-educated doctors were by the late eighteenth century, their understanding of how diseases formed and were spread was in some cases still fairly rudimentary. At the same time, this focus on environmental causes of disease led physicians to emphasize the importance of well-orchestrated sanitation policies to help guarantee the health of the city's population. This connection between sanitary practices and the spread of disease strongly influenced the types of urban renewal projects in Mexico City that the state attempted in the eighteenth century. For example, the belief that stagnating water emitted foul smelling vapors that made people sick influenced Viceroy Revillagigedo in the early 1790s to institute a series of programs designed to renovate and expand the city's existing, but limited, water and sewage systems. Placing greater emphasis on cleaning up the city would result, as Revillagigedo and other city leaders hoped, in not only a healthier population, but also one that would participate in daily life in a more productive manner.

The wide differences in medical knowledge and practices between Spaniards and Indians provide yet another context from which to view the clash between perceived European and indigenous worldviews. The Spanish deemed some elements of Mexica medicine acceptable, and actually admired them, such as their commitment to medical research and their successful use of indigenous plants and minerals. Other elements, however, they rejected. The basis of Mexica medicine in the world of religion, superstition, and magic, and its rejection of the classic theories of Western medicine, made it uncivilized, irrational, and useless to the Spanish and led to a two-tiered medical profession, as discussed below. The increasing importance of the connections between the physical environment, as manifested through public sanitation, and the propagation of disease, became a new context in which city officials framed ideas about urban renewal and public health. At the same time, the intersection between elite attitudes about the poor, and their desires for reforms directed at the environmental problems the city faced, become a proxy for elite anxieties about the state of their city and the presence of the poor within it.

Health Care and Its Institutions

From the Spanish encounter with the Mexica medical world came two different levels of medical care for residents in colonial Mexico City: one, more formal, based in European methods with trained and licensed physicians; and one informal, involving the remnants of Mexica medical practice—the use of herbs, traditional healers, superstition, and magic. In practical terms, the division was between "popular medicine" and "professional medicine." Because of the small number of doctors, the high cost of professional treatments, and differing philosophies, nonelite residents tended to favor popular forms of treatment and care. In drawing conclusions about the healthcare system in colonial Mexico, a note in regard to methodology is warranted. It is often difficult to quantify the effects of disease. Unlike today, colonial officials did not keep systematic records on rates of disease, numbers of deaths attributed to specific diseases, and the presence of endemic illnesses on a day-to-day basis. Nevertheless, some conclusions emerge, especially regarding the class dimension of healing and the different approaches to health care between elites and the plebeian classes. While European trained physicians dominated the ranks of the medical intellectual community, especially the Protomedicato and the administrations of the city's various hospitals, in reality, most residents of the capital sought out their medical care from the informal sector. This situation stemmed from a variety of causes. First, the number of licensed physicians, even by the end of the colonial period, was small, given the size of the city. In 1811, the ratio of licensed physicians to the general population was roughly 1.81 per 10,000 inhabitants.[37] For a population estimated at approximately 130,000, the shortage of physicians was quite severe. Second, the Indian population of the city was generally wary of European medicine and preferred to consult curanderos. Third, physician's fees were high, pricing the working poor out of their care. Finally, therapies practiced by curanderos, especially the use of indigenous plants, herbs, and minerals, often provided quicker and more substantial relief than the more expensive European counterparts. For that reason, it was common for the urban elite, along with their poorer Indian and casta counterparts, to frequent the neighborhood healer.

Attitudes over the role of medical practitioners also separated the formal and informal sectors. Most formal physicians did not focus on promoting preventative medicine; rather, it was their reactionary role as caretaker that was most important.[38] The art and craft of medicine included the long and sometimes drawn out process of evaluating the patient and recommending a regime to follow. Elites, of course, had both the time and money not only to take advantage of this system, but also to indulge doctors in their craft. For doctors trained in the European tradition, they considered the care of the poor irrelevant, because they did not have the economic means financially to support physicians and their extensive therapies. In this sense, economic status affected access to health care. In the case of colonial Mexico City, this was certainly in official attitudes regarding the place of the poor in the web of illness, disease, and medicine. Formal medicine was in many ways a sanitized version of the medical situation of urban life, ignoring the day-to-day realities of the poor and the direct connections between poverty and disease. Doctors generally felt more comfortable among the proprieties of elite culture, not in the vile and dirty world of the urban lower classes.

The dominance of the church in colonial society also influenced the development and patterns of health care in the New World. Since caring for the infirm was historically part of Christian charity, the state deferred responsibility in this arena to the church. Consequently, the church played an important role in health care, through its divine mission to care for the sick. Its presence was generally felt in the institutional setting, primarily the hospital. The city's six major hospitals—Hospital de Jesús, Hospital Real de los Naturales, Hospital de Espíritu Santo, Hospital de San Juan de Dios, Hospital de San Antonio Abad, and Hospital de San Andrés—were all founded and run by various orders of the Catholic Church.[39] The hospital setting, however, reflects the larger racial and class divisions that were present within the colonial healthcare system. First, all the city's major hospitals resided near the city center, away from the poorer and predominantly mixed raced populations of the outlying barrios. The exception to this was the Hospital Real de los Naturales built in the Indian barrio of San Juan. This should not be surprising, of course, since it was the only hospital in the city devoted entirely to the indigenous population. However, the colonial location of hospitals made the access of medical care for the urban poor more difficult.[40] Second, only certain urban groups tended to utilize hospital care. Elites, because of their material resources and philosophical connections to European medicine, had doctors treat them at home. Indians, on the other hand, avoided hospitals whenever possible. They even resisted using the Hospital Real de los Naturales, because the care they received there so contradicted their cultural preference, that they believed it was a place that people went to die. In that sense, it is easy to understand why Indians favored the informal medical sector, where they could get more concrete, and often more successful, help for their physical ailments. Poor castas, mestizos, and Spanish were most likely the largest group of hospital "consumers" in colonial Mexico City.

Despite the status and legitimacy that European trained doctors held in colonial New Spain, in reality their numbers were very small, and their services beyond the reach of most residents of the viceregal capital. The number of people hospitals could care for was also fairly limited.[41] These practical realities overtook ideology in the world of medicine. Most people did not rely on institutional care, but rather resorted to more popular forms of medicine and healing, especially the curandero. They persisted, and in general continued to practice in response to the lack of physicians in Mexico City, the limited access that most urban populations had to hospitals, and the continued adherence to non-European medical philosophies.

Initially dominated by those of Indian background, the arrival of Africans into New Spain introduced new cultural elements to the practice of curanderos. By the end of the colonial period, the ranks of curanderos represented Indians and Africans, mulattos, mestizos, and a wider mix of casta populations, which increased their attraction in the eyes of a racially heterogeneous urban population. Women also held an important position within the ranks of curanderos. Unlike the structure of professional medicine dominated by men, curanderos could be commonly found treating patients, offering medical advice, and generally taking on a more significant role in the popular arena. This is partially reflective of a tradition in Mexica medicine that encouraged women to participate in the medical sphere, beyond the role of caretaker. It also reflects how women parlayed their domestic tasks of food production, gardening, and nurturing into the world of medicine and health care. While these traditional healers, who drew their knowledge from both the Native American, African, and European worlds, were officially ridiculed by the Spanish and subject to prosecution by the Inquisition, they provided the bulk of health care and medical expertise to the poorer segments of colonial society.[42]

Public Responses to Disease and the Poor

Since the church dominated the day-to-day practice of medicine in colonial Mexico City in the formal sector and curanderos in the informal sector, endemic disease did not generally elicit broader concern by colonial officials, simply because medical practitioners and those that they cared for operated independently of any state apparatus. Epidemic outbreaks, however, were different and prompted a number of responses from various institutions in colonial society. For example, during the typhus epidemic of 1737, five provisional hospitals were established specifically to care for those suffering during the outbreak. These five—H.P. de Nuestra Señora de Guadalupe, H.P. de Nuestra Señora de los Milagros, H.P. de San Rafael, H.P. de San Sebastián, and H.P. de Santa Catarina, opened during the winter months of 1737 and closed when the epidemic faded later that summer. For the most part, these hospitals operated under funding from the archbishop and donations from wealthy residents of the city. The response was unique to this particular epidemic and was not repeated later in the century during other epidemic outbreaks.[43] Examining the treatment of the poor in the context of both epidemic and endemic disease focuses attention on the place of disease in the urban context, illuminating its role in the relationship between elites and the urban poor. It also reveals the variety of attitudes elites held toward poorer residents of the capital, and how these attitudes shifted with the perceived threat of blame for disease. The potential danger epidemics posed, especially to both legitimacy and power of the church and the state, forced both institutions to deal more swiftly with these crises. These responses also point to how different institutions shifted blame on disease to the activities of the poor and focused on the idea of individual actions causing contamination. If only the lower classes could control their behaviors, they would not be as at high a risk for illness.

During epidemic outbreaks, city and ecclesiastical leaders directed more attention toward the care of the impoverished. They were the most numerous victims of epidemics, and certainly the most pathetic, thus garnering the sympathy of both elites and the state. Even though Enlightenment scientists had begun to introduce scientific explanations for the development and perpetuation of disease, as discussed earlier, the church, with its focus on charity and piety, still was extremely influential in the types of responses to epidemics and other public health crises. Although there was a marked decline in viewing catastrophe as vengeance from God during the eighteenth century, the church's role in defining the cause of disease, especially during crises, did not disappear altogether.[44] Religion still influenced the ways in which people conceived of disease and systems of care. Epidemics provided a public stage to demonstrate the quality of one's faith and standing in colonial society, and the poor were at the center of this stage. This was a key characteristic of elite identity during the late colonial period. The importance of Christian charity compelled elites to help in times of crises, and the public nature of large-scale epidemics encouraged visible public responses to help the poor. Once these crisis periods passed, however, the city's poor became invisible and soon forgotten, left to fend for themselves.

Examples of the types of elite public responses to epidemic crises are illustrated in the outbreak of smallpox that struck Mexico City in late summer and early fall 1797. Viceroy Branciforte was acutely aware of the need for public assistance even before the epidemic actually struck the city. On February 28, he issued a directive describing his plans for coping with the impending epidemic.[45] He anticipated that funding care for the sick would generate intense struggles. As the epidemic approached, the city council wanted to halt all public works projects and divert those monies to poor relief. The viceroy, however, rejected that idea.[46] He argued that suspending these projects would put more people out of work, thus creating a new group of vagrants who would compete for aid with needy victims of the epidemic. He also argued that royal monies should not be used to fight the epidemic; rather, Christian piety and humanitarian sentiment should both be tapped in the name of public health and public welfare.[47] The viceroy's position is indicative of the prevailing notion at the time that health care should primarily be a function of the community at large, not the state. These themes also highlight the continuing reality of how elite identity formation was tied to the institutional church and acts of Christian charity. Economic and material differences were reenforced through these kinds of acts and served to reify colonial social hierarchies. Tensions existed between the need for the poor versus poor as active in their own medical demise. The discord present between colonial notions of social order and status versus the desires of the individual to control their bodies challenged prevailing colonial notions of corporatism. It also points to the fact that as colonial rule inched closer to its demise, less money was available for social services, such as epidemic control.

Branciforte encouraged donations by publicly commending those who complied. He used praise liberally, knowing that its recipients would not forget the favor they received from him. In a society where outward appearances and reputation were especially important among elites, public praise from the viceroy could go a long way in buttressing someone's standing among the upper echelons of colonial society. During the epidemic, various members and institutions in the capital donated close to 90,000 pesos on behalf of the sick.[48] Not surprisingly, representatives of the church contributed the most generous donations: the Archbishop of Mexico City gave 12,000 pesos; the Convento de la Encarnacíon 2,000 pesos; the Convento de la Concepcíon 4,000 pesos; and the Convento de Jesus María 2,000 pesos. *Cofradías*, or lay religious societies, accounted for donations totaling 1,900 pesos. Other notable donations came from the Viceroy himself, the cabildo, and Don Francisco de Zúñiga, who gave 12,000 pesos, the largest individual donation other than the archbishop.[49] Branciforte and church leaders agreed that giving money was a tangible way of demonstrating good Christian virtue and charity during a pressing time of need, and those who donated also benefited through the increased social prestige that came with praise from the viceroy.

Branciforte created municipal charitable societies, or *juntas de caridad*, to organize the administration of the monies donated, and the archbishop oversaw the efforts of these neighborhood councils.[50] Generally, they were headed by highly respected and well-established members of colonial society, who were responsible for allocating food, clothing, and medical care to the poor.[51] Each *quartel mayor*, or city district, was subdivided into these committees; ranging anywhere from eleven to thirty-three committees per district.[52] These societies did extremely important work, as the city's existing hospitals were woefully inadequate to deal with the scope of the epidemic. The city's six major hospitals—the Hospital de Jesús, Hospital Real de los Naturales, Hospital de Espíritu Santo, Hospital de San Juan de Dios, Hospital de San Antonio Abad, and the Hospital de San Andrés had a total of approximately 1,275 beds, far short of the number of sick that the charity societies aided.[53] In the end, these charitable societies provided food, clothing, and medicine for 44,516 victims of the epidemic, of whom 4,451 died.[54] Just as those who donated money, the members of these committees won public recognition for the good works they did in bringing comfort and relief to the poor.

City leaders used public processions, or *novenas*, as another important tool to rally public support against epidemics through prayer and pious acts. Branciforte himself argued that "Aside from measures derived from human wisdom...nothing will do more to stop the epidemic than fervent prayers to God, His Holy Mother, and His Saints, imploring their mercy and protection by public and private supplications."[55] To that end, he announced novenas to honor the image of Santísimo Cristo Renovado de Santa Teresa and the Virgin of Guadalupe. The novena for Santísimo Cristo began on November 17, at the height of the epidemic. Some of the most prominent and distinguished members of colonial society joined the procession as it wove itself through the streets of the city.[56] The novena for the Virgin of Guadalupe followed on December 4, but it was reserved exclusively for worship by Indians. Both events allowed for the public display of prayer and consolation for the victims of the epidemic. As the cabildo wrote to Branciforte regarding these events, "not a moment should be lost in carrying out the measures relative to imploring, in the name of public welfare, the mercies of the Most High, as a remedy for the present epidemic."[57]

Urban elites and the state, who feared the socially and economically destabilizing force of epidemics, were intimately involved in initiatives designed to help the urban poor. During epidemic outbreaks, wealthier residents of the city viewed the poor as victims deserving of help. It was also the Christian duty of those more fortunate to make sure that aid reached as many people as possible. The same could not be said once the crisis was over. As the natural span of epidemics shifted from fear to relief at their end, the urgent need to contain and eradicate the disease waned. Endemic disease did not invite the same sort of opportunities for public recognition and praise as its epidemic counterpart, nor did it inspire elites or the state to offer the same kinds of compassion toward the urban poor. Unfortunately, the need for continued medical care and resources did not disappear, as maladies such as fevers, respiratory problems, and gastrointestinal ailments were all too common among all residents of the viceregal capital. What did change after epidemic outbreaks was the way in which elites managed disease. Without the crisis of an epidemic looming, the responsibility for care shifted back into the private realm. In periods between epidemics, public discussions of health care focused on ways in which people could deal with illness daily, with their own resources at hand. Care for the sick now became an issue for the individual; it was not the responsibility of wealthy individuals or the state.

One exception to this rule, however, was the founding of the first secular hospital in the viceregal capital, the Hospital de San Andrés. As the last major hospital built during the colonial period, it was modeled after European hospitals at the time, around the idea that public service and preventative medicine superseded the doctrine of charity and focus on the spiritual well-being of the patient. Founded initially as a military hospital, and modeled after the Hospital General de Madrid, it became an important source of public medical care during the smallpox epidemic of 1779. As part of the larger strategy of revitalizing the state's control of the colonial politics, economics, and society, the establishment of the Hospital de San Andrés represented the Bourbon's attempt to move medicine and health care into a more modern era, less dependent on the perceived "superstitions" of the church.[58] An examination of reactions between endemic and epidemic periods helps to highlight early transitions toward modernity, as health care slowly began to shift away from the church and toward the state.

Much of the popular medical advice was published in various forms in the *Gazeta de México*, Mexico City's only daily newspaper at the end of the colonial period. Indeed, the emergence of the *Gazeta* marked the beginning of increased public interest and use of popular medicine, detached from both the formal and informal sectors. While editors directed the content of the *Gazeta* toward the literate—which meant the colonial elite—it is probably safe to assume that much of the information in the periodical found its way down to the masses through daily conversation, gossip, business transactions, and the domestic interaction of city residents. Instructions on treatment ran the gamut from simple fevers, to gout, to more serious illnesses, such as measles.[59] In some instances, information provided was precautionary and intended to help stop the spread of disease. For example, to help protect against contracting measles, a boiled and cooled mixture of water and sulfur was sprinkled on bed sheets and clothing.[60] In other cases, the *Gazeta* singled out specific environmental factors contributing to disease, in an attempt to help educate colonial residents on the connections between public sanitation and disease. In 1784, an anonymous contributor to the *Gazeta* wrote that an overabundance of dead insects, especially flies, in and around stagnant pools of water was a sign of illness present. In fact, he argued, an inordinate amount of flies in and around stagnant areas of water and filth, especially in the poorer neighborhoods in the northeast and southeast areas of the city preceded the typhus epidemic of 1772. He cautioned residents of the city not to forget how easily mortality rates rose due to diseases associated with the above (typhus, pneumonia), and to take the necessary steps, primarily keeping doors and windows closed, to protect themselves from the impending health risk.[61]

Information on domestic health, such as the benefits of breastfeeding and care for infants, also appeared in the *Gazeta*. Mothers seemed to understand the importance of adequate prenatal and postnatal care. In conjunction with various directives discussing care during illnesses, urban residents had access to tracts on the importance of breastfeeding infants to protect them against infection, as well as the importance of keeping children clean. The promotion of breastfeeding is of particular note since infants and small children readily succumbed to diarrhea and other gastrointestinal parasites; breastfeeding dramatically reduced the instances of these problems.[62]

The *Gazeta* contained nontraditional medical practices as well. The edition dated January 19, 1790, addressed in part growing concern within the formal medical profession over the rise of what was termed "nervous illnesses," which manifested themselves in a population with "acrid blood, a weak constitution, and easily unnerved."[63] Doctors attributed this to the rising incidence and presence of venereal diseases in colonial society. The *Gazeta* deplored the ways in which venereal disease not only worked to destroy those infected, but also passed on deficiencies to the next generation through conception. The use of mercury, despite its poisoning side effects, was sanctioned by "legitimate" doctors, who at the same time criticized indigenous remedies, which were safer, but to them provided no cure.

A closer examination of the *Gazeta* also points to the established medical community's priorities regarding public health and early attempts to influence the realm of popular medicine with more European-based remedies. An extensive supplemental issue published in 1795 titled "A compendium of cures for various illnesses," focused most of its information on cures for what was collectively known as "fevers."[64] The supplement examined treatment in three areas: the occasional infection, the chronic illness, and preventative measures, with treatments ranging from bleeding to dietary restrictions, the use of opiates, and hygienic practices aimed at preventing infection.[65] Popular health tracts also began to reflect a need to emphasize preventative medicine, or in the very least address some of the most common, endemic aliments that residents faced, but in a more informal manner. In 1788, a handbook of practical medicine was also published in Mexico City. In his *Compendio de la Medicina*, Juan Manuel Venegas listed remedies for a wide variety of common illnesses, such as venereal diseases, diarrhea, constipation, skin disorders, fevers, and gout. He also covered more unique problems, such as anorexia nervosa, bulimia, hypochondria, hysteria, and infertility. Venegas also devoted portions of his guide to the importance of a complete diet, sufficient rest, and moderation to help avoid sickness.[66] These suggestions emphasized a trend toward more responsibility on the part of the individual in their own care—with a focus on things such as rest, diet, and personal environment. It reflected an emerging shift toward a more modern approach to public health issues and challenged more traditional means of dealing with outbreaks, such as the novenas sponsored by the church.

Although both his work and articles published in the *Gazeta* provided the reading public with valuable information regarding home remedies, it is difficult to know how widespread and accessible this advice was to the average resident of the viceregal capital. For the most part, published recipes did not rely heavily on traditional herbs and minerals used more commonly by curanderos and self-medicators. Rather, patients had to buy the components at the local pharmacy. Residents were not only frustrated by the lack of efficiency and cooperation on the part of pharmacists, but the medicines required for home remedies were often an expense that was difficult for many to take on. A letter of complaint to the Mexico City cabildo in June 1788 illustrates some of the problems residents had with pharmacies, or *boticas*. In the case of the pharmacy adjacent to the Hospital San Juan de Dios, patients complained that access to medicines was limited, the quality of said medicines was poor, and that the costs of the medicines were too expensive. Hospital administrators countered by saying the opposite. Despite limited funds, the hospital was committed to providing medicine for the sick at whatever hour they needed it, that the medicine was fresh and of good quality, and that it was offered at a low price. As with so many other issues of material life and culture during the colonial period, dramatically contrasting viewpoints existed side by side.[67] The material components of many of these remedies, including specific dietary requirements, uncrowded and well-ventilated living quarters, and specific medicines from the city's pharmacies, were out of reach for the urban poor. Poverty kept them from dealing effectively with the diseases that plagued their daily existence. Many turned to curanderos who often provided less expensive and more successful remedies, since simple herbs and plants could be grown at home. Curanderos, through their use of superstition and magic, could also address cultural beliefs and fears that Spanish physicians would dismiss as too traditional and irrational.

Elites, however, resisted acknowledging that poverty perpetuated and exacerbated disease. They argued that the poor, through their reckless behavior, had no one else to blame when they got sick. The focus of elite ire was on the individual, not on the limitations of poverty. This made it easier to absolve themselves from any role as a member of a larger colonial community. In 1786, the president of the Protomedicato, Dr. José Ignacio García Jove, writing on how to cure various diseases, argued that the poor were particularly susceptible to illness because of both the delinquent conditions they lived in and the numerous offenses they committed. They abused alcohol, ran around the city naked, used "vulgar" medicines, and generally did not take care of themselves.[68] Viceroy Revillagigedo echoed García Jove's comments in his instructions to his successor, Branciforte. He believed that the poor were far more likely to get sick during epidemics, because they were regularly sick anyway. They failed to take care of their clothes, furniture, and other personal items, and they often spread diseases through pawning infected goods. Branciforte also believed that the pawning of the clothes of infected patients was such a problem that he issued public directives against it during the 1797 smallpox epidemic.[69] To both of these men, it was the personal choices of the poor that made them sick, not the circumstances of poverty that were out of their control. This attitude reflects a more subtle stereotype in the recklessness of the poor, and the belief that the behaviors perpetuating poverty were the same ones that precluded taking precautions against disease. Unlike epidemic periods when elites labeled the poor victims, in the years between large-scale outbreaks they feared them as incubators of disease and a gateway to the weakening of colonial society.[70] In nonepidemic years, elites and the state viewed the poor as chiefly responsible for their own misfortune, and the response to their care reveal a curious mixture of Christian concern during epidemics and general indifference during the periods in-between.

Concluding Thoughts

In understanding the context of disease and its connections to urban planning and renewal, the types of responses to both epidemic outbreaks as well as elite management of endemic disease in Mexico City invite some important conclusions as well as questions. First, the variety of responses to the care of the urban poor in the context of disease reflects a struggle that existed regarding the definition of public health during the late colonial period. Dissonance existed between traditions of religion and the church, whose emphasis was on caring for the poor—part of Christian charity that especially for elites marked identity as well as reenforcing colonial difference versus responsibility of the individual to make the right choices to protect themselves and those who willingly did not suffered the consequences. While the disease environment remained unchanged, ideas and attitudes inspired by Enlightenment thinking prompted physicians and officials to alter their ideas regarding the propagation and spread of illness. In broadening their understanding of disease, doctors and city leaders also reoriented their perception of the relationship between disease, sanitation, and public health. They shifted away from ecclesiastical assumptions of sickness as a punishment for human sin, to an increased awareness that certain diseases had noncosmological causes, causes that humans could influence if not control. By framing issues of public health in this way, colonial leaders began a subtle shift toward conceptualizing what a modern city and modern urban populous was to look like. Just as debates regarding political and economic modernity were emerging toward the end of the colonial period, this debate could also be seen within the contexts of urban planning. It was here that late colonial leaders like Viceroy Revillagigedo differed from their earlier counterparts. By connecting disease to the urban environment, they chose, at least on the surface, to deal with some of the tangible contributors to urban disease—dirty water, poor sanitation, flooding, and poorly constructed public spaces. However, a deeper motive regarding the connections to urban renewal emerged as well, motives connected to the actions and activities of city residents. The polluting actions of the individual came into play.

The state favored environmental approaches to disease containment and eradication than any attempts at alleviating poverty in the lives of city residents. Although it is clear that the consequences of poverty perpetuated disease, political leaders in the viceregal capital seemingly refused to acknowledge this, placing the blame on the poor themselves. They argued that disease was primarily the product of dirt and decomposing matter, and that once city planners solved these problems, a more healthful environment would result. In fact, some of the most extensive urban renewal initiatives developed in Mexico City during the colonial period took place from 1789 to 1794, between the epidemics of 1784–1787 and 1797. When it came to containing and eradicating disease, public matters, such as garbage collection, sewage systems, drainage, paving, and potable water were considered important and worthy of state attention and funds. A good example of this is Branciforte's refusal to shelve temporarily public works projects in order to redirect funds to health care during the smallpox epidemic of 1797. It should also be noted that the emphasis placed on these types of urban renewal projects is a reflection of general understandings of the development and spread of diseases that were common at this point. It was still believed, to a certain extent, that polluted air, *miasmas*, was to blame for the presence of disease in the capital. People became sick through breathing infected air. Factors such as overcrowded housing, inadequate diets, and unemployment were considered private matters and thus inappropriate objects for state action. Environmental responses were probably also more appealing to elites in that they took the victims of disease—the urban poor—out of the equation altogether. The state could argue that they were focusing time and energy on programs that cleaned up public spaces, thus benefiting all colonial residents. As much as order and rationality had been applied to more formal political and economic structures through the Bourbon Reforms, these ideas were also reflected in the spatial, environmental, and health contexts of the viceregal capital.

    Second, while elite focus on treating and aiding the poor increased dramatically during epidemic periods, it seems that epidemics seldom, if ever, produced long-term or radical solutions for the ordinary poor. For example, the city council redirected money donated during the smallpox outbreak of 1797 for crisis management and emergency planning. No money was set aside for long-term projects designed to alleviate poverty; better housing, higher quality food, or access to health care. Once the public crisis was over, the focus on the poor as pitiful victims in need of assistance shifted to the poor as reckless individuals who threatened the health, and consequently the stability, of society in the viceregal capital.

The presence of diseases and the types of responses they generated vis-à-vis the poor also reflects a conflict that existed between groups in colonial Mexico City over health care. While the motives behind charitable giving varied, it appears that the poor were merely objects in elite and state responses made during epidemic crises. When it benefited them socially, the wealthy were more than willing to devote time and money to help the victims of disease. Even the state understood that responding in some fashion to epidemic crises was necessary to maintain legitimacy in the eyes of their constituents. However, once epidemics ended, the poor once again became subjects of fear and loathing. Just as with other activities, such as excessive drinking, work habits, and popular diversions, disease became another arena in which elites sharply criticized the behavior of the poor.

Alongside legislation passed to alter the behavior of the city's plebeian classes, elites also turned their focus to ways to regain control of the urban environment, in a sense reclaiming it from the masses. While Revillagigedo and others couched many of these programs in terms of protecting the public from the devastating consequences of disease, in reality they served elite desires to reshape Mexico City into a more accurate reflection of Enlightenment ideals of rationality, symmetry, beauty, and most importantly, control. Elites articulated the problem of disease not only from a health perspective but also from an urban planning and a cultural perspective. In their eyes, disease kept the viceregal capital from functioning in an efficient, systematic, and organized way. What follows is the story of how elites and the state tried to mold Mexico City into a spatial representation of Bourbon ideals, through new sanitation programs, improved drainage and paving, access to potable water, and alterations of public space, namely construction of new markets, renovations to the Plaza Mayor, and bathhouse reform.

CHAPTER FOUR

A Basic Necessity: Water and the Urban Environment

Of all of the changes to the urban environment Viceroy Revillagigedo advocated, perhaps none was more important to the health of city residents than his program to renovate and repair the existing public water system. On the western fringes of Mexico City were two sources of potable water, providing enough water to sustain the population throughout the colonial period. Two main aqueducts served the city, thousands of feet of pipe transported water, and a series of public fountains existed as public sources of water. Outside the boundaries of the public system, wealthy residents and colonial institutions such as the church could pay to have a private fountain built within residences, connected directly to the public lines. On the surface, it appeared that the system was logical in its organization, and accessible to most, if not all, city residents.

However, this was an ideal picture; reality was fraught with problems. First, the system as it existed before Revillagigedo was limited largely to the city center. Both aqueducts stopped on the western edge of the city, and the infrastructure in place to transport water to the rest of the city, in terms of existing piping and public fountains, did not extend into the northern and eastern districts. Residents in the Indian barrio of Santiago Tlateloco, in particular, had to spend large amounts of their income on purchasing water from aguadores, who often sold the precious resource at inflated prices. This burden weighed heavily on poorer residents, whose incomes were extremely limited to begin with. Families who chose to collect water themselves struggled to find time to do so and often put themselves in harm's way. Young girls and women risked verbal and physical harassment, while boys were known to get into trouble; gambling and fights were the greatest hazards. Second, many parts of the public system were in bad physical condition. Residents complained that fountains were inoperable due to structural damage, and sections of piping were broken. Other fountains were overused and did not maintain a constant supply of water. City residents sometimes misused public fountains, which became places to wash clothes and bathe animals, while others became places to dump garbage and wastewater.[1]

Revillagigedo's desire to improve the public water system was due in part to health concerns; the cabildo fielded continuous complaints over sicknesses residents had to endure because of drinking polluted water. However, the viceroy was also concerned with public safety. Similar to other public spaces—pulquerías, markets, parks, and main thoroughfares—the plazas housing public fountains were popular sites for the homeless and vagrants to congregate, presenting a public eyesore, harassing residents, and perpetuating the vice-ridden activities that compromised the tranquility and security residents demanded. Revillagigedo also addressed the problem associated with the city's public baths. Popular among the plebeian classes, public baths were sites of general disorder and lack of restraint that marked the urban lower classes. As part of his larger project to bring order, comfort, and safety to the urban environment, Revillagigedo passed an elaborate series of laws and regulations aimed at controlling both those who ran the bathhouses as well as those who frequented them.

In the end, like the other public works projects undertaken by urban reformers—projects meant to reflect Bourbon ideals spatially—plans to improve and repair the potable water system fell far short of original intentions, and in a greater sense reflected the larger inequalities existing within colonial society. To understand the inherent problems that existed in the water supply, as well as the difficulties colonial officials faced in solving these problems, it is important first to examine the water distribution system throughout the city.

Organization of the Public Water System and Supply

During the colonial period, a public water system existed to provide relatively fresh, potable water to city residents. Two major aqueducts brought water into the city limits from freshwater springs in the surrounding area. The first originated in Santa Fé, with springs from the Desierto de los Leones feeding into it as it flowed toward the city. Construction of this aqueduct, composed of 900 arches, began under the viceregal administration of the Marqués de Montes Claros (1603–1607) and finished under the Marqués de Guadalcázar, the viceroy in 1620. It entered the city at the neighborhood of San Cosme, running along the northern edge of the Alameda, and terminated for distribution at the intersection of Calles de San Andrés, Santa Isabel, and the Puente de la Mariscala.[2] By the later part of the eighteenth century, however, demand was starting to exceed supply, so Viceroy Bucarelí completed another aqueduct in 1779. The source for this system also came from the springs of Chapultepec, the waters of which were stored in a large stone reservoir. The aqueduct, composed of 904 stone arches, followed the same route of the historical Mexica aqueduct. It ran into the southern part of the city, from the Tacubaya causeway, through the Arcos de Belén, and ended for distribution at the Fuente del Salto de Agua. However, it was not as clean as the waters from the Santa Fé aqueduct, and often referred to as *gorda* (fat) or *gruesa* (thick) because it was brackish and prone to muddiness during the rainy season.[3]

These two sites transported water throughout the city via a series of pipes, or *cañerías*, to any number of public fountains (*fuentes públicas*). Because of the irregularity of records kept earlier in the colonial period, it is difficult to know exactly when and where public fountains were constructed. Documentation for the period of this project, however, is complete and gives us a somewhat accurate picture of the locations of public access sites. Table 4.1 lists the location of new public fountains built during the second half of the eighteenth century. According to a listing taken in 1806, besides the above, public fountains could be found in the following areas: Portal de las Flores, Plazuela de Loreto, Plaza de la Concepcíon, Plazuela de Santa Ana, the corner of Calle la Cerbata and Plazuela de San Sebastían, Calle de Revillagigedo, Calle de la Candelaría, Puente del Fresno, Plazuela de las Vizcaínas, Plazuela de la Barata, Plazuela de San Salvador, Plazuela de Monserrate, and Plazuela de Regina.[4]

Along with these common sources of water, many public buildings had their own private fountains connected to the city supply (see table 4.2). Again, documentation is sketchy for the period leading up to the eighteenth century, but lists existing in city council records from 1700 onward give us a general idea of access beyond public fountains. Not surprisingly, most of those who had special access to water acted in an official capacity with the institutional church, especially through

Table 4.1 List of *Fuentes Públicas* built in Mexico City, 1740–1805

Location	Date Constructed
Plazuela de San Gregorio	1740
Barrio de Santa Cruz y Soledad	1745
Plazuela de Santa Trinidad	1753
Plazuela de San Lázaro	1753
Plazuela de Santa Cruz	1753
Pila de Puente de San Lázaro	1753
Plazuela de Santa María	1772
Plazuela Del Factor	1778
Plazuela de Santo Domingo	1780
Plazuela de San Juan de la Penetencia	1783
Molina de la Polvora	1785
Plazuela de Santiago	predates 18th century
Plaza Mayor	predates 18th century
Plazuela Del Colegio de Niñas	1793
Puente de Fierro	1793
Plazuela de Santa Catarina	1794
Plaza de San Pablo	1795
Plazuela de Ave María y Santa Cruz	1795
Puente de Blanquillo	1801
Parroquia de Santa Cruz	1805

Source: AHCM, Aguas: *Fuentes Públicas*. Vol. 58.

Table 4.2 List of public buildings with private access to public water supply in Mexico City

Location	Dating from
Hospital del Divino Salvador para Mujeres Dementes	1703
Hospital de San Juan de Dios	1721
Hospital de San Lázaro	1728
Hospital de Terceros del Orden de San Francisco	1748
Hospital de Naturales	1763
Fabrica de Puros y Cigarillos en la Lagunilla	1770
Colegio de San Juan de Letrán	1772
Casa Cural en el Calle de San Miguel	1772
Hospital de San Andrés	1774
Casa de los Niños Expositos	1788
Jardin Botánico en el Palacio Real	1790
Colegio de Miniera	1797
Hospicio de Pobres	1801
Casa Cural de Santa María de Redonda	1808
Hospicio de San Nicolás	1815

Source: AHCM, Aguas: *Edificios Públicas*, Vol. 32.

hospitals, schools, and hospices. Important economic institutions such as the Royal Tobacco Factory also benefited from the key role it held in providing jobs and revenue for the Crown. Economic necessity even stipulated that smaller enterprises have better access to water. For example, the city's textile manufacturers clustered around the fuente pública at Salto de Agua, as well as silversmiths on Calle Plateros and blacksmiths on Calle Tacuba always enjoyed a steady supply of water for their activities.[5]

This special access did not guarantee a continual supply of water, however. The hospital of San Lázaro, which cared for those suffering with leprosy, had public access to water starting in 1728, but in a petition sent to the city council in 1762, complained that their water service was intermittent at best. Quite often, the staff of the hospital had to go out and buy water, which cut into the funds available to treat patients. Because of the lack of reliable water in their fountain, they could neither bathe patients nor wash their clothes and linens as frequently as they would have liked. Hospital administrators asked the city to provide the funds for new piping connecting their fountain to the public supply, and the city agreed to provide the new lines, at a cost of 2,085 pesos, 5 1/2 reales.[6]

Those who could afford the cost of construction also tapped into the public water supply through private cañerías and *fuentes particulares*, or private fountains built within homes that linked onto the existing city water system. Table 4.3 lists the source and general location of these fountains.[7] The mainline of Puente de Mariscal and adjacent branch lines serviced the northern half of the city, while Salto de Agua and its corresponding lines covered the southern half. Some of the more notable locations included the following: viceregal palace, with nine private

Table 4.3 Source and location of *Fuentes Particulares* in Mexico City, 1806

Mainline	Branch Line and Length	Fuentes Particulares
Pte. de Mariscal	San Francisco (1342 *varas*)	122
	Palacio (1458 *varas*)	43
	San Lorenzo (1458 *varas*)	110
	de la Santísima (1665 *varas*)	105
Salto de Agua	de la Alameda (1544 *varas*)	11
	de la Merced (1968 *varas*)	66
	San Pablo (1412 *varas*)	48

Source: AHCM, Aguas: *Cañerías*, Vol. 19, Exp. 29.

sources; the Convento de las Capuchinas with four; the Convento de Santa Clara with five; the Convento de Casa Profesa, also with five; and the Convento de Santa Isabel with three.[8] This certainly represents the power and material wealth of government officials and the church during the colonial period. By 1806, 505 "private" fountains existed within city homes and businesses.[9]

Despite the seemingly comprehensive nature of the public water system in colonial Mexico City, it suffered from some fundamental problems. First, city residents complained that many existing fountains were dry; the piping providing water was either broken or extensively clogged with garbage and debris. Residents used fountains to dump garbage, which could work its way down into the piping system. For example, in 1762 residents near the Convento de San Juan de la Penitencia sent a complaint to the cabildo arguing that their neighbors were using the cañeria that they shared as a place to dump garbage. Consequently, it had become clogged, limiting the flow of water into the Convent.[10] In May 1777, one of the priests in the parish of Santa Cruz informed city officials that water was not reaching the public fountain—the main source of water for the neighborhood. He attributed the problem to "maltreatment of the piping" and asked that repairs be made.[11] In both cases, repairs were completed. In May 1784, in a lengthy petition to the city council, residents of the parishes of Santa Cruz, San Pablo, and La Palma, all complained that the fuentes públicas in their neighborhoods were inoperable, primarily because garbage had clogged the corresponding piping. They argued that their only access to drinking water was from a very dirty nearby canal that had made some of the residents sick. Therefore, they had to either buy water from local aguadores, which was expensive, or to go out themselves to get water from other public fountains, which was time consuming. City leaders did respond to this petition, recognizing their responsibility in attending to problems connected with public services, and agreed to clean and repair the piping.[12] Indeed, one of the reasons behind Viceroy Revillagigedo's extensive overhaul of the drainage system, and the implementation of new sanitation programs in the 1790s, such as the formalization of garbage collection and the criminalization of public defecation and dumping of animal waste, was to protect what he saw as compromised access to clean water. To him, it was as much a public health issue as it was a question of adequate city services.

Sometimes, residents offered to repair or rebuild public fountains themselves. In June 1787, Don Julian Lezaun, a resident of the barrio of San Pablo, wrote in disgust to the city council about the problems related to a broken fountain. He stated that it was no longer serviceable, and in fact, it attracted vagrants who committed acts "against God" and threatened the security of the neighborhood. Families also needed access to water to meet their daily needs, so he offered to tear down the old fountain and build a new one, with the financial support of his neighbors.[13] Numerous letters of support accompanied his petition, but it is unclear whether he and his fellow residents followed through with their plan.

Other fountains were in serious need of repair due to age as well as overuse. In September 1772, the priest of the church of Santa María de Redonda sent a letter to the cabildo informing them that the neighborhood fountain was in need of serious repairs. He argued that apart from the residents who lived adjacent to the church, people from surrounding neighborhoods also came in to use the water. Apparently, this small fountain was the only point of access to water for an extensive area. Consequently, heavy public demand was causing it to fall apart. By the time of the petition, it appears that the fountain had not been functioning as efficiently as it needed to. The cabildo agreed to assess the situation and eventually approved limited repairs.[14] However, these repairs did not solve the problem in the long term, for in 1794 alcalde mayor Don Antonio Valdes sent another petition to the city council, informing them that the fountain was again not working.[15] Unfortunately, the petition ends there.

Second, as both the tables and maps illustrate, the geographical scope of the water system was limited largely to the city center, in and around the historical traza boundaries. It is particularly obvious that well into the eighteenth century, major areas of the city, most notably the eastern neighborhoods and the Indian barrio of Santiago Tlateloco to the north, had no reliable and direct access to potable water. This is strikingly similar to the geographical issues that plagued other public works projects, namely sanitation and garbage collection, and drainage and paving programs. Since it makes sense to a certain extent that the state would want to protect its economic enterprises and felt a certain alliance with elite interests, it comes as no surprise that the public water system as it existed before Revillagigedo's tenure represents the fundamental imbalances between the city center, which housed business and the upper classes, and its outlying neighborhoods, dominated by the plebeian classes. Changes made under the leadership of Viceroy Revillagigedo ultimately did not make a significant difference in the lives of those in outlying barrios.

Clean Water for All or Just Some? Changes under Revillagigedo

Just as Viceroy Revillagigedo placed a new emphasis on garbage collection, public sanitation, drainage, and paving of public space, he also made tangible improvements to the public water system, extending the length of available piping, or cañerías, and constructing and refurbishing a number of fountains in the city. Ignacio Castera, who held the position of *Maestro Mayor de Arquitectura*, or master architect for the capital, took the lead in orchestrating and carrying out these improvements and took personal interest in the physical design of many of the fountains. This position also placed Castera in charge of all city-planning projects, including the design and upkeep of the city's public services, the establishment and maintenance of building codes, and the organization and renovation of public spaces.

In March 1790, José Antonio de Alzate Ramiréz, a respected architect and city planner, undertook a review of public water services. He identified the areas of the city where the scarcity of potable water was most acute. First, two fuentes públicas serviced the eastern districts of the city: one at the Puente de Fierro, and the other in the Plazuela de la Santísima Trinidad. The first one was dry, while the second had irregular water supply. In the southern part of the city, around the Iglesia de la Beatisima Trinidad, the public fountain was serviceable only part of the year. From February through June, the water was "scarce" according to residents, although Ramiréz gave no reason for this. It was in the southeastern barrios of San Sebastían and Santa Cruz, and the northern barrio of Santiago Tlateloco, however, where the water situation was the worst. In the case of Santa Cruz, it can be assumed that the fuentes públicas that had been constructed in the 1740s and 1750s were no longer functioning.[16] In the case of San Sebastían and Santiago Tlateloco, there were no public fountains at all.

Ramiréz was particularly concerned with the situation in Santiago Tlateloco. Residents of this area had to spend the bulk of their income on necessities such as food and housing. Because there was no local source of potable water, he argued, residents also had to spend large amounts of money on the most basic necessity of all—water.[17] This situation had a more profound effect in this area than in the city center, since Santiago Tlateloco was, for the most part, a poor neighborhood. Residents had to either purchase water from aguadores, or collect it themselves. The latter option not only took time away from income-earning tasks, but also put children, especially unaccompanied girls, in potentially dangerous situations.[18]

Ramiréz was not the first person to raise the issue of a lack of potable water in Santiago Tlateloco. Two years before his assessment, in October 1788, there had been discussions regarding the construction of public fountains and piping linking the principal plaza in Santiago Tlateloco to the city water supply, ensuring easier access to clean water for the neighborhood.[19] City planners had argued that this project was important for the health of residents in that area; because of the lack of potable water, many had resorted to drinking contaminated water from the surrounding canals and had gotten sick. They also had touted public safety as a reason for the project. Some people had moved out of the neighborhood because of the water situation, and they had left their homes to ruin, which in turn invited crime and violence into the area. Members of the city council had proposed a plan that would link a public fountain in the main square of Santiago Tlateloco directly to the Puente de Mariscala aqueduct, adjacent to the Alameda.[20] The line was to run 1,816 varas in length, at a cost of 7,688 pesos.[21] Apparently, however, this project was never undertaken. There is no other reference to it in the city council records, and Ramiréz makes no mention of it in his evaluation of 1790.

Ramiréz concluded his assessment with a list of suggestions to remedy the water situation. First, he argued that the ultimate source of water was not the problem. The springs from Santa Fé and Chapultepec produced more than enough water for the entire city population.[22] Rather, the problems were due to inadequacies in the existing distribution system. Despite his earlier concern for the residents of Santiago Tlateloco, he believed that the greatest problem did not exist there, but in the eastern districts of the city. His solution was not to expand piping and public fountains to the area, but rather to encourage aguadores to expand their services. Second, he stated that even areas that had good access to the city's water supply often ended up with dirty and undrinkable water, so there was a need to focus greater attention on cleaning and repairing existing piping.[23] Reaction to Ramiréz's report was not exactly positive. Bernardo Bonavilla, a member of the city council, responded by disputing that barrios such as Santiago Tlateloco and San Sebastían had depopulated because of the lack of public services. Rather, he argued that it was the nature of the Indian residents of these neighborhoods to be constantly on the move, primarily so that they could avoid their tribute payments. Rather than maintaining a fixed address, Indians were more likely to avoid areas of the city with large non-Indian populations, and search out neighborhoods where they could blend in. While agreeing with Ramiréz about the necessity of providing clean water, he believed that any widespread improvements to the distribution system would disrupt water service to a large part of the city's residents.[24]

The public works projects that followed would indeed reflect Ramiréz's assessment and Bonavilla's response. Even though there was a real need to expand the water system to areas outside the city center, as we will see, projects initiated by Revillagigedo focused on the traza and not on poorer, outlying barrios, such as Santiago Tlateloco, and thus did not make a dramatic difference in the areas of the city where change was most necessary. His plans included both the construction of new water piping as well as the construction and refurbishing of public fountains. Table 4.4 lists the location and dates of construction of new piping.

The construction and repair of fuentes públicas were the other focus points of Revillagigedo's plans for the public water system. Table 4.5 lists these projects, along with the nature of the construction and corresponding dates. As illustrated in Map 4.1, the geographical scope of the construction and repairs leads us to a few observations. First, despite Revillagigedo and Castera's best intentions, the newly refurbished water system still fell

Table 4.4 List of *Cañería* construction in Mexico City, 1792–1795

Location	Date
Calle de San Francisco	January 1792
Puente de los Gallos	April 1792
Calles de San Andrés, Santa Clara, y Tacuba	May 1792
Plaza de San Juan, Calle de la Victoria, Convento de San Juan	June 1792
Hospital de San Lázaro	August 1792
Calles de Santa Brígida, Puente del Espiritu Santo (to the corner of Calle del Angel)	October 1792
Calle de San Francisco to the corner of Calle de las Damas	January 1793
Calle de Santa Brígida	February 1793
La Plazuela de Santa Catarina	December 1794
Calle de San Lorenzo	August 1795
Calle de la Garrapata (near the Colegio de San Pedro y San Pablo)	October 1795

Source: AHCM, Aguas: *Cañerías*, Vol. 20, Exp. 57, 60, 67, 77–79, 82, 87, 95, 100, 103.

Table 4.5 Construction of *Fuentes Públicas* in Mexico City, 1793–1796

Location	Type of Construction	Date
Convento de Merced	New fountain	March 1793
Colegio de las Niñas	Old fountain torn down and replaced	March 1793
Plaza del Volador	New fountain	March 1793
Plaza Mayor	New fountains (4 in all)	April 1793
Plaza del Factor	Old fountain torn down and replaced	April 1793
Plaza de Santo Domingo	Old fountain torn down and replaced	April 1793
Plaza de Santa Catarina	New fountain	February 1794
Plaza de San Pablo	Old fountain torn down and replaced	1795
Plazuela de San Sebastían	Existing fountain repaired	April 1795
Parroquia de Santa María	Existing fountain repaired	April 1796

Source: AHCM, Aguas: *Fuentes Públicas*, Vol. 58, Exp. 32, 33, 37; AGN *Obras Públicas*, Vol 36, Exp. 18, fs. 404–420.

far short of solving the water problems for residents outside of the city center. Indeed, one of the key arguments that can be drawn from the statistical information is that the majority of spending and "repair" continued to focus on certain areas of the city: those populated by the wealthy, especially on Calles de San Francisco, San Andrés, Santa Clara, and Tacuba, and the "industrial" district of the city, south of the Alameda.[25] Economic interests in the city center were more important in the long run than remedying the material problems of poverty in outlying neighborhoods. No doubt the Bourbon state was more interested in the economic benefits it gained from colonialism rather than the welfare of the colonized, and it understood that economic security and protecting economic interests influenced the larger relationship between economic and social stability. The potentially destabilizing effects of a lack of public services, especially access to clean water, did not seem to capture the concern the city leaders quite as much as maintaining its economic agenda.

The northern barrio of Santiago Tlateloco, along with poorer eastern and southern neighborhoods, continued to suffer from a lack of clean, affordable water well after the end of Revillagigedo's term in office. In a letter to the viceroy in April 1797, Balthasar Ladrones de Guevara, argued that if bread and meat, two important necessities in the lives of residents of Mexico City, received so much attention from the government, then water (and access to it), should be equally, if not more, important. He noticed that many days public fountains, especially those serving the poor, supplied little to no water. Buying water

Map 4.1 Location of *Cañerías* and *Fuentes Públicas* built by Viceroy Revillagigedo.

continued to put an additional economic stress on an already precarious standard of living.[26]

Despite renovations in 1795, chronic problems continued with the public fountain in the Plazuela de San Sebastián. In April 1796, Castera received complaints, informing him that the fountain was again lacking water. His subsequent investigation showed that the piping supplying the fountain was broken and he called for new construction at a cost of 1,650 pesos.[27] It is unlikely, however, that these repairs were undertaken, as another complaint followed exactly one year later, in April 1797. Water still was not accessible from the fountain, but at this point, there was no mention of any subsequent repairs.[28]

A third complaint was filed in 1799, this time to the head of the city's water projects, or *juez de cañerías*.[29] In it, residents expressed their frustration that while the *pila* (fountain) originally had been built to serve the public, it had not functioned for a considerable amount of time, causing grave problems for the families who lived there. It was a poor neighborhood, so working parents often had to send their children to find water, sometimes quite a distance from their homes, with unfortunate consequences. In one case, a vagrant raped a young girl. The police often caught boys getting into mischief, sometimes quite serious, such as gambling. The community argued that it was not right that they should have to suffer such grave dangers just to gain access to water, and felt the city government should provide this necessity to them.[30] Unfortunately, the document ends there, so we do not know the consequences of this petition. However, the following year, in December 1800, the fountain received some minor repairs, at a cost of 290 pesos. Don Francisco Saenz de Escobosa, one of the members of the cabildo that year, wrote that the repairs to the fountain were especially important since this was a relatively poor neighborhood, and it was difficult for its residents to afford purchase of water from sources outside the area. He believed that providing benefits to the public would lead to creation of happy supporters of the state.[31]

San Sebastián was not the only poor neighborhood complaining about its situation. In 1800, one of the priests from the eastern barrio of Santa Cruz wrote about the lack of water in the fuente pública in the Plazuela de Santísima Trinidad y Santa Cruz. He argued that people in his parish spent so much time trying to acquire water from other areas that it cut into time that needed to be spent working. Those who could not possibly find time away from work had to hire someone, which often tripled the cost of the water. According to him, even the baptismal fountain inside the church had dirty water. Consequently, many people got sick from drinking contaminated water, and some even died.[32] In addition, according to the priest, an even more serious problem existed with this public fountain. Since it was not serviceable, it attracted numerous vagrants and other idle and worthless individuals, who often fought with each other, gambled, verbally assaulted women, and generally added a perverse and immoral element to the neighborhood.[33] Besides the health and economic issues connected to a lack of water, the priest's concerns extended to the safety, security, and peace of the neighborhood residents he ministered. According to a general listing from the city council records, a fountain was built in the plaza in 1805; it is unclear, however, whether this was merely a repair to an existing fountain, or the construction of one entirely new.[34]

Residents in the barrio of la Palma reported similar problems. The parish priest asked for repairs to the public fountain, as water was a necessity for those who lived there. Just because it was a poorer neighborhood, he argued, it did not mean that residents there should go without clean water. He went on to point out that Viceroy Revillagigedo had done many wonderful things for the city and made many important reforms: completing new public projects that were of great use to residents; establishing a good police force, as well as justice administration; and making the city a nicer place to live. So then, he concluded, why should the poor in his neighborhood also not benefit from these improvements?[35] We do not know, however, what became of his petition.

Even wealthier areas of this city, those that had benefited most directly from Revillagigedo's programs, were not immune to difficulties in maintaining water supplies. In April 1797, Manuel Velazquez de León stated that three of the four public fountains built in the Plaza Mayor four years earlier were now dry.[36] The city council recognized that the public was very upset over this. After all, the Plaza Mayor represented the heart of the city and had undergone major renovations during Revillagigedo's tenure. Close to 5,000 pesos had been spent on constructing these fountains. Built in a massive, symmetrical, and austere style, they were the ultimate physical representation of the new Bourbon order, efficiency, and attention to material improvement. Any faults existing in the Plaza Mayor reflected poorly on the organization and design of the city as a whole. Indeed, the cabildo viewed the dry fountains in the Plaza Mayor as indicative of larger citywide deficiencies in the public water supply.[37]

New Regulations for Public Baths

Besides providing potable water for city residents, the public water system also supplied water for the many bathhouses throughout the city. Historically, bathing had been an important ritual to the Mexica before the arrival of the Spanish. From the emperor down, residents of Tenochtitlan were encouraged to bathe daily. However, when the Spanish first encountered Native American populations in the sixteenth century, they were convinced that frequent bathing contributed to the massive smallpox deaths occurring among indigenous peoples. From their experiences during the *Reconquista*, Spaniards identified all bathing as a ritual preceding a Muslim's act of worship.[38] In addition to the prohibitions on all-over bathing that were specific to the Iberian Peninsula, Europeans generally held that dousing the body in water opened the pores to evil forces, which might come in and upset the balance of the four humors, causing illness or death.[39]

Mexica populations at the time of the Spanish conquest, however, were accustomed to bathing quite often.[40] The highest levels of Mexica society, starting with the emperor, supported this practice. For example, Moctezuma II, head of the empire when the Spanish first arrived in 1519, was known to bathe up to four times a day, and he encouraged daily bathing among the rest of the population.[41] While the homes of the Mexica nobility and middle classes were constructed with private bathing quarters, bathhouses were established throughout the imperial capital for the poorer classes.[42] Ample access to water through the city's extensive public water works, dominated by two large clay-piped aqueducts, guaranteed that citizens of Tenochtitlan would continue to enjoy their daily baths.[43] Besides traditional bathing, the Mexica were also particularly fond of steam baths and saunas, and they enjoyed the typical Mexica steam bath, or *temazcal*, for a variety of different reasons: ritual purification, general hygiene, or for relaxation. In that sense, steam baths were important in maintaining not only physical health, but mental health as well. The Mexica considered these baths as especially important rituals for soldiers, pregnant women, and new mothers, for their relaxing effects, as well as those who suffered from fevers and venomous insect and snakebites. It was believed that taking a steam bath would "sweat out" the dangerous poisons and toxins that threatened the victim's health.[44]

Personal hygiene also went beyond the limits of bathing. The Mexica had concoctions, such as a crude toothpaste derived from wood ashes and honey to treat halitosis, and a body deodorant made from pulverized animal bones, the juice of herbs containing antiseptic properties, and "sweet-smelling" flowers.[45] Unlike their European counterparts, who typically masked body odor with powders and perfumes when available, the Mexica population took pride in their physical appearance, and rather than trying to hide offensive body odor, took great pains to alleviate it in the first place. Consistent and thorough personal hygiene practices also contributed to an extremely low occurrence of epidemic disease within the Mexica Empire. This changed, however, with the arrival of Spanish troops and settlers and their diseases in the sixteenth century.

In the context of initial smallpox outbreaks in Mexico City in the 1520s, Spaniards interpreted Indians who washed their infected bodies in hot or cold water as appealing to the healing powers of a pagan god. Justly punished by the Christian deity, these bathers could expect to die in large numbers.[46] Fully convinced of the evilness of bathing, the Spanish were ruthless in their attempts to stamp it out. The European preference for infrequent bathing continued into the eighteenth century. The lack of adequate water systems in colonial Mexico City probably also discouraged daily bathing, as many residents of the viceregal capital had poor access to water. They either had to buy it, which proved to be expensive for some, or carry it away from one of the city's public fountains. Some resorted to bathing in public in city canals, a practice that colonial officials found particularly offensive and potentially dangerous, and an impetus to more serious social disorder. Although the Spanish did not follow the same rigor as their indigenous counterparts when it came to personal hygiene, bathhouses nevertheless existed in Mexico City to meet the needs of residents. Since most well-off families in the capital had connections to the public water system constructed in their homes, they could bathe at home. Public bathhouses, therefore, generally served the poorer casta and Indian populations in the city.

Bathhouses also gained a reputation, in part because of prevailing elite perceptions regarding the class of people they served. Various urban sectors, including the church, considered bathhouses the site of scandalous activities: *temascaleros*, the men who brought water into the baths, lingering too long where the women bathed; men and women bathing together; lounging around naked or half dressed; taking meals together; and consuming large quantities of pulque. Just as with elite perceptions regarding the connections between lower classes and crime, the bathhouses were perceived to be the sites of much immoral and dangerous activity because the individuals they served, members of the plebeian class, were inherently so. Elites blamed the lower classes for most of the problems that befell the city: disposing of garbage in city streets, canals, and fountains; the commonplace practice of public defecation and urination; public drunkenness; sexual indiscretions, and the variety of criminal activities that accompanied all of the above. Sexual indiscretions in the public baths were of special concern.

The investigation of Baño del Padre Garrido, in the southeastern part of the city, illustrates some of the most common problems associated with the public baths. In February 1793, Don José Molina, a resident of the neighborhood, testified that when he frequented the bathhouse, he encountered naked women, as well as women and men bathing together, while consuming large quantities of alcohol. This was particularly bothersome to him, as he had no private bath in his home; he used this bathhouse out of necessity, not as a luxury, and thus felt he should not have to encounter such embarrassing and immoral behavior.[47] Apparently, city officials agreed with Molina and closed down the bathhouse to resolve these "disorders." The proprietors, Lorenzo Francisco Antonio, Indian *tributario*, and his wife, María Dioncia Gertrudis Gonzales, mestiza, contradicted Molina's testimony, stating that men were present, but none had taken baths with the women there. Gertrudis also added that on occasion men and women showed up and had lunch together, but this did not extend into the baths, and after lunch the men left. It seems their testimony was not convincing enough. Although there is no record of Gertrudis receiving a punishment, the city fined Lorenzo eight days' labor on a public works project.[48]

In a frontal attack against those who ran public baths, as well as those who frequented them, Revillagigedo introduced a series of regulations on August 21, 1793, aimed at diminishing the social and physical disorder accompanying bathhouses. He argued that the most scandalous behavior associated with the baths was the common practice of men and women bathing together. Therefore, bathhouses had to provide separate quarters for men and women, to be clearly labeled and strictly enforced. The construction of bathhouses must emphasize this separateness. Construction of walls was to physically divide men and women, hiding them from each other's view and making communication between them impossible. Owners were to provide separate dressing areas as well. If a proprietor wanted to include a room for poorer customers to wash their clothes—as was a common custom in many bathhouses—it must be separate from the baths. Revillagigedo instructed that no more than twenty-four licensed bathhouses were to operate in the city at any one time, twelve for women, and twelve for men. Those choosing to operate a bathhouse without an official license, failing to follow the proper channels when it came to obtaining a license or refusing to comply with occasional inspections faced a fine of twenty-five pesos. Those who allowed men and women to bathe together received fines of twenty-five pesos for the first offense, fifty pesos for the second, and for a third offense, whatever penalty seemed just for the individual involved. Patrons who remained naked while washing clothes faced fines of twelve pesos. Finally, those individuals who recklessly entered bathhouses to cause trouble and harass those inside faced twenty-five lashes, and a month's labor on public works projects. City government fined proprietors who failed to curtail this type of activity fifty pesos.[49] The severity of the punishment for general "disorder" may have represented the seriousness with which colonial officials regarded this type of activity. It is another good example of how the state used corporal punishment as a corrective tool, one used to rehabilitate members of society who did not fit the Bourbon mold of order, modesty, efficiency, and productivity.

There were also regulations on the construction of bathhouses, apart from keeping men and women separate. To protect the surrounding neighborhood, wastewater must be disposed of completely. Piping leading to the public drainage system was to remain operational; bathhouse owners could not dump wastewater directly into the street; and they were to construct latrines away from the streets and with proper ventilation to avoid odors. Bathhouses must be lit up completely at night, and doors must remain closed and locked after hours of operation. Failure to observe these regulations would result in a fine of twelve pesos. As Revillagigedo argued, all these orders existed as an attempt to guarantee safety and security for the neighborhoods housing public bathhouses.[50] Whether owners and patrons followed these regulations is difficult to ascertain, as the documentation regarding public baths is sketchy at best for this period. Nevertheless, the very introduction of regulations points to the fact that city leaders viewed the bathhouses as sites of social disorder, especially considering those that they served (or perhaps because of them). Bathhouse reform thus became part of the larger programs established by Revillagigedo to transform the city into an urban spatial representation of order and control.

Concluding Thoughts

Documentation concerning the public water system drops off almost entirely after 1805, so it is difficult to understand what challenges city officials faced in the waning years of colonial rule. However, a number of important conclusions may be gleaned from this examination of the public water systems of late eighteenth-century Mexico City. First, like all the other sanitation and public works projects, the renovations done to the public water system concentrated heavily on the urban center at the expense of the poorer neighborhoods that surrounded it. Certainly, economic activities demanding a steady supply of water had guaranteed access to it. Elites secured access through their personal wealth, which allowed them to live in the urban center, as well as to construct private water lines and fountains within their residences. In many ways, the priorities in renovating the public water system in the capital reflected the class and race hierarchies that underlie colonial society. Areas demonstrating the greatest need for new connections to the public water supply, especially Santiago Tlateloco, never saw those needs fulfilled. Others, such as San Sebastián, while initially receiving help from Revillagigedo, struggled in the years that followed and suffered from the aftereffects of seemingly shoddy work and incomplete repairs.

The discrimination experienced by poorer residents went beyond insufficient access to potable water. The lack of access to water took a heavy economic toll on them since they oftentimes had no other option but to purchase water at inflated prices. They put their children in potentially dangerous situations when they sent them out to collect water. They compromised their health when they drank dirty and polluted water. Despite the fact that improved access to water, probably the most promise for improving the health of city residents, that justification seemed to affect only a certain segment of colonial society, as reflected in the limited geographical and class-specific scope of the project itself.

Finally, just as with attempts to curb public defecation, as well as the social problems that inhabited the Plaza Mayor and its market before the establishment of the Volador, new plans for improving the public water system had elements of social control and safety woven in. The repair of inoperable fountains served as part of a full frontal attack on the city's poor, since they were popular sites for vagrants and the unemployed to congregate. City leaders wished to curb this use by reestablishing the original purpose of these fountains, as places where people could get water. Reforms on the public baths were another attempt by Revillagigedo to limit the social and physical disorder that these sites represented. Indeed, when the voices of the urban poor were part of the discussions about the existing public water system, it was interpreted in a negative fashion. Either they complained because of insufficient or nonexistent access to water in their neighborhoods, or they were the protagonists in perpetuating the horrible and disorderly activities that elites so closely associated with them.

CHAPTER FIVE

Restoring Order Out of Chaos: Garbage Collection in Theory and Practice

In 1807, Don Mariano Colasso, who lived in the southwestern part of the city, on Calle de Mesones at the corner of del Tompiate, was fined twelve reales for dumping human waste into the street. When asked why he continued with such activity, even though there were public laws against it, he replied that the house in which he lived did not have a latrine or a rubbish pit that he and his neighbors could use to contain their waste. Besides, he argued, as long as he could remember, residents of the city always left garbage in the street. This was part of popular custom, unchallenged by the residents of the viceregal capital. For him, the fine was a mere inconvenience that would not deter him from continuing to use public space as his personal dumping grounds.[1]

The case of Don Mariano points to the conflict that existed between residents of Mexico City and city leaders regarding the disposal of garbage, one which perplexed political leaders when it came to developing coherent and enforceable sanitation programs. Local unwillingness to cooperate with new sanitation plans emphasized the fact that there were differing views and perceptions within late colonial urban society as to what constituted "cleanliness and order." Elites, particularly state agents like Viceroy Revillagigedo, tried to push their vision of sanitation through local programs designed to eliminate what they considered polluting behavior. They viewed the dumping of garbage and human waste, along with the practice of public defecation, as threatening both the order and stability of Mexico City on a number of levels. Therefore, improving sanitation and hygienic practices did not only encourage the type of modesty that went hand in hand with civilized society, but was necessary to reestablish the notion of Bourbon self-control and discipline in an urban population considered by city leaders as unruly and undisciplined. Although aesthetic and health issues were important benefits of these programs, elites wanted to mold the activities of residents to their ideas of what constituted proper, namely civilized, behavior.

A key impediment to the success of new sanitation programs rested with city residents themselves, and how they both understood and classified space. Many defined the streets as the domain of the public. The idea of having private space in which to retreat was not the reality for the majority. As discussed earlier, only the extremely wealthy could afford the luxury of privacy, or had the ability to separate themselves from the filth everybody faced on a daily basis. Most other residents rented small, cramped rooms adjacent to the street, built rudimentary structures wherever they could find space, or had no permanent residence at all, simply living in the streets themselves.[2] In most cases, the streets were simply an extension of personal living space. Many perceived plans to alter this space, and regulations on its use, as state intrusion into their private activities. At best, city residents reacted with indifference to state programs supposedly implemented on their behalf. As will be seen in the examples of a local tavern, el Águila, and the use of alleyways to dump garbage, residents often defined space in ways that made most sense to them and met their practical needs. Indeed, when examining the lack of enthusiasm for state-sponsored sanitation reforms, it is important to recognize tensions that emerged over issues of autonomy and control. Many urban residents favored traditional definitions and uses of public space, uses of their own design, which allowed them to claim a sense of control and agency in their daily lives. This was especially important given the relative lack of control that most residents of late colonial Mexico City had, in terms of economic opportunities, and the realities of race, class, and gender discrimination.

While on the surface the goals of sanitation reform were meant to create a more healthful city and populous, part of the dynamic of new sanitation regulations underwritten by men like Viceroy Revillagigedo included punishments for breaking the "rules"; mechanisms put into place to criminalize certain polluting behaviors, and thus forcing residents through fear to comply to new state regulations on their daily activities. These punishments, infused with racial and class assumptions, were designed to deter citizens from both dumping garbage and defecating in the streets. Using monetary fines for haphazard dumping practices, and corporal punishment for the more egregious activity of public defecation, city leaders made it clear that they connected different urban groups to various behaviors. Race and class were also woven, if indirectly, into where sanitation reforms were carried out. The scope of city programs often was limited to the central areas of the city, especially wealthier neighborhoods. The poorer outskirts, such as the Indian barrio of Santiago Tlatelolco, and the southern and eastern neighborhoods of the city, were never the focus of systematic campaigns to rid the streets of waste. In fact, they became the areas of the city where urban planners placed garbage dumps to contain waste. Neighborhoods dominated by the urban poor, by Indians and mestizos, blacks and mulatos, bore the brunt of Mexico City's sanitation problems; not only did they lack the same kind of sanitation systems as the city center, they collectively became the city's dumps. Indeed, this aspect of urban renewal—the collection and containment of waste—prioritized beauty and convenience, rather than utility and the consequences of poverty. The groups in colonial society who needed relief the most, the urban poor, did not receive it.[3] The exceptions to this, of course, were epidemic crises, but even these were relatively short-lived periods. Completely absent from the discussion and debate about the causes and effects of urban pollution was a consideration of the role of poverty in the lives of the majority of the urban population; the planning surrounding the development of urban sanitation programs did not inspire city leaders to examine how poverty perpetuated the presence of pollution in the daily lives of poorer residents. In fact, many within the elite circles of colonial society argued that it was the conscious actions of the poor, and not the consequences of poverty, that created urban squalor and decay.

Revillagigedo's programs, which were designed to contain and eradicate garbage and waste from the streets, is yet another example of the struggle in which elites and the popular classes engaged over definition, use, and control of public space, as well as the struggle between old customs and new ideas. "Enlightened" elites viewed the streets as public space that was in disarray and the garbage and filth, along with the diseases they perpetuated, represented the masses of "traditional" poor who populated the city. Elite desires to pull Mexico City into the modern era included efforts to "civilize" the masses. This process, however, went beyond the political, economic, and even cultural spheres. It also included a refinement of manners and the setting of standards as to what some considered appropriate public behavior. Executing private acts in public, such as urinating and defecating, other "polluting" activities such as the dumping garbage in public space, bathing in public fountains, sleeping in streets, markets and abandoned structures, public drunkenness, and public nudity were the antithesis of civilized behavior. Seen as such, these acts constantly challenged elite sensibilities, and they considered these a threat to molding Mexico City into an urban milieu exemplifying beauty, hygiene, safety, efficiency, order, and reason.[4] In a broader sense, this focus on conscious actions as driving the problem of urban filth and decay served as a symbolic proxy for elite anxieties over the socioeconomic conditions of the city. While Mexico City had always had its fair share of vagrants and economically disadvantaged since the arrival of the Spanish in 1519, economic tensions in the viceregal capital increased dramatically throughout the eighteenth century, as more and more migrants from the countryside fled to the city seeking economic opportunities. Physically, the city infrastructure was unable to deal with this onslaught, and elites watched in horror and disgust as they saw their environment collapse under the weight of the urban masses.

Earlier studies of class interaction in colonial Mexico City have focused on elite attempts to control the behaviors and activities of the poorer classes, such as their work habits, places of residence, religious celebrations, street diversions, and consumption of alcohol. However, evidence about urban planning in colonial Mexico City shows that elites, such as Revillagigedo, did not stop there. More mundane activities, such as the dumping of garbage and bodily waste, also became sites of struggle between elites and the urban lower classes. Elites used the streets as a stage in which to promote their agenda of a clean, ordered, and rational world. Unfortunately, for them, the urban poor understood order and rationality differently from their wealthy counterparts. As Don Mariano pointed out at the beginning of this chapter, their daily realities and customs, rather than threats from the state, shaped their attitudes toward public sanitation.

Early Attempts at Sanitation Reform

State attempts at establishing sanitation controls in the city during the colonial period were fairly limited, both in scope and in funding, and it was not until the mid-eighteenth century that more consolidated attempts at dealing with increasing urban sanitation problems came into focus.[5] However, city leaders faced tough challenges with this task. Throughout the colonial period, residents of Mexico City, regardless of their social standing, used the streets as their personal toilets and continued the commonplace practice of dumping garbage in public spaces. In November 1758, cabildo discussions regarding the state of cleanliness in the city focused on the many deficiencies that existed. Residents generally disregarded ordinances passed in the 1740s, in an attempt to regulate public cleanliness. Of particular concern was the poor state of paving in the city's main thoroughfares. This problem made it difficult for residents to get around the city, to conduct their daily business, and generally caused many inconveniences. As a result, the cabildo and city planners advocated new paving projects, calling not only for new paving to be put in place, but also to slope streets slightly to allow waters to drain away properly when necessary.[6] These new public works projects would help to rid the city streets of their "deformities," providing order, beauty, and convenience in their place.[7] Waste disposal measures, however, were not part of this plan.

Sanitation came up again in February, 1762, when Don Pedro Fermín Mendinueta, *corregidor* (council member) of Mexico City, and Don Joseph de Gorraez, Don Luis de Monroy, and Don Mariano Malo, all deputies of the *Junta de Policía*, issued public orders addressing cleaning the city. They reported large amounts of garbage littering city streets, causing localized flooding, and compromising the daily activities of city residents. All property owners were required to clean up the garbage within fifteen days of publication of the orders, with special attention paid to the following occupations: butchers, bakers, meat sellers, factory owners, tanners, blacksmiths, and general store owners, whose activities the Junta de Policía viewed as particularly careless due to the polluting nature of the waste they produced.[8] Indian garbage collectors were also lumped into this group, accused of collecting garbage and excrement from homes in one neighborhood, and dumping it in the streets of another, rather than taking it to specified public dumpsites. The fine for failure to adhere to the new regulations was six pesos. Indians and servants of all racial backgrounds who were caught dumping garbage into the streets faced twenty-five lashes rather than a monetary fine.[9] This was probably a reflection of the fact that many Indians and domestic workers in Mexico City were poor, and most likely did not have the cash resources to pay such a fine; physical punishment was therefore seen as a more appropriate deterrent for this particular group.

The use of corporal punishment for Indians who broke the new sanitation laws also points to larger connections between Indians and social disorder. Elites often connected disorderly behavior, in this case the illegal dumping of garbage, with lower-class groups, including Indians, whom they described as lazy, immoral, and lacking in reason and self-discipline. The types of punishments, therefore, which the state preferred in dealing with the urban poor aimed at changing their behavior. Since monetary fines were not realistic given the lack of income among the poor, physical punishments were the only logical, and realistic, alternative. In the case of the new sanitation laws discussed earlier, the public humiliation connected with the twenty-five lashes was supposed to be enough to change behavior.

Apparently, these regulations, and the punishments connected to them, did little to improve sanitation conditions in the viceregal capital. In October 1769, Viceroy Carlos Francisco de Croix called for a citywide evaluation. The viceroy also issued his own plans on how to remedy the city's sanitation problems. He argued that older ordinances aimed at "eliminating the abuses by city residents that resulted in the deformity of the city" were of little success, and that the continued practice of dumping garbage in the streets resulted in "the production of rotting air, which altered the blood, causing an imbalance in the humors of the body and resulting in bad health."[10] Some of his solutions required property owners to construct latrines, stiff fines for those who dumped garbage or excrement in city streets and canals, prohibitions against washing clothes in public fountains, and controls over various professions well known to dump trash in and around their businesses.[11] He also argued that abandoned buildings throughout the city were popular sites for dumping garbage, and he gave owners six months to fix any problems associated with their properties.[12] Enforcing these regulations must have proven difficult, especially those regarding the dumping of bodily waste, as the city council republished some of the laws in 1771.[13]

Another evaluation in 1773 followed the one in 1769, with more specific details on how to go about cleaning up some of the worst-off areas. The cabildo planned to set aside 8,000 pesos per year for street cleaning. Twenty-eight specially designed carts, using indigenous drivers, collected waste, at least as a temporary solution until city planners established a more permanent workforce.[14] In the past, convicts had been the more popular choice for the onerous job of collecting garbage and human waste, but in 1771, Viceroy José de Galvez suggested that Indians from the two barrios of San Juan and Santiago Tlatelolco provide the labor for this purpose. Until 1737, a portion of Indians annual tribute had been set aside for cleaning the city's canals. That same year, however, a devastating smallpox epidemic broke out in the city, and officials diverted monies designated for sanitation projects elsewhere. After the epidemic subsided, officials never reinstated the tribute monies used for public cleaning. Galvez believed that since tribute monies no longer funded the cleaning of canals, Indians should contribute their labor instead.[15]

Despite the details contained in the 1773 plans, many complaints arose over the failures of the program. First, residents throughout the city described street cleaners as lazy, providing irregular service at best. Whether this was a realistic evaluation of Indian workers or merely a reflection of racial stereotypes is difficult to ascertain. Certainly, it would not be surprising if Indian garbage collectors were unwilling to do the work, given the nature of the job. Second, garbage and waste from various businesses, workshops, and stores continued to pile up in the streets, despite existing regulations aimed at alleviating the practice. The money and labor earmarked for city cleaning were simply inadequate for the scope of the problem. Finally, it seemed that the sanitation ordinances of 1773 were too narrow in scope. Besides the collection of garbage, other problems that were in dire need of attention included the washing of clothes and animals in public fountains, compromising the clean water supply.[16]

When it appeared that local political institutions failed to improve Mexico City's sanitation problems, private individuals were keen to offer their advice and ideas. In 1776, Pedro Josef Cortez wrote to the city council, arguing that despite the various proclamations, plans, and attempts by different institutions to combat the deficiencies in urban sanitation, they never implemented a program to clean the streets of Mexico City. He himself submitted a proposal to the city council, which called for both the construction of structures where people could dump garbage and excrement, as well as the collection and transportation of the waste to the city's outskirts. In his plan, Cortez would oversee both programs. To pay for the cost of building the dumpsites, as well as providing for the carts, mules, and personnel for garbage collection, he proposed a tax of one real on each household in the city. He foresaw four potential benefits of his proposed system. First, improvements in drainage, as trash would no longer block sewers and canals. Second, the tiles and cobblestones used to pave streets would last longer. Third, there would be aesthetic improvements; the "general convenience and brightness" of the city would be enhanced. Finally, these improvements would protect residents from sicknesses that resulted from the decay of materials such as animal carcasses and human waste. Such illnesses, Cortez emphasized, were very common in the city.[17] Unfortunately, for Cortez, the cabildo rejected his plan, citing already existing city ordinances dealing with standing garbage and body waste. The problem, according to them, was not the lack of a citywide sanitation program, but rather compliance with laws that already existed.[18]

Plans to clean the capital resurfaced once again, when in 1779 a major smallpox epidemic broke out in Mexico City, renewing concern over provisions to improve sanitation services. While the cabildo focused its attention on providing medical instruction through published pamphlets on the nature and treatment of smallpox and on how to avoid succumbing to the disease, the Junta de Policía argued that cleaning rotting piles of garbage off city streets was one possible remedy for the propagation of the virus.[19] They believed that money devoted to public works projects should not be redirected into other emergency measures to deal with the epidemic.[20] City officials and the medical community both agreed that the care of epidemic victims, many of whom were poor, was best handled by religious institutions and wealthy individuals, but the larger program of first controlling the spread of epidemics and later of eradicating disease from the city was best served by state sanitation and public works projects aimed at cleaning up the urban environment. The notion that alleviating poverty might also be an important step in helping people avoid infection in the first place seemed lost in the larger debates over how to fund epidemic relief.

In the wake of the 1779 epidemic, the Junta de Policía once again elaborated on plans to deal with the city's sanitation problems, arguing that keeping the urban environment clean would help in controlling disease and discouraging the outbreak of epidemics. Members stated that while all areas of the city suffered from the disorder of standing garbage, the traza area demanded attention and funds first. Calle de San Francisco, along with the Plaza de San Francisco, Callejón de la Condesa, and Calle de Canoa were in immediate need of cleaning and repair.[21] In 1780, these were very wealthy areas of the city, and that special attention should be devoted to them reveals perhaps a particular bias in the implementation of sanitation programs. City planners devoted the most comprehensive plans, as well as the most money, on the city center, where the wealthy of colonial society lived. However, the emphasis on these particular urban spaces also belies the reality that it was in these areas that you had the most direct, and daily, interaction between the city's wealthy and the city's poor. It was in this context that wealthy residents came face to face with what they called the "polluting activity of the poor," and where the sharp reality of poverty and decay (versus their wealth and splendor) was painfully, and dangerously, understood. While all areas of the city reflected concerns about the destabilizing nature of vagrants and the impoverished, they took on an elevated urgency within the traza.

For these very reasons, outlying neighborhoods and districts of the city rarely were included in citywide plans.[22] Nevertheless, in 1780, plans called for the use of forty cleaning cars to canvas the city from 6 a.m. to 12 noon, and again from 2 p.m. to 6 p.m. The Junta also argued that the traditional ways of classifying and using public spaces were no longer acceptable, namely the dumping of garbage into the city streets, and that city residents must adopt new attitudes regarding personal hygiene.[23] Placing the blame for urban pollution on city residents, rather than deficiencies in state programs, made it easier for institutions such as the Junta de Policía to obscure the failures and inadequacies of the system. It absolved state agencies from providing a solution; if residents could be more responsible and change their "traditional" way of doing things, sanitation problems would not be so severe. However, general indifference to new regulations, coupled with continued adherence to popular custom regarding personal and public hygiene, represented the main obstacles to the success of state legislation aimed at alleviating sanitation problems in Mexico City.

Indeed, the system had its failures and inadequacies, as plans to clean up garbage in the city up to the late eighteenth century were haphazard at best. While it seems apparent that city leaders understood the scope of the problem, as well as the health hazards it posed, effective plans never came to fruition. Those put in place were clearly insufficient; programs were too narrow in scope and poorly funded, and enforcing regulations proved difficult. The latter was of particular concern. The fact that programs designed to clean up the city did not make a perceptible dent in the problem reveals two particular problems: state agents lacked the legitimacy or political influence to carry out their plans, and common practices of dumping waste in city streets were deeply entrenched in the behaviors of some city residents. While institutions such as the Junta de Policía tried to shift the blame over to the actions of city residents, it was unrealistic to expect decades of common practices to change overnight. More concerted efforts at forcing new policy on city residents developed with the arrival of Viceroy Revillagigedo in 1789.

The Plans of Viceroy Revillagigedo

Significant changes to Mexico City's sanitation programs came with the tenure of Revillagigedo. For perhaps the first time, the capital had a well-conceived and multifaceted plan for public sanitation. Revillagigedo envisioned a number of benefits attached to improved sanitation: aesthetic improvements, increasing the order and symmetry of public space, improving the living conditions of city residents, and limiting the presence of disease. On August 31, 1790, he issued a fourteen point royal decree (*bando*) that laid out rules for public cleanliness and order. Included in the decree were regulations regarding the dumping and collection of garbage, stating that they were not only for the comfort and convenience of city residents, but also to protect their health. The first set of instructions dealt with the collection of garbage and waste. Garbage collection happened daily, even on festival days, from one hour before sunrise to one hour after sunset, with separate cars for garbage and human waste. Residents were instructed to set out garbage by 7 a.m. (from October 1 to February 28) and 6 a.m. (from March 1 to September 30), and only on Wednesdays and Saturdays; all other times it was to remain within the residence. Rather than dumping garbage in piles in front of their homes, people were to use city-designated receptacles. Cleaning carts would be equipped with bells, so that residents would know in advance of their arrival, and those who impeded the collection of garbage faced fines of twelve reales for the first offense, twenty-four for the second, and thirty-six for the third.[24] Revillagigedo also wanted to institute plans to carry systematically the city's garbage well beyond the guardhouses, or *garitas* that ringed the city and represented its defacto boundaries. Unfortunately, city officials did not institute this plan, as it was too difficult due to the poor condition of roads outside the city, and the long distances mule trains would have to travel daily to make the plan effective.[25]

Live animals and animal carcasses contributed to the city's garbage, and Revillagigedo devoted specific points in his instructions to this issue. First, residents could not leave dead animals in the streets to rot; rather they were to notify the proper authorities within twelve hours so that prompt removal could take place. Second, owners who let their animals roam freely and dirty the streets faced a fine of ten pesos for the first offense, twenty for the second, and thirty for the third.[26] This second regulation aimed especially at people who let their dogs run wild. Besides the feces that dogs left in their wake, rabies was a significant health concern at this time, and these rules were an attempt to bring the disease under control.[27]

The difference between Revillagigedo's plan and the ones that preceded it had to do with the level of detail. Revillagigedo wrote in very specific terms about how people were to dispose of garbage and its collection. He also differentiated between regular garbage, such a food scraps, and the more onerous problem of human and animal waste, as well as giving special instructions to the disposal of trash from the variety of businesses that made up the city's economy. While many of his predecessors focused on the need for sanitation controls, Revillagigedo actually put this vision into practice. Regulations singled out two groups in particular for their "polluting behavior." The first were butchers. Butchers had faced the wrath of colonial officials before: bandos in 1756 and 1775 discussed the numerous problems that were caused by their activities, including the illicit selling of meat, the dumping of carcasses in streets and canals, and the dumping of animal wastes from butchering (including blood) in sewage gutters and canals. Neighbors often brought complaints against butchers; the rotting flesh not only smelled bad, but was also a breeding ground for bacteria. Don Victoriano de Rivero, whose neighbor was a pig butcher, complained that the rotting carcasses left in the street made his home uninhabitable, due to the unbearable stench.[28] When the preferred dumping grounds were canals, these practices impacted the surrounding water supply, blocking the canals used to carry wastewater out of the city, and causing adjacent streets and buildings to flood. On February 17, 1792, Revillagigedo seized on early ordinances against butchers and expanded them, arguing that a reinstating of these regulations was necessary to eliminate the illnesses butcher's random dumping caused, as well as to bring order back to the streets. His tone in the document seems to be one of anger, especially at the offenders who so cavalierly compromised the health of their neighbors through their disorderly activities. He called for eliminating such dumping, as well as requiring butchers to control their animals and keep them from wandering the streets and other public places.[29] Stiff fines accompanied these offenses: fifty pesos for each time the law was broken.[30]

Similar to the discourse surrounding butchers, city leaders accused other plebeians who dirtied the streets and plazas of the city on compromising the health of their fellow residents through their disgusting behavior. For a city with a large homeless population, it should not be surprising that peeing and defecating in the streets was a common practice. Elites, however, viewed this public display of an intimately private activity as the ultimate in disorderly behavior. The outward and casual manner in which many of the lower classes treated their bodily functions marked them as less civilized in the eyes of elites, and the willingness to not only relieve oneself in public, but also accept it as common behavior, challenged elite cultural norms and divisions between public and private space and socially acceptable behavior.[31] In a certain sense, this clash of cultures provided a daily reminder to wealthier residents of what they were up against in bringing order and propriety back in again. Of course, the health hazards this activity created were also reasons elites cited when explaining how public urination and defecation contributed to social disorder. Bodily wastes, left lying in the streets, were breeding grounds for the stench that medical professionals believed encouraged the spread of disease. During the rainy season, they mixed with standing water, making many streets impassable on foot, and again contaminating the air. During the dry season, winds picked up excrement and set it aloft.

Revillagigedo denounced those who dirtied city streets and plazas as "indecent...committing an abominable excess."[32] Neighborhoods throughout the city were witness to this activity daily, as he wrote:

> The abuse, disorder, and liberty with which the neighborhoods of this Capital are accustomed, with all classes of people ridding themselves freely of their natural functions, dirtying whatever place, lacking in modesty and with damage to the public health, must be remedied with vigilance.[33]

Revillagigedo considered such people as totally lacking in discipline and self-control—two important characteristics that he was trying to instill in city residents. To him, this type of activity represented the uncivilized nature of the urban masses. It also represented the danger that this activity posed in challenging both the cultural norms upon which elites based their social superiority as well as the potential to transgress established boundaries. If they could not control their bodily functions, and they did not have the moral decency to tend to themselves in private, they had the potential to lack control in other situations. To elites, the all too common practice of public defecation had the promise to digress into other types of public disorder, especially crime. More importantly, it could reflect badly on the state, illustrating their lack of political control over the residents of the city, and thus undermining its legitimacy. Elites also connected public defecation to a variety of other activities that they argued perpetuated illness in the lower classes. Notables such as Dr. José Ignacio García Jove, and Revillagigedo himself, attributed high disease rates among the urban poor to practices such as the abuse of alcohol, public nudity, and the delinquent conditions poor people lived in. This attitude reflects a more subtle stereotype of the poor, implying that the behaviors perpetuating poverty were the same ones that precluded taking precautions against disease, such as poor hygiene.

In an attempt to restore order back into the streets, article thirteen of the August 31 decree singled out public defecation, with time in the city's stocks as punishment.[34] Just as his counterparts who used corporal punishment against Indian garbage collectors who improperly disposed of garbage, Revillagigedo did not institute monetary fines for public defecation. He associated this activity with the plebeian classes, especially those who were extremely destitute and forced to live on the street. As with earlier decrees from the 1760s and 1770s, monetary fines were as inappropriate for this particular urban group, as it was impossible to enforce this type of punishment to change behavior. Physical penalties seemed more appropriate, since that did not assume any type of financial stability. The public, as well as humiliating, nature of the stocks would not only send a message of the intolerable nature of this type of activity, but it would also encourage the perpetrator to change his or her unacceptable behavior.

To contain the problem of bodily waste in the city streets, the viceroy also advocated the aforementioned establishment of communal sites, places set aside strictly for public use and disposal when the need arose, as well as where residents could dump excrement collected within their homes. Property owners would build them adjacent to existing sewage ditches in the city, so that the disposal of waste would be quick and uncomplicated. He gave them three months to comply with the ordinance.[35] By October 1792, it was clear, however, that residents were ignoring the ordinances. The Junta de Policía complained to Revillagigedo that people continued to pollute public areas, and plans for common receptacles for waste had fallen by the wayside.[36] Part of the problem was that the earlier bando had been vague in defining the system of communal spaces, and there had been no punishment for noncompliance in the legislation. The viceroy republished article thirteen of the 1790 royal decree, this time adding much more detail regarding the organization of neighborhood dumps. He gave property owners four months to comply, or be faced with a 100 peso fine.[37] No longer did he speak in vague terms regarding the logistics of waste disposal; now he advocated the specific building of latrines, rubbish bins, and deep pits all lined in masonry. All were to have top openings for easy dumping of waste, and covered spouts at the bottom for quick removal by the rubbish carts that picked up garbage and excrement numerous times during the week. These receptacles were to be covered, to contain the smells that built up and threatened the cleanliness of the surrounding air. Ultimately, argued Revillagigedo, this system would keep the streets clean of offensive waste, would keep the canals that supplied drinking water to the city clean, and most importantly, would discourage the spread of disease through contaminated air, providing for both order and cleanliness and bringing the streets back under control.[38]

While on the surface Revillagigedo's plans focused on containment of waste as a mechanism toward the betterment of public health and welfare, other underlying motives speak to a more complex web of goals and outcomes. This new system also had the potential for containing dangerous behaviors of the urban poor, whom elites blamed for perpetuating the problem in the first place. By establishing sites throughout the city where people could tend to their personal needs in private, Revillagigedo hoped that he could force public defecation back into the private realm. Rather than tending to personal hygiene in a very public manner, these communal sites would reintroduce ideas of modesty, which he felt so many residents lacked. Through his sanitation programs, Revillagigedo tried to force the cultural expectations of the upper classes into the realm of the lower classes. In addition, by criminalizing the act of public defecation, Revillagigedo hoped to instill in city residents a notion of containment and self-control reflected in personal hygiene habits.

Despite his best intentions and well-formulated plans, traditional practices and ideas about the use of public space compromised the success of Revillagigedo's system from the very beginning.[39] Throughout the colonial period, the lines between private and public space for most city residents was decidedly blurred, and they controlled many of the choices about use of space. Over time, systems of waste disposal had developed in accordance with the needs of residents and barrios alike, systems that were convenient to the user, if not the best designed. Many residents viewed the new legislation inaugurated by Revillagigedo as inconvenient at best, and at worst, insufficient for the sanitation needs of most neighborhoods. At times, other popular activities, such as the consumption of alcohol, exacerbated the problems connected to sanitation practices and provided another avenue by which colonial elites tied lower-class culture to urban blight.

A good example of this, tied directly to the sanitation issues connected to the over consumption of alcohol, is the case of the pulquería *de la Águila*.[40] On June 15, 1796, Don Joaquin Alonso Alles, a city judge and member of the city council, reported that the public space adjacent to the pulquería was continually dirty and overflowing, especially with human waste, and that people had resorted to dumping it in a nearby canal.[41] This should not be surprising. Pulquerías were notorious for their dirty and unhealthy environments. Even though Revillagigedo passed major tavern reforms between December 1792 and February 1793, in an attempt to deal with the social and environmental problems connected to alcohol abuse, it was common for drunken patrons to relieve themselves wherever they pleased.[42] Residents in the neighborhood surrounding the pulquería stated to Alles that people continued this practice because the communal site set up near *la Águila* was always full; the cleaning cars that passed by were never able to pick up all the waste that accumulated; and that in general the new regulations were inconvenient for most.[43] This was not a new problem for the tavern. Similar complaints of excessive garbage and bodily wastes had been lodged against the establishment in October, 1794.[44] The other problem relayed to Alles was that along with the newly established communal sites, people also continued to use the old accustomed dumping sites that were more convenient and closer to their homes.[45] What had changed, however, was that the garbage carts were now instructed to collect debris from the state established sites; this took up so much time that garbage collectors were unable to focus on the older, traditionally recognized spaces people continued to use.

The last piece of the story of *la Águila* emphasizes the growing rift between the colonial state and colonial subjects over issues of legitimacy, autonomy, and control when it came to day-to-day activities. Rather than bringing the residents of Mexico City into the discussions of urban sanitation by organizing a system based on the well-entrenched traditional practices of dumping waste, city leaders tried to establish an alternative system, with new dumping and collection sites, running head first into public opposition and dismissal. One challenge leaders like Revillagigedo faced was how the public defined communal space in the first place. Throughout the colonial period, neighborhoods had developed their own systems for waste disposal. For many, the proposed sites were no different from those already existing; places where people dumped bodily waste and other garbage. Only this time, city leaders were forcing wealthier property owners to spend their own money to build receptacles for their poorer tenants to use. While the state focused attention on the problem, and created elaborate rules and systems to follow, they demanded city residents pay for the solution. Of course, this set the stage for noncompliance.

The struggle over who had control of the definition and use of space proved to be another problem city leaders faced in enforcing these new policies. Especially important was the way in which neighborhoods reclassified space for dumping waste. Other areas that were popular sites for dumping garbage, besides streets, were abandoned buildings and dark alleyways. Because these were spaces that were not actively being used by the public—markets, public thoroughfares, plazas, sites of business, ecclesiastical properties—they were reclassified by neighborhoods as places to dump garbage and waste water.[46] However, for homeowners whose properties ran adjacent to alleys, or whose homes were next door to an abandoned structure, this type of activity caused many inconveniences, and they often petitioned the city council to remedy this issue.[47] Standing garbage was a magnet for rats and other disease carrying animals, and hidden away from the main thoroughfares, it was often missed as part of the city's official cleaning programs.[48] Complicating the problem, these were public spaces popular with those who had nowhere else to go; vagrants could use the darkened corners of plazas and alleys to hide from colonial officials, left alone to go about their business. For them, it was the only place affording them an element of privacy in a daily life lived out in public. However, homeowners found the presence of these groups particularly dangerous, threatening the safety and tranquility of their neighborhood. In 1793, Don Ignacio Oreyana, a resident and local entrepreneur, wrote to the municipal government, urging that they close an alleyway adjacent to his home. He stated, "I have a beautiful home on one side, and the other is ugly due to vagrants."[49] In 1794, Don Ignacio Lucero, also in a letter to the city council, asked for help, stating that vagrants were using the alleyway outside his house as a rendezvous for "married women and single men."[50] To combat growing public concern about the social dangers posed by unregulated spaces, Revillagigedo commissioned Ignacio de Castera, the city's head architect, to organize a plan to close up numerous alleys, tear down abandoned structures, number homes, and post street names in view of the public.[51] This, he hoped, would make urban spaces more orderly. It also would eliminate many of the private recesses that were difficult to monitor, discouraging the disorderly activities polluting the dark corners of the city.

Yet with all of this legislation and punitive measures to force people to comply, waste continued to pile up. City leaders and Revillagigedo in particular, failed to realize people's attachment to convenience and popular custom than new regulations. This was due in part to how residents viewed public space. For elites, their material wealth allowed them to carve out private space for themselves, primarily in the construction of their homes. For the rest of the population, a lack of private space meant that they lived many of the mundane activities of life in public. Public space, such as streets, alleyways, and plazas, were merely an extension of their living space and treated as such. The larger question is why were most residents not preoccupied with the consequences of their actions? If the lack of sanitation was so bad in Mexico City, as the viceroy, city council, and various members of elite society argued, why did people put up with it, or more importantly, contribute to the problem? Was it outright resistance against the state or merely indifference? City officials, including Revillagigedo, saw themselves as enlightened, embracing new ideas and theories regarding modernity, and putting them into action. They viewed one of their roles in colonial society as bringing order, cleanliness, stability, and tranquility to urban life through such things as improved sanitation. The fact that residents either openly resisted attempted changes or merely ignored them only reinforced elite's perceptions that most people in the colonial capital did not share the enlightened vision of their leaders. They preferred to continue their daily activities, such as dumping garbage in streets and public plazas, as they had always done. Apparently, living with the stench and mess was an acceptable price to pay for control over one's personal activities and decisions. Noncompliance with new sanitation regulations was not so much a question of a power struggle, or even open defiance and resistance. It was more reflective of the lack of authority and legitimacy that state officials had in the daily functioning of the city. However, elite desires to improve sanitation in the city placed new emphasis on people's personal behaviors. Elites wished to reshape the practices and attitudes of the plebeian classes into one closer to their own.

Race and Class Dimensions of Sanitation Reform

Removing garbage and debris from the city center was an important part of Revillagigedo's plans, and to accommodate the large amount of waste the city produced, he established a series of city dumps in neighborhoods surrounding the traza (see map 5.1).[52] Most of these dumps predominated in areas heavily populated by working- and lower-class

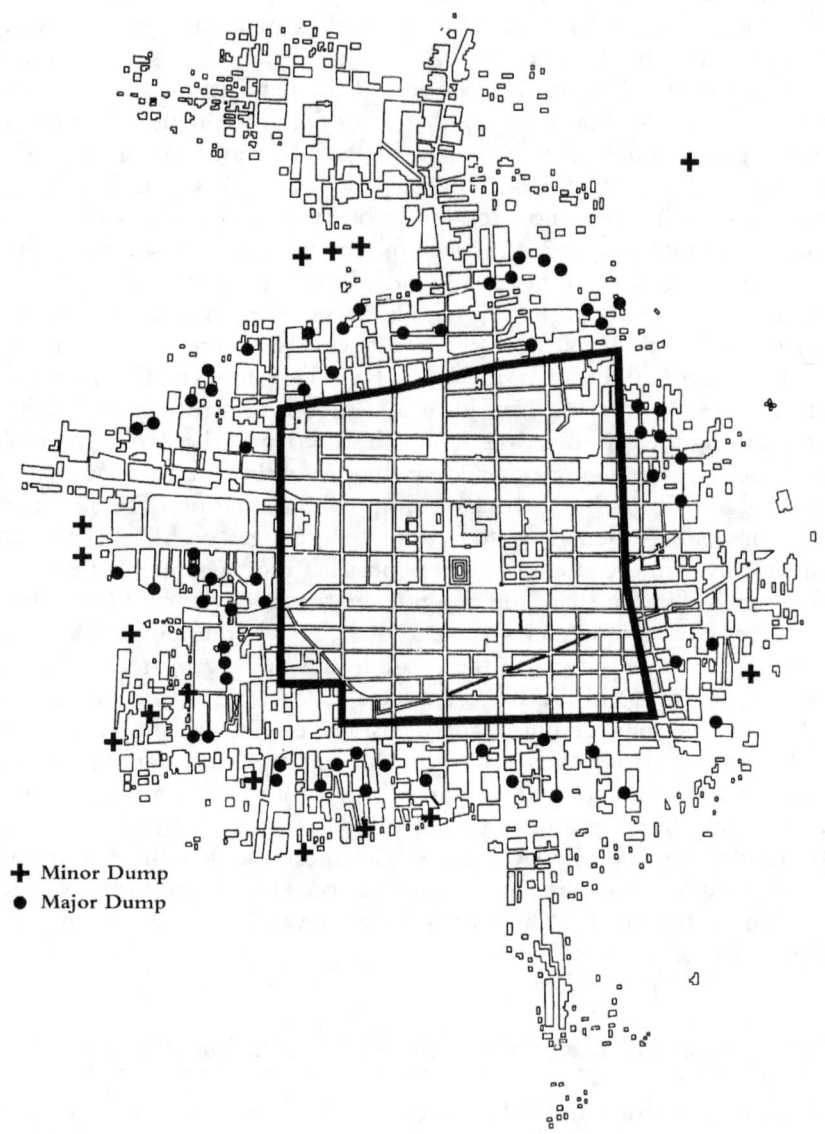

Map 5.1 Location of city dumps, 1790s.

groups, including the Indian barrios of San Juan and Santiago Tlateloco. For a variety of reasons, the one area seemingly spared from dumps was the southeastern quadrant. A major transportation canal flowed into the city from the southeast, bringing with it foodstuffs and other goods for the city's markets, and for health reasons garbage dumps were not appropriate. Second, one of the city's major public thoroughfares, the Paseo de Revillagigedo, ran through this area. This was a popular recreational site for city residents, rich and poor, so regulations attempted to keep it free from city waste. Finally, this area was the site of many of the city's religious festivals and celebrations.[53]

Examining the spatial placement of city dumps suggests that poorer neighborhoods became the dumping grounds of the wealthy. Cleaning the city's outlying barrios was always a problematic proposition, for a few reasons. Collecting garbage through the cart system, while inadequate for the city center, was virtually nonexistent for the outlying suburbs. In addition, receptacles designed to contain human waste were dependent on existing sewage lines, which neighborhoods outside the city center did not have.[54] Most importantly, however, were attitudes regarding residents of neighborhoods surrounding the traza, especially those dominated by Indians. City planners gave little thought to pollution in indigenous zones, or its effects on the health of residents there. The greater concern was the potential for this garbage, and the air it infested, to bleed into the traza, where elites lived. City officials viewed Indian barrios as the place where, according to Revillagigedo himself, "all the horrible things of the city originated."[55] However, rather than making sanitary improvements a priority in these areas, to contain the very problems people who lived outside the Indian neighborhoods feared, the bulk of the money and infrastructure devoted to waste disposal was focused on the city center. Another example of the preeminence placed on cleaning the city center at the expense of the suburbs, it raises questions regarding which urban groups in Mexico City public works projects were to benefit in the first place. While residents of the outlying barrios had reason to complain, those who actually benefited from sanitation services, residents of the city center, were surprisingly critical. Focus of criticism centered on the following issues: the mules used to pull the carts were dirty; garbage collection was slow and irregular; the carts and mules damaged the pavement; the coverage of services was too limited; and the program lacked adequate funding.[56] Generally, existing sanitation services was an impractical solution for the city's problems with waste.

Despite the many failings of his programs, Revillagigedo was quite positive in evaluating his accomplishments at the end of his term as viceroy. Generally, he felt that they had greatly improved sanitation in the capital, with visible progress in reducing standing garbage and bodily waste that had once filled city streets. He also argued that the health of the city's population had benefited from his incentives.[57] He was quick to point out, however, that even with improvements, the situation was not completely under control. For example, even though the city budget allotted close to 12,000 pesos to city cleaning projects in 1794, many areas still were not being cleaned.[58] Neighborhood leaders in quarteles menores four, fifteen, and twenty-six, on the northern edge of the city center toward the Indian barrio of Santiago Tlateloco, complained to the Junta de Policía that cleaning carts were not passing through their neighborhood, per Revillagigedo's royal decree of 1790. Particularly disturbing to them was the presence of human corpses, including the bodies of infants, among other trash and waste.[59] Similar problems existed in quartel menor two, on the eastern edge of the city near the Plaza de Santa Catalina.[60] One of the priests from the parish of San Sebastían, also on the eastern edge of the city center, echoed similar concerns; the lack of garbage collection had resulted in flooding and stagnant waters around the church. However, more important than the threat to public health that this situation could cause, he was worried that people in the neighborhood would not be able to get to mass.[61] While the problem of excess trash may have been somewhat contained through Revillagigedo's incentives, the viceroy himself argued that the fundamental problem of traditional and popularly sanctioned dumping practices had not been solved. As long as residents continued to view city streets as normal places to dispose of garbage, Mexico City would never rid itself of the problems public dumping caused.[62]

Perhaps in an attempt to make sure his policies continued in place after his departure from New Spain, Revillagigedo left elaborate instructions to his successor, the Marqués de Branciforte. Of particular concern was making sure the city air remained clean and pure, that streets remained clean, and that waste and floodwaters drain freely out of the city. Attention to these concerns, according to the outgoing viceroy, was key to maintaining public health and containing diseases such as hepatitis and dysentery.[63] Revillagigedo also placed special emphasis on the cleaning and maintenance of public spaces, for instance in front of the viceregal palace and the Cathedral in the Central Plaza, the markets of the Plaza del Volador, the Plaza de Santa Catarina, and the Plaza del Factor, and the various *paseos* (public thoroughfares) used by city residents for recreation.[64] Finally, he warned Branciforte about the continuing problems of public nudity and public defecation and urination.[65] The men who followed Revillagigedo as viceroy did not match the comprehensive nature of his concerns, reflecting poorly on subsequent state leaders who lacked his initiative, ingenuity, creativity, and passion for improving the living conditions of city residents. However, his ideas resurfaced numerous times and formed the basis for Mexico City's sanitation programs until the end of the colonial period and beyond into the nineteenth century.

Revillagigedo's Ideas Revisited

Visitors and residents alike argued that Mexico City was cleaner during the tenure of Revillagigedo than any other time during the colonial period.[66] With his sanitation programs arguably the most comprehensive of its time, they succeeded to a limited extent due to the power and will of the viceroy himself. Once Revillagigedo left office, despite his pleas to Branciforte to continue his public health programs, progress slowed. Those who followed Revillagigedo as viceroys lacked the vision and commitment necessary to contain Mexico City's sanitation problems. The continued problems of dumping waste in public spaces, the reliance on old ordinances rather than developing new and innovative ways of dealing with sanitation, and failure to make public sanitation a priority dominated the post-Revillagigedo period. The only time solutions to sanitation problems were a priority of the state, in terms of infrastructure and money, was during epidemic outbreaks in 1797 and 1813.

One of the biggest complaints continued to be the filthy conditions existing in many public spaces throughout the city. City officials and residents repeatedly cited the Plazuela del Conde de Santiago, located just south of the central plaza near the magnificent home of the esteemed Conde de Santiago de Calimaya, as one of the worst examples of public sanitation gone awry.[67] In 1795, a year after Revillagigedo left office, resident complained to the city council that the plazuela—the little plaza—was being used by both men and women to relieve themselves in full public display, without concern for modesty and civility. Convicted of disorderly activity, offenders faced corporal punishment; male offenders were to spend time in the city's stocks, while female offenders were sent to jail.[68] In 1798, an ongoing discussion between the Junta de Policía and Viceroy Branciforte over new fines for dumping garbage in public spaces singled out the plazuela again. Garbage in the plaza continued to pile up, and the earlier problems of public defecation continued. With this in mind, the Junta advocated increased fines for dirtying public spaces; four reales for the first offense, eight reales (one peso) for the second, and twelve reales for the third offense.[69] As with earlier punishments meted out to those dirtying public space, the fact that the Junta used physical punishment for public defecation and monetary fines for those dumping garbage suggests that different urban classes were connected to both public defecation and indiscriminate dumping of garbage; poorer urban classes to the first, being unlikely to have the cash resources to pay a fine, and middle/upper classes to the latter, where financial incentives to change activity seemed more appropriate. It also points to the continued use of corporal punishment as an attempt to change plebeian behavior more in line with elite norms.

Using the city stocks for male offenders, a public and humiliating form of punishment also reflects the fact that colonial officials were particularly worried about the impact of people urinating and defecating in public on both the order and stability of society. The Plazuela del Conde de Santiago was not the only place in Mexico City where this was a problem; it was just one example of many. In 1807, major streets in the city center, such as Calles de San Bernardo, Capulinas, Cadena, and Zuleta, as well as the area around the Hospital San Andrés (the city's largest hospital) continued to have problems with people either dumping bodily waste in the street, or simply relieving themselves when the need arose.[70] What concerned elites the most about this activity was their perception that it tended to go hand in hand with other types of offenses. Those dirtying public spaces also slept in and around the plazas, public fountains, churches, and abandoned buildings that dotted the city. They also used the cover of night to participate in all sorts of "offenses against God," a term used for a variety of activities, but most often referring to sexual acts. On May 16, 1809, José María Gómez wrote to the viceroy, Pedro Garibay, regarding the problem of people defecating and bathing around the Puente de la Merced, one of the major streets running east out of the Plaza de Volador and fronting the Convento de la Merced:[71]

> likewise, men and women at all hours come around [the street] without modesty, to attend to their bodily needs, and after washing or bathing they stay partially or entirely naked...they cause serious harm to those who see them, I feel inflicting the worst on

the eyes of the *cantos* like those of the Convento de la Merced, the women who open their windows to this activity, the many young women who travel by and live in the area, and ultimately the many young people who are around during the day.[72]

Punishment in the stocks, designed to send a message to other members of colonial society; lack of modesty and decency was threatening the moral sensibilities of more vulnerable residents of the city, would be dealt with through public example.[73]

Wealth and status did not protect areas of the city from continuing problems. In April 1796, a petition to the Junta de Policía mentioned problems on Calle de Cadena, home to some of the richest families in the viceregal capital. Br. Manuel de Riezu, rector of the Hospital de San Pedro, wrote complaining of the poor sanitary conditions existing in the streets surrounding the hospital, including Cadena. City cleaners never came to pick up garbage and other waste, allowing it to block the sewage canals and creating stagnant pools of sewage and other wastewater.[74] The Junta immediately responded, sending cleaning cars to the area to deal with the problem. One can argue that the quick response to the crisis reflected the status of colonial society involved. The fact that the inconvenience centered on both a hospital and wealthy residents of the city certainly did not hurt their case.

While wealthier sections of the city often experienced quick results when it came to sanitation problems, this does not mean that city officials did not completely ignore poorer neighborhoods. Certainly, the central sector of the city was, for the most part, the focus of most of the sanitation programs that developed during the eighteenth century. However, similar to the increased emphasis on the physical care of the poor during epidemic outbreaks, the scope of Mexico City's sanitation system changed as well. An outbreak of smallpox in 1797 and one of "mysterious fevers" in 1813 encouraged city leaders to incorporate neighborhoods outside the traza into urban sanitation plans, as the urgency of epidemics placed more emphasis on the necessity of sanitation controls in halting the spread of illness.[75] As some of the epidemics' most pathetic sufferers, residents of poorer neighborhoods became victims in need of charity and help, and so efforts to improve sanitation included them as well.[76] While doctors and state leaders favored inoculation and quarantine measures in dealing with smallpox, they also saw improving existing sanitation measures as an appropriate use of state funds in the fight against epidemics.[77] The church and donations from private individuals formed the material foundations of medical relief.[78]

This was certainly true of Branciforte, who was viceroy during the smallpox outbreak in 1797. On February 28, he issued a directive explaining his plans for dealing with the impending epidemic.[79] One of the key struggles he anticipated was funding care for the sick. As the epidemic approached, the cabildo wanted to halt all public works projects and divert those monies to poor relief. The viceroy, however, rejected that idea.[80] He argued that suspending these projects would put more people out of work, creating a new group of vagrants who would compete with needy victims of the epidemic for aid. It would also compromise the sanitation programs key in keeping the streets clean and discouraging the spread and perpetuation of disease.[81] In the ensuing discussions regarding sanitation standards during the epidemic, the Junta de Policía emphasized once again the importance of maintaining street cleaning programs to control the spread of disease and argued that a number of places in the city were not following regulations regarding the disposal of garbage. They also placed the blame for the lack of enforcement squarely on the shoulders of Ignacio Castera, master architect of the capital, who remained in control of sanitation programs after Revillagigedo's tenure in office.[82] Because of the presence of an epidemic, city officials dealt with these particular sanitation problems immediately, as the *alcaldes de barrios* (ward chiefs) from the thirty-two districts in the city reported to the Junta verifying that the stated cleaning had been done.[83]

The fevers epidemic of 1813 provides another example of the emphasis city leaders placed on maintaining sanitation programs in the attempt to control the spread of disease. Like others, this epidemic disproportionately affected the urban poor. Dr. Luis José Montaña, a doctor asked by the city council to evaluate different aspects of the epidemic, offered a variety of explanations. Besides attributing part of the problem to inadequate diets and shelter, he also pointed to the environmental conditions dominating the barrios outside the city center. He described the poor as people who "live like prisoners in shacks hidden away in a maze of alleys and [vacant] lots, which are surrounded by rubbish, manure piles, and puddles."[84] In June, during the height of the epidemic, observant individuals notified members of the cabildo that street cleaners were dumping garbage in the poorer neighborhoods of the city, rather than taking it out to the city dumps, thus exacerbating an already dreadful situation.[85] In their response, the viceroy, cabildo, and Protomedicato all emphasized the importance of maintaining stringent sanitation conditions in an attempt to stave off disease, especially in poorer neighborhoods. Viceroy Felix María Calleja del Rey argued that one of the best ways to impede the spread of the disease was to maintain, as best possible, clean city streets and public spaces. To this end, he called on the city council members to commission a resident from each street in the city to evaluate the state of cleanliness and then report any problems.[86] The Protomedicato concurred and argued in favor of burning rubbish heaps rather than allowing them to decompose, thus infecting the air and encouraging the spread of disease.[87] Don Rafael Morales, who was in charge of maintaining the city's sanitation programs at the time, understood the increased importance of keeping the city clean. He argued that, for the time being, the focus of combating the epidemic, from a sanitation perspective, should be on poorer neighborhoods, where the gravest situation existed.[88] One of the problems, he argued, was that there were not enough cleaning cars to handle the amount of garbage produced. To that end, the city council allocated 22,000 pesos to Morales' efforts. The other major problem that existed was that the Junta de Policía was too lax in enforcing the fines accompanying continued dumping of trash and bodily waste into city streets.[89] There was little incentive for people to change their behavior, even during a crisis such as the current epidemic.

Increased attention to sanitation controls during epidemic periods reveals that while the general state of city cleanliness may have declined after Revillagigedo's limited success, local leaders still understood, at least part of the time, the importance of keeping the capital clean, both in terms of not only medical benefits, but also social benefits. While the need to control disease made collecting and disposing of garbage necessary in 1797 and 1813, various institutions, including the city council and viceroy, struggled continuously to control urban pollution during the intervening years. Elite perceptions over the role of city residents, especially the poor, in perpetuating sanitation problems vacillated between contempt for people's actions in nonepidemic years, to helping the poor rid themselves of the polluted environments, which made them sick during the height of epidemic crises.

In the end, this struggle did not encourage or invite new, innovative, or long-range approaches to Mexico City's garbage problems. City sanitation guidelines issued in 1804, 1805, 1807, 1815, 1819, and 1820, rather than introducing new approaches and greater enforcement, merely built on Revillagigedo's bando of August 31, 1790, at times simply republishing his legislation.[90] City residents also increasingly became the scapegoats for the inadequacies and failures of city programs. Instead of trying to remedy shortcomings, such as poor funding, the limited scope of garbage collection, and the lack of enforcement of fines and punishments meant to discourage damaging activity, those in charge of cleaning the city blamed poor sanitary conditions on residents' activities. Pedro Prieto, manager of sanitation projects in 1815, argued that his workers should not be held responsible for the continuing garbage problem in the city. Residents were to blame, since they continued to dump garbage haphazardly in the streets, ignoring the containers set up in neighborhoods that garbage collectors used to pick up and transport waste out of the city center.[91] Francisco Bustamante, head of city sanitation in April, 1823, summed up elite frustrations when he argued that cleaning the city was the responsibility first and foremost of its residents. It was up to them not to sweep garbage into the streets and to use the city canals as toilets. City leaders had done their job by providing a system to clean the streets, and they were not responsible for its deficiencies if residents chose to ignore regulations aimed at improving their living environment.[92]

Concluding Thoughts

Examining the development, implementation, and ultimate lack of success of waste collection programs in Mexico City during the late eighteenth century raises a number of important observations and conclusions. First, responses to new sanitation programs emphasizes the contested visions of "cleanliness and order" between elites and plebeian residents of the viceregal capital. The common practice of dumping garbage in the street, along with the open display of bodily functions, such as urination and defecation, illustrated to elites that many in colonial society did not follow their cultural norms when it came to certain aspects of human behavior and bodily propriety. While elites supported state programs that attempted to change the behaviors they viewed as uncivilized and a threat to their established social and cultural norms, some residents of the viceregal capital, such as Don Mariano, or the neighbors surrounding the pulqería *la Águila*, viewed cleanliness and order through their own lens. While favoring practices that were more traditional when it came to dumping garbage, they also juxtaposed their preferences against state systems that they saw as inefficient and unsuccessful at dealing with the problems of urban sanitation. Therefore, there was little incentive for them to change their behavior.

Despite the comprehensive nature of ordinances surrounding collection and containment of garbage and waste, enforcing these regulations proved difficult, if not impossible. First, enforcement often fell to the police, a group who did not have much legitimacy in the eyes of city residents. Making about eight pesos a month, they faced an ambivalent position. On one hand, it was their responsibility to uphold unpopular mandates that aimed to control people's activities. On the other hand, they themselves were members of the communities and neighborhoods in which they worked. If they were too vigilant in their job, neighbors treated them with contempt and viewed them as being too intrusive. If they were too lax, the regulations were not enforced and the problems continued. For the most part, police enforcement was ineffective, as communities resisted their attempt to enforce the law, viewing them as another example of state intrusion into their private lives and activities.[93] In many ways, this lack of compliance on the part of residents belies a lack of authority on the part of both the city government and the viceroy himself.

This issue of the legitimacy of city/state leaders in the waning years of the colonial system can be seen in the intersection between elite concerns about disorderly conduct, state goals to eradicate this conduct (as illustrated in Revillagigedo's plans), and alcohol consumption on the part of the lower classes, as discussed earlier in the case of the pulquería de la Águila. Political leaders in Mexico City were indeed concerned about the destabilizing consequences that the overconsumption of alcohol inflicted on society—public drunkenness, peeing and defecating in public spaces, vagrancy—and articulated programs aimed at moving the popular classes more in line with elite cultural sensibilities. However, city leaders walked a fine line and had to be careful that they did not push the public too far. Colonial society was structured around a careful social balance, and while elites may have feared the masses to a certain extent—their potential for inciting urban unrest, their majority in numbers, the social stresses that their poverty enabled—the very nature of elite identity and superiority depended on the seemingly disorderly lower classes. This was true to a certain extent with the larger state structures as well. In a colonial world ordered by the Bourbons, the state needed the existence of the lower-class groups to justify their new systems of order, efficiency, and control. While they may have wanted to, and saw benefits in, creating a cleaner, safer, and more orderly city, representatives of the colonial state had to be careful not to alienate or anger people too much, lest they upset the delicate balance upon which daily life rested on.

As historian Michael Scardaville has pointed out, the structural reforms directed at taverns were a profound failure, and attempts at reshaping popular practices, connected to drinking, public urination, and defecation, can be understood in the same light. There was indeed a certain amount of ambivalence regarding the uses and abuses of alcohol, and its impact on both society in general, and public spaces in particular. Many wealthy families in the viceregal capital had direct ties to the production and sale of alcohol, and the state gained tremendous revenue from the taxes generated by this production.[94] Reigning in alcohol abuse, as troubling and negative as some of the consequences of its use were, had profound economic impacts that elites and the state did not want to cross. So in the end there continued to exist an uneasy tension between the popular use and abuse of alcohol by the urban masses, and anxiety on the part of the upper classes in regard to the physical disorder and perceived chaos, which they believed this consumption produced.

There were other ways in which city leaders themselves were somewhat ambivalent about enforcing the programs. Employing garbage collectors proved to be difficult. The dirtiest and most disgusting of jobs, the collection of human waste, often fell to indigenous workers, who still occupied the lowest rung on colonial society's ladder. Even though race was no longer the prime social marker by the late colonial period in Mexico City, it still played an important role in defining different groups in society, in justifying Spanish superiority, and in maintaining control over the vast majority of colonial residents.[95] It seemed obvious to elites to employ Indians in the position of cleaning up everyone else's waste, a job considered unfit for just about anyone else. Nevertheless, even they were considered inefficient workers, often accused of being lazy, simply collecting garbage in one neighborhood, and then dumping it in another.[96]

Programs instituted by Revillagigedo and his supporters were also infused with racial and class elements. Clearly, certain transgressions were associated with different social groups, and punishments designed to deter dumping garbage and human waste varied. Dumping garbage met with monetary fines, because this activity was associated with groups of better economic means. Meant to deter the activity, the fines instituted did not often work, since generally they were easily paid. They did not offer much incentive to change behavior. On the other hand, public urination and defecation by plebeians was viewed by elite groups as both uncivilized behavior, as well as a challenge to elite cultural and social norms. This activity represented the inability of certain groups in colonial society to control themselves, and this disorder and lack of modesty had the potential to spill into other areas of colonial life, namely crime. Punishments instituted for the failure to contain one's outward bodily propriety were physical in nature, since the lower classes did not have the material resources to pay fines. More importantly, however, physical punishments, such as time in the city's stocks, or a series of lashes, humiliated and shamed the offender into changing his or her activity, at least in theory. The way in which these punishments played out, in public for all of colonial society to witness, added to the humiliation, and made the offender a public example to others.

The scope of sanitation programs also reinforces racial and class divisions that existed in late colonial Mexico City. Poorer districts of the city, such as the Indian barrio of Santiago Tlateloco, as well as the neighborhoods to the east of the city center, were never included in the city's plans. In fact, they became the sites where city government established dumps to contain urban waste. Neighborhoods that housed the urban poor, Indians and mestizos, Africans and mulatos, bore the brunt of Mexico City's sanitation problems. Not only did they suffer from some of the worst problems associated with a lack of urban sanitation services, but the physical reality of these neighborhoods worsened when they effectively became the city's dumps. This aspect of urban planning—the collection and containment of waste—was more concerned with beauty and convenience, rather than the utility and the consequences of poverty. The groups in colonial society that needed relief the most, the urban poor, did not receive it. The ways which city planners conceived solutions to sanitation problems did not inspire them to examine how poverty perpetuated the presence of pollution in the daily lives of poorer residents.

Despite the many failures of sanitation programs instituted during the latter years of the colonial era, there are some significant long-term legacies to the programs of Viceroy Revillagigedo. First, they illustrate the continued importance of the viceroy in the day-to-day life of Mexico City. As questions about the nature of the colonial system increased, and individuals began to view independence as a viable option, men like Revillagigedo found themselves, and what they represented, increasingly under fire; the colonial state struggled to maintain relevance and legitimacy in the lives of its subjects. The relative success that Revillagigedo achieved through his sanitation programs, along with the longevity of these programs well into the postcolonial period, illustrates that in some contexts, state leaders could prevail and maintain some influence. For a late colonial era viceroy, Revillagigedo was extremely popular, and part of this popularity reflects some of the successes he achieved in the realm of urban sanitation. Second, late colonial attempts at reinforcing state authority through urban planning projects anticipate latter discussions and debates over the nature of modernity and urban development that emerge throughout Latin America in the late nineteenth and early twentieth centuries (1870–1930). Revillagigedo's policies continued to dominate the realm of urban planning in Mexico City well into the nineteenth century, as the newly independent Mexican state struggled to gain its footing. The anxieties that late colonial elites expressed about the uncivilized nature of the urban masses became part of the discourse over the development of modern Mexican culture and identity.

CHAPTER SIX

Mastery over the Streets: Drainage, Street Paving, and Renovation of Urban Space

Standing garbage, and the health hazard it posed, was but one of the sanitation problems that concerned leaders in the viceregal capital. There were also concerted efforts to deal with the continuing issue of street flooding, an inadequate sewage system, and disorganized public spaces. In 1826, British traveler G.F. Lyons, upon his arrival in the capital, commented on his initial impressions of the streets of Mexico City:

> The principle charm of Mexico consists in the width and regularity of the streets, which cross at right angles, and in almost every instance traverse in one unbroken line the whole extent of the city; affording a fine perspective of nearly two miles, although the natives allow them a much greater length. They are all well paved, with pathways on either side, while through their center, beneath a line of broad slabs, runs the common sewer. It is a far cleaner town than might be expected, well lighted, and now under a good police. Many of the houses are on a large or even magnificent scale, and the whole of those in the principal streets are fine buildings, but, as in many towns on the continent of Europe, the custom of letting the ground floor as shops, stores, and manufacturing is very prevalent, even with those who possess the most splendid residences.[1]

Despite the problems of standing garbage, dump heaps of animal waste, and the all too common practice of public defecation, Lyons portrays the capital, and especially the city streets, as well organized, spacious, and clean. While there were some parts of the city he was critical of-the main theater, Chapultepec Castle (which he described as "immense and neglected"), and the city's markets ("crowded and lamentably dirty")—on the whole he seemed rather impressed throughout his visit.[2]

Certainly, the image Lyons depicted was one colonial elites and state officials supported and agreed with. However, a closer examination of the formation and implementation of public works projects connected with flooding, sewage, and public space seems to challenge Lyons's description. Well-intentioned public works programs aimed at alleviating sanitation problems and the health risks produced by flooding and inadequate sewage defined the scope of urban planning in Mexico City at the close of the eighteenth century. The tenure of Viceroy Revillagigedo, in particular, saw major projects undertaken in the area of new drainage gutters and piping, widening and paving of streets, construction of sidewalks, and the renovation of public spaces, namely the Plaza Mayor, both to encourage the drainage of water, and to limit the spread of illness and general inconvenience to city residents.

In the final analysis, however, these solutions proved grossly inadequate for the problem at hand. First, they were limited in scope. Although the need for a more systematic sewage system and protection against flooding encompassed the entire city, these improvements were realized only in the city center. Indeed, in poorer neighborhoods, such as Santiago Tlateloco, urban services did not improve. In many ways, these changes were merely aesthetic, rather than more widely connected to public health issues. Second, public works programs lacked the funding necessary to guarantee their completion. Just as many other public institutions in late colonial Mexico City, city planners had to fight for an increasingly smaller piece of the colonial pie. Most monies directed at drainage projects went to renovations of the Plaza Mayor, and projects along major, and economically valuable, thoroughfares adjacent to the Plaza Mayor. Many projects relied heavily on convict labor not only because it was inexpensive, but also because it fit into the Bourbon mission of rehabilitating colonial citizens from lazy and ignorant to more rational and productive members of society. Finally, the nature of these projects, as we will see below, support the argument that Bourbon changes aimed more to contain urban problems and preserve the status quo rather than produce radical change, social or economic. Rather than confronting the material aspects of poverty, such as adequate drainage in poorer districts, city officials focused their efforts and resources on providing public services in the city center, where economic interests and needs of the wealthy prevailed. In doing so, they attempted to alleviate elite anxieties about the disorder and instability that stemmed from plebeian abuses of these services and spaces. Before discussing and examining the projects in greater depth, however, a brief discussion of flooding as an urban problem and theories of sanitation associated with the movement of water will be considered.

Flooding and the Movement of Water

From its inception, Mexico City suffered from flooding. Its geographical location, an island of partially reclaimed land in the middle of a lake, guaranteed that rising waters during the rainy season would invade the capital city. This was not always the case, however. The forerunner of Mexico City, the Mexica capital of Tenochtitlan, had a series of well-designed canals, which carried dirty water out of the city limits and dumped it into Lake Texcoco. Excrement and other garbage was also carried out of the city nightly on a series of barges, and more than 1,000 men were employed to sweep and wash down city streets every day. Other canals, designed to handle the seasonal rising and falling levels of the lake, helped to alleviate flooding as well. Attention to public sanitation and personal cleanliness made Tenochtitlan a very healthy city.[3]

When Tenochtitlan became the colonial capital of Mexico City in 1521, the Spanish immediately began campaigns to reshape it physically, by draining the surrounding lakes and reclaiming land. While they kept intact a few of the city's major waterways, primarily for transportation and as a link between the city and outlying rural agricultural districts, they also began projects to drain many of the canals that existed within the city, replacing them with a familiar street system based on European models. One of the immediate consequences of these campaigns was that it destroyed the natural drainage system that Mexica had brilliantly developed through the canal system. Canals had always served as a way to drain excess water and sewage out of the city in an organized and healthy manner.[4] By eliminating many of them, Spanish colonizers ensured that flooding became a constant problem for city residents. Every rainy season brought difficulties, with the first major flood occurring in 1555.[5] Other floods of notable mention occurred in 1604 and 1622.

However, perhaps the most catastrophic flood to hit Mexico City occurred in the late summer and fall of 1629, when heavier than normal rain, along with a fierce thirty-six hour storm beginning on September 20, paralyzed the city, causing considerable ruin for the city's residents. Flooding resulted in many shops and markets losing their entire inventory; destroying the living quarters and rudimentary structures of the urban poor, leaving thousands hungry and cold; and contaminating the city's water supply, making many sick and opening up the potential for the spread of water-borne diseases.[6] While this flood forced a renewed focus on drainage projects for the valley, the problem did not go away. Every rainy season brought with it water that flooded people's homes, uncovered bodies in the city's graveyards, and made unpaved streets a muddy mess, while destroying existing paving on others. From a sanitary perspective, flood waters mixed with garbage left in city canals, blocking them and making drainage much more difficult. Standing water mixed with garbage and excrement not only smelled bad, but it was also a breeding ground for bacteria and disease.

Flooding continued to be a problem well into the eighteenth century and as the city's population grew, produced more waste, and continued haphazardly to dump garbage, sanitation problems and common diseases increased at an alarming rate. At the same time, the eighteenth century also brought with it new environmental theories affecting the ways in which city planners conceived of and dealt with urban sanitation issues. Theories of movement in conjunction with ideas surrounding sanitation and disease gained newfound importance. Key was the belief that stagnant air and water were to blame for illness and unhealthy living conditions. The noxious smells emanating from standing garbage infected the air, and it was the air people breathed that consequently infected them. Standing water that did not drain out of the streets and canals had a similar effect. In many places, the environment people lived in became the focus for legislation, as medical practitioners and city leaders increasingly emphasized ways to encourage the movement of dirty water away from the city, as well as eliminating piles of garbage that putrefied the air that resident's breathed.[7]

In the case of Mexico City, that meant first containing the things polluting the city air: decomposing carcasses, standing garbage, and excrement left in the city streets. As will be examined in this chapter, it also meant advocating the building of new sewage systems, separate canals for drainage, and street paving to encourage the movement of water, especially during periods of heavy rains and floods. By the late eighteenth century, cleanliness and sanitation in Mexico City was most closely associated with drainage and the movement of water. The historical problem of flooding in the city certainly influenced this focus; floods had caused substantial damage, both physical and economic, in the past. No group in colonial society was immune from its damaging effects, so it is not surprising that this issue drove much of the legislation on sanitation and disease control from the late colonial period onward. One of the results of city improvements, however, was that projects universally favored wealthy residents and economic interests over residents in poor neighborhoods, who desperately needed improvements in their living conditions. Therefore, while flooding affected all colonial residents to a certain degree, some were more equipped than others to deal with it.

Along with new theories redefining debates surrounding sanitation, elites increasingly tried to blame sanitation problems on the urban poor. As previously examined, political leaders, church officials, and prominent residents often conflated filthy urban environments with the urban poor who inhabited these spaces. While Enlightenment scientists were beginning to understand that dirty living and working conditions, especially polluted air and water, encouraged the spread and perpetuation of disease, those who held power in Mexico City blamed many aspects of the foul urban landscape directly on the poor. The immoral activities of lower-class groups perpetuated their poverty, according to elites, as if to say the poor chose to stay in their dismal conditions. Wider sanitation programs reflect these attitudes, in how they were conceived—aesthetic over substantive—and where they were implemented—focusing on the city center and not outlying areas of most pressing need.

Practical Solutions to the Problem of Flooding: Drainage and Paving

Viceroy Revillagigedo exhausted considerable effort in trying to establish a well-organized and systematic garbage collection system, to relieve the city's continued waste problem. However, containing garbage alone was not enough to combat the health problems connected to poor sanitation. Another element of his larger plans included construction and repair of existing sewage and drainage lines, the expansion of street paving, and building sidewalks. All of these improvements would help encourage the movement of water, and would "achieve beauty and comfort in transit, cleanliness necessary to carry out the health of the public, and for the splendor and good order of this most famous capital"—all circumstances demanding immediate and total attention.[8] These projects would also help to alleviate the continual flooding that imperiled the city, especially during the rainy season.

Revillagigedo placed his ideas in the hands of Ignacio Castera, Mexico City's master architect.[9] Assisting Castera was Miguel Contanzo, a military engineer, and Joseph Damían Ortiz a well-respected architect.[10] Within the context of Enlightenment era influences, especially the emphasis on order, symmetry, logic, and reason, the role of architect and military engineer became much more important in urban planning. Strict adherence to applied science began to drive the training of these professionals, first in Europe and later in Spanish America. Surveying and engineering methods advanced rapidly. Graphic artists learned to depict topographical and spatial features in map and plan form with greater accuracy and control. Mathematicians studied probability and statistics, analytical geometry, and advanced algebra. The methods and emphases that emerged during this period were an antithesis to the uninhibited Baroque style that had dominated in the sixteenth and seventeenth centuries. Bourbon architects and engineers trained with a greater emphasis on the sciences, mathematics, and logic found the Baroque aesthetic too irrational and tangled in confusion. It did not represent the simple, austere, and efficient Bourbon aesthetic they sought. Indeed, the Bourbons increasingly called on military engineers and formally trained architects to devise a variety of public works projects to renovate urban space. The goal was to make the viceregal capital more symmetrical, better organized, and cleaner, in keeping with the Bourbon focus on a rejuvenated and efficient colonial environment. This meant a newfound emphasis on improvements such as public sanitation, sewer lines hidden from public view, paved and well-lit streets, the construction of sidewalks and new leisure thoroughfares, and the opening and regulation of public spaces such as the Plaza Mayor. As any good Bourbon leader, Revillagigedo called on the most skilled and rationally trained professionals to aid him in this task.[11]

It is surprising; however, that Revillagigedo gave Castera, a classically trained architect, preeminence over the city's many talented engineers when it came to organizing and implementing many of the new public works projects. In eighteenth-century Europe, a growing rift emerged between engineers and architects, with the former called on more frequently to provide solutions for urban problems because investors and administrators recognized that they possessed valuable expertise. Engineers were considered more able than architects to determine whether government should sponsor a lot of construction or achieve redevelopment through regulation; whether urban services should be centralized or diffused throughout the city; how much of a city's physical plan should be predetermined; what the relationship of important buildings to the street plan should be; and how the costs of urban development could be written off. Architects, on the other hand, designed primarily for aesthetic effect, focusing more on form than function.[12] In the case of Mexico City, however, the choice of Castera to head planning and construction of Revillagigedo's public works projects emphasizes the continued predominance of architects in colonial Latin America over engineers, and shows how Latin America lagged behind its European counterparts in terms of the engineering profession taking control over public works projects, namely sanitation, drainage, paving, and the water supply. Unlike in England and most European countries, by the end of the colonial period in New Spain the profession remained controlled by a guild. Training began as an apprentice, or journeyman, under a master. After considerable practical experience, an exam was taken to obtain a master's license, which covered not only mastery over the planning of structures, but also more mundane skills, such as the laying of tiles and mixing of mortar. Architects also had to demonstrate their ability to calculate masses and areas, so that they could conduct appraisals on land and existing properties.[13] Once one received master status, that person fell into one of two classifications: *de lo blanco*, masters of European background, and *de lo prieto*, masters of colored background. The former was free to participate in any type of planning, construction, and appraisal. The latter was limited to the planning and construction of adobe structures and was prohibited from making appraisals.[14] As in Europe, the emergence of engineers in New Spain was within the structure of the military. More mature military institutions in eighteenth-century Europe meant that the role of military engineer within urban planning emerged earlier than in colonial Mexico. While military engineers supported Castera in bringing Revillagigedo's plans to fruition, this body did not enjoy the same kind of dominance that their European counterparts did. While architects in Mexico City had a well-established history and training mechanism within the guild, this was not the same for engineers.

The focus on form was evident in the way Castera understood Mexico City's problems. His main criticism of the urban environment was its irregularity. Whether in the haphazard construction of houses and public structures, the narrowness of city streets, or the garbage and filth that littered the neighborhoods, Mexico City did not reflect an image in accordance with its role as the capital of the Spanish Empire. Rather than reflecting everything the reforming Bourbon's stood for—order, efficiency, symmetry, austerity, restraint—the capital became mired in a hodgepodge of inadequate social services, cluttered public spaces, and incongruous physical structures. Castera argued that various public works projects Revillagigedo proposed, the public would see, including drainage and paving projects, as "immensely beautiful, comfortable and convenient, useful, economical, and perfect in all of its structure and organization."[15]

Drainage Initiatives: Gutters and Piping

Under the guidance of Castera, drainage construction began in earnest in 1790, a year after Revillagigedo assumed office. Although there is a large amount of information regarding the plans to drain Lake Texcoco, upon which Mexico City rested, existing city council records do not give us a clear picture of the scope of citywide drainage projects for the decades preceding the 1790s. There were some sporadic projects, especially on main thoroughfares such as Calle de San Francisco in the 1760s. Surprisingly, data for the 1770s and 1780s are completely missing, so it is difficult to know what was happening before Revillagigedo began his term.[16] Nevertheless, there is excellent documentation for the 1790s (see table 6.1 and map 6.1).[17]

Generally, these drainage projects consisted of constructing open gutters, or *targeas*, which lined the streets, gutters built underneath *banquetas*, or sidewalks, or in some cases underground lines into which surface water fed. Sometimes these projects coincided with paving and sidewalk projects (as will be discussed later in the chapter); at other times, their construction coincided with the laying of pipes for the city's public water system. Indeed, one of the goals of Revillagigedo's overall city improvement project was to ease the problem of polluted water contaminating the potable water supply.

The viceroy published official guidelines for constructing drainage gutters and piping, as well as street paving in April 1794. While this publication is well after the completion of most of the projects organized by Castera and his associates, it probably reflects the types of construction practices and regulations that officials adhered to in earlier projects. First, city leaders recognized their responsibility to provide the infrastructure to drain city streets of rainwater, as well as

Table 6.1 Listing of drainage projects during the tenure of Viceroy Revillagigedo, 1790–1794

Location	Date
Calle de Don Juan Manuel	1790
Calle de Estampa de Regina	1790
Front of Real Aduana and Iglesia de Santo Domingo	1791
Puente de Santa Barbara	1791
Calle de Cadena	February 1791
Calle de Empedradillo	February 1791
Calle de San Bernardo	May 1791
Calle de Zuleta	May 1791
Calle de Espíritu Santo	July 1791
Calle de la Azera de los Flamencos to the corner of San Bernardo	February 1794
Calle de Zuleta	March 1794
Calle del Parque de la Moneda	April 1794
Calles del Relox, San Ildefonso, and del Rastro	May 1794
Calles Santa Isabel, Santa Brígida, Puente de los Gallos	April 1792
Calle de San Andrés (to the Puente de Mariscala)	April 1792
Calles de Tacuba, Santa Clara, and Vergara	April 1792
Calle de San Bernardo (to the Puente de la Merced)	April 1792
Calle de Arzobispado	May 1792
Puente de Espíritu Santo (to the corner of Calle de Angel)	July 1792
Calle de Capuchinas	November 1793
Calle de Perpetua (past the Plazuela de Santo Domingo)	December 1793
Puente de los Gallos to Calle Galán	December 1793
Calle Portaceli to the Puente de la Garita de San Antonio de Abad	February 1794
Calle de Escalerillas	February 1794

Sources: AHCM, *Licencias: Artájeas* (limpia), Vol. 3238, Exp. 7, 9–13, 15–16, 18, 21, 23–25, 27, 32–33, 37, 40–43, 45, 48, 50.

dirty water from within homes and businesses. It was the responsibility of residents, however, to construct and maintain the drainage systems within their homes. The width of piping within homes was not to exceed one-half of a vara, or approximately sixteen inches.[18] Drainage gutters built along streets were to measure four and one-half *pies*, or roughly four and one-half feet, in depth, and two and one-half pies in width. They were to be lined with an especially slick dark rock that was found in and around Culhuacan, located south of Mexico City on the shores of Lake Xochimilco.[19] Sidewalks were to run at least six *pulgadas*, or inches, above the drainage gutters (street level) to allow residents to walk around safely and comfortably, and the construction of a buffer between the paved street and the actual gutters, to protect them against the damage from passing coaches. To encourage natural drainage,

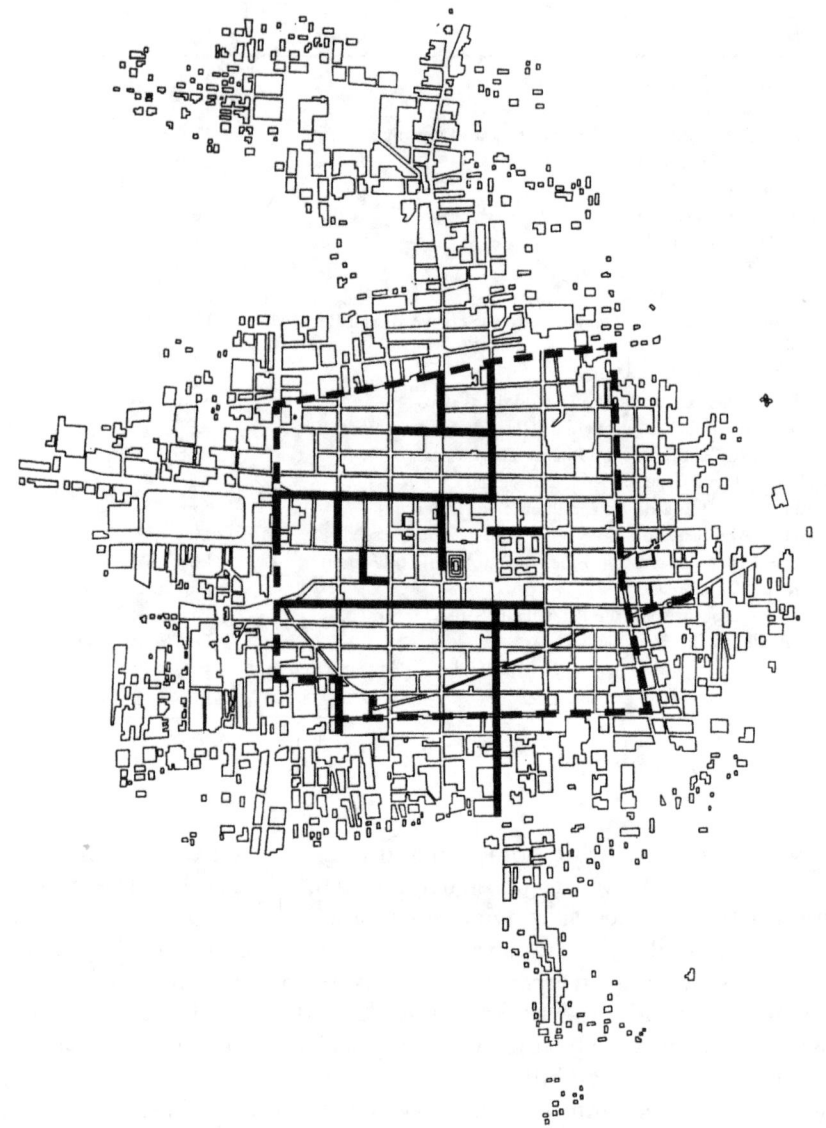

Map 6.1 Location of drainage projects during tenure of Viceroy Revillagigedo, 1790–1794.

architects angled streets, from the center downward, at approximately fifteen inches. Paving was to be as uniform as possible.[20]

The different reports included in city records that discuss these projects in detail almost universally acknowledged that one of the most important benefits would be improved public cleanliness and health. Standing water and excrement, as examined earlier, contributed to the spread of infection and disease, especially in areas of the city where people lived in close surroundings. Given the propensity of city residents to dump waste water in the streets, it was all the more important to construct systems which encouraged that water to drain away, rather than stagnate in pools close to living quarters, shops, taverns, and other public spaces. Besides the public health issues, residents also argued that repairing and expanding the drainage systems would make neighborhoods more comfortable, and beautiful, so there was an aesthetic element to the projects as well. The other key benefit articulated was the protection of property from flooding due to excessive rains. Mexico City, built on a lake, suffered from periods of flooding during the rainy season, as lake levels naturally raised. In the pre-Conquest period of Tenochtitlan, the Mexica had constructed a sophisticated series of canals that managed seasonal water fluctuations. However, one of the long-term consequences of the Spanish preference to fill in these canals and replace them with paved streets was the loss of an important form of flood control. As a result, it was common for people's patios, along with the rooms on the first floor of the structure, to flood during the rainy season. In the case of residential structures, homes became, at least temporarily, uninhabitable. On May 24, 1791, Don Victor Yturraran, who owned a home on Calle Zuleta, stated in a letter to the cabildo that the first floor of his home was uninhabitable due to flooding. He called on the city to construct a drainage line, so that he and his neighbors would not have to suffer from the prejudices they faced due to the flooding.[21] Since most storefronts were also located on the ground level of structures, merchants often risked the loss of valuable inventory in the event of surface flooding due to rains.

One project in particular was justified not in terms of public health or as an issue of flooding in particular. Rather, it had to do with the festival and celebration of Corpus Christi.[22] In April 1792, Castera headed up the project to provide drainage gutters and underground piping on Calles Tacuba, Santa Clara, and Vergara.[23] He organized this project primarily to make sure that the procession would be able to take place in a clean and comfortable environment, both for those participating and those observing. The cost of the drainage portion of the project was 9,197 pesos, while the paving was 1,305 pesos, and the sidewalks 1,568 pesos, for a total project expenditure of 11,801 pesos.[24] Easily one of the more significant projects during Revillagigedo's term, in the scope of both the project as well as the cost, it emphasizes the important role the church continued to play in colonial life, in terms of not only religious instruction and support, but also less-obvious ways, such as urban planning.

Since public works projects were very labor intensive, they provided valuable job opportunities in a city where most people did not have reliable employment and struggled to survive. Despite this, one of the more important sources of labor on public works projects in general, and in the repair and construction of drainage canals and piping in particular, was the use of convicts. In his study on criminality in late colonial Mexico City, Gabriel Haslip-Viera examines the use of convict labor as a form of punishment. For example, in 1796 and the period 1800–1817, approximately 14 percent of all punishments handed down for criminals in Mexico City were in the form of laboring on the city's public works projects. More specifically, in quartel mayor number seven, the district that essentially covered the Indian barrio of Santiago Tlateloco, 25 percent of convicts were sent to serve on public works projects. While individuals from the upper- and middle-economic strata (merchants, administrators, barbers, pharmacists, scribes, and vendors) and high-skilled artisans (coachmakers, silversmiths, and goldsmiths) constituted close to 12 percent of all arrests at this time, the overwhelming number, roughly 70 percent, came from low-status artisans and the laboring classes (bakers, brass workers, candle makers, carders, carpenters, hat makers, ironsmiths, masons, rosary makers, shoemakers, spinners, tailors, tanners, tinsmiths, tobacco workers, weavers, and workers at the Royal Mint). The remainder of arrests, close to 16 percent, came from the service sector (coachmen, cooks, muleteers, porters, and servants).

Haslip-Viera also found that the types of crimes varied between socioeconomic classes. The upper and middle strata were most commonly arrested for property crimes, fraud, and sexual offenses; high-status artisans for property crimes and fraud; low-status artisans for violent crimes, property crimes, nonviolent family disputes, vagrancy, drunkenness, and gambling; and service sector workers for property crimes and escaping from jail. Not surprisingly, racial categories generally correspond to the above. Spaniards were most-often arrested for property and sexual crimes, and adultery; mestizos and mulatos for property crimes, vagrancy, drunkenness, and gambling, and escaping from jail; and Indians for violent crimes, adultery, vagrancy, drunkenness, and gambling, and escaping from jail. Although these numbers postdate Revillagigedo's tenure as viceroy, and the period of most active public works construction, it is highly unlikely that they differ much from the period under study here. From the standpoint of the state, criminal labor was popular, practical, and cost effective, as a way to lessen the total costs of construction.

Perhaps more important than the economic aspects of penal labor, however, were the social reform aspects that penal labor engaged. Social disorder, especially crime, in colonial society was generally associated with lower-class groups, described as lazy, prone to immoral and illegal activity, and generally lacking reason. In essence, the poor were the cause of general disorder because they were naturally and inherently prone to it. In reality, the poor in colonial society committed crime both out of economic necessity and as a way to negotiate increasingly insecure and desperate lives. Robbery was sometimes necessary to provide food for one's family. Drinking and gambling provided an escape from lives lived on the edge. Violence was a common response to stress and lack of economic and social options. Begging represented the refusal of some to accept denigrating work routines and low wages. Low-class groups broke the law not out of any inherent desire, as elites and colonial officials believed, but rather for a variety of social and economic reasons.[25]

As discussed earlier, city officials used physical and public punishments against offenders in response to public defecation. Rather than instituting fines for such behaviors, city leaders argued that the nature of the offense, along with the people who committed it (for the most part those of low economic and racial status) demanded that a more "corrective" form of punishment take place, in hopes of changing the person's behavior. In the case of minor criminal offensives, authorities believed that time spent providing labor for public works projects would serve as a corrective measure as well; that participating in an activity that would ultimately bring a measure of good to city residents would help in molding former criminals into more productive members of colonial society.

The support for drainage projects, as with public works projects in general in the viceregal capital, came from a variety of sources, including funds from the coffers of the Junta de Policía and the *fondo de Real Desagüe*.[26] The state also had limited support from private individuals and institutions. Of course, city officials allocated this type of funding to drainage projects in the wealthier parts of the city, where individuals and families had disposable income to direct at improving their local environment. Residents along Calle Cadena provide one of the better examples of personal donations made toward infrastructure improvements. In February 1791, the contract outlining the construction of drainage and paving for Calle Cadena listed the following personal contributions: Señora Marquesa de Selba, 1,000 pesos; Don Manuel Sanchez de Tagle, 200 pesos; Don Manuel Santa María, 500 pesos; Don Rodrigo Sanchez, 500 pesos; Don Matías Guitérrez de Lanzas, 500 pesos; and Don José Damían Ortiz, 500 pesos.[27] In a city where the average yearly income ranged between 60 and 300 pesos, these amounts, while not significant to those who donated them, would have represented an extremely large amount of money to most residents of the capital. Convents also provided funds from time to time. In May, 1791, the Convento de San Bernardo provided 1,000 pesos for the construction of drainage piping on the street of the same name[28]; in February, 1792, the Convento de Regina donated 1,785 pesos toward both drainage gutters and sidewalks on Calle Estampa[29]; and in April, 1793, the Convento de Santa Clara contributed 1,500 pesos for a drainage gutter on the Callejón de Santa Clara.[30] While private donations in general did not provide enough money to offset lack of funding on other projects, they served as an important source of revenue when offered.

In September 1794, city leaders announced that the drainage projects recommended by Revillagigedo and instituted by Castera were completed. It was now the responsibility of the state to keep the drainage gutters, piping, canals, and streets throughout the city clean of standing water and waste.[31] Nevertheless, this was rarely the case, and despite the new investment in drainage projects for the city, problems persisted well after Revillagigedo left office. One of the most common complaints brought to the attention of the cabildo was the lack of flood protection drainage gutters provided, despite the new construction. Garbage was part of the problem, due to the continued practice of dumping waste directly into the targeas. However, residents also complained that the actual dimensions of drainage canals were insufficient to handle the amount of wastewater and rains produced. This was especially true on the main thoroughfares of Calle de San Francisco, Calle de San Bernardo, Calle del Parque de la Moneda, and the streets in and around the Royal Palace.[32]

Complicating this situation, private sewage pipes, located within homes and connected to the city system, often overwhelmed even the newly built drainage lines. As early as 1794, the city recognized that the amount of wastewater private residents produced was often too much for the city lines to handle. This situation was especially problematic in the city center, on the following streets: Calles de San Francisco, Coliseo, Palma, Coliseo Viejo, Espíritu Santo, Refugio de Angel, Monterilla, San Bernardo, Capuchinas, Cadena, San Juan de Manuel, Vergara, Santa Isabel, Zuleta, and Brígidas.[33] With the exception of Calles de San Francisco, Coliseo, Palma, Refugio el Angel, and Monterilla, the rest of the streets had undergone substantial repairs and improvements as part of Revillagigedo and Castera's public works program.[34] This should not be so surprising, however, as these streets constituted one of the wealthiest areas of the city. Residents here could afford to construct their own private sewage lines, as opposed to dumping wastewater in the street. This "luxury" was one of the issues contained within broader attitudes toward sanitation, which separated the city's wealthier residents from their poorer counterparts.

Another problem was the limited scope of these improvements. Neighborhoods virtually excluded from the new projects included the northern Indian barrio of Santiago Tlateloco, along with the eastern and southern neighborhoods of San Carmen, San Sebastián, Santa Cruz, Santo Tomas, and San Pablo. Unpaved streets and insufficient drainage systems typified these outlying neighborhoods. Periods of heavy rain made streets a muddy mess, and the dumping of waste by residents complicated this situation. Indeed, as examined earlier, these neighborhoods also lacked regular garbage collection, despite legislation promoting otherwise. In many cases, they became the dumping ground for garbage. Therefore, while these projects brought limited improvements, they did not affect the areas of the city that needed them most urgently.

Complaints to the cabildo in August 1802, after a particularly heavy period of rain, emphasized many of the deficiencies that still existed within the public drainage system despite the improvements made less than a decade earlier. Residents reported that many of the streets in the city center were seriously flooded. The following streets were most affected: Calles Tacuba, de la Profesa, San Francisco, la Iglesia de Espíritu Santo, de la Santísima Trinidad, Coliseo, de la Palma, Portal de Espíritu Santo, Carmen, Cocheros, Capuchinas, and San Bernardo. While not all of these streets had been the subject of repairs and construction, a few had undergone significant improvement: Calles Tacuba, Espíritu Santo, Capuchinas, and most importantly, San Bernardo.[35] Indeed, merchants along Calle San Bernardo, one of the main shopping thoroughfares, complained that customers could not get to their stores because of the floods, thus slashing their profits. Others lamented the loss of valuable merchandise: 780 boxes of cigarettes, 20 *arrobas* of sugar, and an unspecified, but apparently large, amount of chiles and cacao.[36] The Monte de Piedad, which handled plenty of pawning business daily, was also flooded, as were many of the churches in and around the city center, making it difficult for residents to observe mass.[37] If anything, this particular event illustrates that there were important economic aspects to urban planning and the construction of drainage infrastructure. While proponents often stressed the health and environmental aspects of these programs, the economic benefits, while perhaps not as obvious, were just as important. Well-drained streets allowed people to move about more freely through the city. They encouraged and made day-to-day activities, such as shopping, easier to accomplish. They also protected merchant's assets—storefronts and stocks—and helped to keep stores open and operational, thus guaranteeing profits. Flooding itself was problematic, not only because it compromised the health and living conditions of city residents, but also because it hampered the day to day functioning of the city, especially at an economic level.

Street Paving and Sidewalks

Revillagigedo and Castera's focus on improving the flooding situation in the city was not limited merely to drainage projects. The paving of city streets was another tool in combating the problem of standing and stagnant water. Historically, the city had constantly dealt with the problem of irregular paving. The popular use of horse drawn carriages caused considerable damage to paved streets; this included the continual use of horses and wagons to haul goods between the large markets and the smaller retail shops. City officials perceived the greater problem to be the leisure use of carriages, which was popular among the elite classes. Carriages represented a means by the upper classes to publicly demonstrate and flaunt wealth, and it was very common to see these families go about town in their carriages. Codes of honor for elite women also demanded that they go about town accompanied by family relatives, ideally within the physical protection of carriages rather than on foot. Hipólito Villaroel, in his critiques of the weaknesses of the city, estimated that there were 637 coaches in use in the viceregal capital, and many of them served the functions of luxury and vanity, but not necessity. He blamed them for most of the confusion and congestion that was commonplace in the city center and felt that carriage owners should have to pay fifty pesos annually into a fund for repairing the paving they damaged.[38] The consequences of this type of excessive use were real. Paving stones were often cracked and displaced under the pressure of horses' hooves and heavy carriage wheels. The dumping of wastewater also increased the gradual decay of existing paving, by trapping water between flagstones, as well as pooling it in the spaces opened up by broken and displaced stones.

These issues, of course, generally applied to streets in the city center; especially along the business thoroughfares such as Calles San Francisco and San Bernardo, as well as streets adjacent to high rent properties, such as Calles Tacuba, Capuchinas, Cadena, Espíritu Santo, and Santa Clara.[39] For the most part, neighborhoods surrounding the traza did not have the luxury of paved streets; dirty streets and alleyway predominated in this area. Streets flooded during the rainy season, and dry and dusty in other times of the year, along with a lack of paving in these poorer barrios contributed greatly to the presence of disease and the general discomfort and inconvenience of residents there.

Perhaps of all of Revillagigedo's sanitation programs, paving projects proved to be the most extensive and comprehensive. However, he was not the first viceroy both to voice concern about the problem and to offer solutions. In 1780, Viceroy Matías de Gálvez and head of the Junta de Policía, Don Francisco Antonio Crespo, issued a bando regarding the overall cleanliness and paving of city streets. In it, they argued that most of the paving deficiencies that existed in Mexico City at this time were due to the damaging practices of city residents, in particular the practice of dumping wastewater and garbage out into public thoroughfares.[40] Therefore, it was required that residents themselves be responsible for the repair of paving on streets adjacent to their properties. They set limits to the amount of cargo wagons could transport and made general transportation of goods at night illegal. This was most likely done to discourage attempts by residents to try to circumvent the new weight requirements under the cover of darkness.[41]

The city council, in 1782, suggested limited improvements for the areas directly north of the Plaza Mayor and the city's southeastern quadrant, as part of an extension of the debate undertaken in 1780, but there is no evidence to show that these projects were completed.[42] In 1785, with the help of funds from the *ramo de Pulque*, the projects on Calles Palma, Coliseo, and San Francisco were completed, bringing with them "beauty, cleanliness, comfort, and public health" to this part of the city.[43] Finally, in 1787, repairs of street paving were approved for the following streets: Santo Domingo, de los Tlapaleros, Meleros, and Monterilla, although it appears that these repairs were not immediately completed and later fell under the larger project instituted by Revillagigedo.[44]

The viceroy did not waste time in tackling the paving problems in the city. In a pronouncement date November 27, 1790, Revillagigedo laid out his plans for this massive project, providing both the justification and the structure. He argued that through his own personal observations, previous projects aimed at renovating city streets were insufficient, and paving throughout the city was in dire need of repair. He suggested immediate attention be paid to this public defect. As with the earlier discussions on sanitation and drainage projects, paving would increase the "beauty and comfort in transit, general cleanliness, proper conduct and health of the public, and would allow the police to better fulfill their role in keeping order in the capital."[45] Table 6.2 and map 6.2 confirm the major paving improvements undertaken during the latter half of the eighteenth century, including Revillagigedo's term in office (1789–1794).[46]

A few points of clarification must be made regarding these projects. First, the documentation that exists regarding paving in the city is sketchy before 1775. At this stage, it is difficult to determine the state of city streets before the scope of this work. At the same time, the number of projects undertaken between 1789 and 1794, the years of Revillagigedo's term, are almost double to those in the preceding eleven years. Clearly, there was an increased emphasis on paving city streets in the early to mid-1790s; an increase that corresponds with the emergence of other public works projects, such as new sanitation initiatives, drainage projects, renovation of public space, and the expansion of the public water supply.

The organization of this large project was based on the division of the city into four separate quadrants, or *quadrillas de Empedradores*. A *maestro mayor* headed each, who was in charge of organizing and carrying out the repair of street paving within their district. Under him were two supervisors, or *sobrestantes*, twelve skilled workers, or *oficiales*, and eighteen *peones*, or unskilled laborers. Also included in the ranks of laborers were twelve each of the following: *barretas* (those who use pick-axes); *pisónes* (those who use heavy mallets for crushing, pounding, flattening); *martillos* (hammerers); *palas* (shovelers); *talachas* (those who cut down trees to provide lumber for the projects); and *huacales* (crate builders). The labor hierarchy established on paving projects was further entrenched through the social and racial background of those involved. Most likely maestro mayores were Spanish; sobretantes were lower-level Spaniards or mestizo; oficiales were either mestizo, mulato,

Table 6.2 Major paving projects in Mexico City, 1767–1796

Location	Year
Calle de Santo Domingo	1767
Calles de San Francisco and Espíritu Santo	1771
Calles de San Francisco, Tacuba, and San José de Real	1777
Calle de Ortega de la Victoria	1778
Calle Tacuba (leveling of existing paving)	1779
Calle de San Felipe Neri	1779
Calle de San Juan	1779
Calle del Calvario (in front of the Alameda)	1779
Calle de Coliseo	1783
Calle de Santo Domingo (until the corner of Santa Catarina Mártir)	1783
Calles de San Francisco, la Palma, y Monterilla	1784
Calles de Santo Domingo and del Relox	1785
Calle de Mesones	1787
Calle de la Estampa de Regina	1788
Calle de Espíritu Santo	1789
Calle de Capuchinas	1790
Calle de Santo Domingo (first and second blocks)	1791
Front of the Real Aduana	1791
Calle Cadena	1791
Plazuela de Carmen	1791
Calle de Necatitlan	1791
Calle de Empedradillo	1791
Calles de Santa Isabel, Brígidas, and Puente de los Gallos	1791
Calle de San Bernardo	1791
Calles Tacuba, Santa Clara, and Vergara	1792
Calle de los Donceles	1792
Plazuela de Santo Domingo	1792
Calle Arzobispado	1792
Calles de Coliseo, Colegio de Niñas, and Zuleta	1793
Calle de la Palma	1793
Calle de Cordobanes	1794
Calle de Alcaiceria	1794
Calle de Monserrate	1794
Calles Ratas and Regina	1794
Calles Relox, San Idelfonso, and del Rastro	1794
Plaza Mayor	1796

Source: AHCM, Empedrados, Vol. 880–882.

or other well-placed casta, and the unskilled laborers came from the Indian population.

To avoid conflicts and disputes, maestro mayores could not exchange labor. If a laborer failed to show up for work without informing the

Map 6.2 Major paving projects in Mexico City, 1767–1796.

boss three days in advance, he risked replacement. The same held true if workers showed up drunk or wasted time on the job. This particular punishment reflected larger societal stereotypes connected to lower-class unskilled labor. Workers were paid the following daily wages: sobrestantes, five reales; oficiales four reales; peones (including those listed earlier) two and one-half reales.[47]

Just as with the drainage initiatives, money for paving projects came from a variety of sources. Revillagigedo's ideas for a resident tax to fund paving projects first emerged in his bando of November 1790. He argued that residents should cover some of the costs of improvements, which in the end would benefit them in numerous ways. He advocated that every homeowner pay one-half real for each vara of street that fronted his or her property, and estimated that with 3,525 homes in the city, this tax would raise roughly 44,070 pesos to fund paving projects. Through this, he also argued that the most any resident would probably have to pay, based on the size of their property would be five pesos per year, a minimal sum. However, the viceroy did not hold Indians and residents of poorer neighborhoods to this standard. Poorer residents were only responsible to contribute what they could manage.[48] While this recognizes the financial difficulties that poorer residents faced daily, it also may have been used as the basis not to extend street paving out into poorer barrios, where the necessity was just as great, if not more so, than in the city center. It is also curious why Revillagigedo, in his arguments, singled out Indians, as opposed to grouping them with the poorer vecinos. This might have had something to do with recognizing that Indians' primary economic responsibility was to provide their yearly tribute payments to the state, and that demanding financial contributions to public works projects could compromise this payment. Another important source of funding came from the fondo de Real Desagüe, from which 100,000 pesos were redirected to Revillagigedo's paving projects.[49] What is significant about this sum is that in 1794, the total balance of the account stood at 297,622 pesos. A transfer of 100,000 pesos would have represented a significant portion of this total. The fact that such a large sum was allocated toward paving illustrates how important these projects were to Revillagigedo's overall mission of making Mexico City a more organized and efficient Bourbon capital.

The specifics of the organization of the labor for these projects, as well as the types of funding used by Revillagigedo, point to some of the inherent problems that the viceroy faced in bringing his urban planning ideas to fruition. First, given the detail in which Revillagigedo described the labor specifications, it is probable that an official department of public works did not exist within the administration of the viceregal capital from which the viceroy could direct his projects. Second, the struggle to find ways in which to fund his projects emphasizes that monies were not put aside routinely for such things as improvements to the drainage system and expanding existing paving. Revillagigedo, as viceroy, did not have *carte blanche* to spend colonial revenues as he saw fit. In reality, it was the city council's primary responsibility to oversee municipal sanitation, the water supply, cemeteries, and so on, not the viceroy's. The city council may have perceived the fact that Revillagigedo emphasized urban sanitation to such an extent as an overall critique of their leadership and legitimacy, a critique they did not take lightly, and which resulted in the withholding of municipal funds to support new sanitation programs. Certainly, the struggle between local and colonial government limited to an extent the success of sanitation initiatives throughout the colonial period, as well as into the nineteenth and twentieth centuries.

While the scope of Castera's project seemed quite ambitious, in reality it was not. Just as new drainage projects focused for the most part on the city center, the same was true for paving projects. As illustrated in map 6.2, the spatial layout of newly repaved streets focused on the high rent districts immediately north, west, and south of the Plaza Mayor. Ignored were the Indian barrios of Santiago Tlateloco and San Juan, along with the poorer neighborhoods that ringed the eastern and southern edges of the city. Some streets also underwent multiple renovations and repairs, perhaps at the expense of extending some paving projects to the city outskirts. This included Calle Santo Domingo, with paving done in 1767, 1783, 1785, and 1791; Calle de San Francisco, in 1771, 1777, and 1784; and Calle Tacuba in 1777, 1779, and 1792.

Residents questioned the quality of the construction and repairs. As early as November 1793, residents reported damage to the paving on many of the streets that had recently undergone repairs, including Calles San Bernardo, Capuchinas, Cadena, San Francisco, Santa Isabel, Puente de Gallos, Coliseo, and Espíritu Santo.[50] Certainly part of this had to do with the continued problem of carriages and annual rains damaging the paving stones, but perhaps shoddy work and poor paving design also had something to do with the failure to provide long-term solutions to the street paving issue.

Finally, certain projects also took priority and demanded extra funds. One such project was the renovation of the Plaza Mayor. Early on, Revillagigedo expressed concern over what he considered the disordered nature of the city's main public spaces, especially markets. Since the Plaza Mayor housed one of the city's largest markets, it became the focal point of his attack. He viewed these spaces in general as poorly paved, prone to flooding during rains, marked by mounds of garbage (generally produced by the market itself), and human excrement (markets generally had poor public sanitation services).[51] The main plazas housing markets, including the Plaza Mayor, attracted vagrants, who harassed patrons during the day and used the cover of night to commit, according to the viceroy, the "worst offenses," including excessive drinking, robbery, public nudity, public defecation, and performing sexual acts in public.[52] The general construction of the market in the Plaza Mayor, in particular, was very haphazard. Organized as a series of tents and movable structures, as opposed to a permanent building, this also added its chaotic nature, argued the viceroy. In essence, the Plaza Mayor was the antithesis of Bourbon order, efficiency, and austerity, in terms of both the structures it housed as well as the people it attracted.

To combat this element of spatial and social disorder, the Plaza Mayor underwent a dramatic transformation. The first change came with the market, moved from the Plaza Mayor into a new permanent building, the Volador in 1791. Located in one of the plazas adjacent to the main square, the Volador represented Bourbon order and logic as applied to marketplaces. Revillagigedo himself described the new market as "the best and most convenient arrangement to allow for ease in buying and selling goods; providing a clean and orderly environment in which to earn a living."[53] The market was organized into a square, with permanent stalls, as opposed to the tents that had once dominated the old open-air market; different types of goods were sold together (see table 6.3).

The upper floors of the market consisted of these permanent stalls. The main floor was set aside as a sort of daily market, where poorer residents could come and sell goods on an informal basis. Some of the more common types of commodities sold at this level might include clothing (new and used), prepared foods, baked goods, artisan crafts, and smaller amounts of any of the goods sold above in the permanent stalls. While Indians had space above the permanent stalls to sell corn, this was generally only in the event that the main level of the market was full. The police heavily regulated this main level; merchants took down their tables each night and returned home. Stalls were not set up around the Volador in the plaza, but rather remained within the building. The market could not be used as a place to gather socially, nor could it be used as the public as a shortcut through the plaza. City

Table 6.3 Organization of goods sold in the Volador market

Stall Numbers	Types of Goods Sold
1 through 24	blankets, woolen shawls, ribbon, hats, cotton cloth
25 through 48	sweets, candied and dried fruit, biscuits, cheese, and butter
49 through 72	iron tools, copper utensils, horseshoes and nails, notions (pins, needles, etc.)
73 through 96	spices, seeds, eggs, chiles
97 through 144	fresh vegetables, fruits, and flowers
145 through 168	meats, live and dead birds, fresh and salted fish
168 through 192	pottery and crockery, luggage, rope and fishing tackle, leather (tanned and untanned), shoes, saddles
194 through 205; 292 through 303	corn (sold exclusively in the market by Indians)

Source: AGN, *Obras Públicas*, Vol. 8, Exp. 5, f. 58–59.

ordinances prohibited open fires, stoves, and restaurants, to protect the wooden structure from fire; therefore, any foods sold in the market had to be prepared off site before sale in the market. Garbage produced by proprietors had to be disposed of in appropriate receptacles and not on the sidewalks in front of the building. Cleanliness of the market as well as the surrounding plaza was of the utmost importance.[54] The market closed at night, and sixty-four lanterns surrounding the structure kept the structure well lit. This helped to keep away vagrants and generally to discourage people from loitering around and sleeping in the plaza.[55] In an effort to regulate market activities, Revillagigedo established a special body, the *Juez de Plaza*, to monitor both the people in the market as well as the activities therein. This body had the right to question both seller and buyers, arrest delinquents and others who harassed the public, and monitor selling activity. It looked for the illegal use of weights and measures, the sale and consumption of illegal beverages, and the sale and purchase of illegal commodities. Its primary responsibility was to guarantee the safety and comfort of both merchants and customers, both in the quality of goods as well as in the environment in which these commercial exchanges took place.[56]

Restructuring the market represented the first stage of renovation of the Plaza Mayor. One of its most important elements was its function to control which social groups had access to the market. Its structure and organization was part of a frontal attack against the homeless and vagrants who, according to the viceroy, caused so many public problems, and whose activities and vices threatened both the safety and health of city residents. Nevertheless, even poor merchants, a group in which castas and Indians dominated, fell into this category. Limited to the heavily regulated lower floor of the market, their activities were more closely monitored than their counterparts in the permanent stalls above were. The very fact that they did not have access to a permanent place in the market represented the existence of generalized suspicion of their activity, as well as their lower and inferior status not only within colonial society, but within the commercial community as well.

Once the main market was removed from the Plaza Mayor, the square was leveled, new paving was put in place, and four new fountains were constructed for public use.[57] Upon completion of the renovation project, Revillagigedo placed inscriptions on each of the four fountains, commemorating the accomplishments. They read as follows:[58]

On the fountain in front of the Cathedral:

> In the glorious reign of Charles IV, being Viceroy
> the most Excellent Juan Vicente de Güemes Pacheco
> de Padilla, Count of Revillagigedo, the plaza was
> lowered in the years 1790 to 1793 and its four
> fountains were erected. The atrium of the Holy
> Cathedral Church was also lowered and redecorated,
> and its façade was completed and beautified

On the fountain in front of the main entrance to the viceregal palace:

> In 1790, during the glorious
> reign of Charles IV, being Viceroy the Most Excellent
> Juan Vicente de Güemes Pacheco de Padilla, Count of
> Revillagigedo, public lighting in the streets of this
> city was introduced, as were the most useful lantern-
> keepers who attend to them and to the public safety

On the fountain in front of the viceroy's private entrance to the viceregal palace:

> In the reign of Charles IV,
> in the viceregency of the Most Excellent Juan Vicente
> de Güemes Pacheco de Padilla, Count of Revillagigedo,

the street plan of the city was laid out, glazed tiles were set in place, the houses were numbered, annexes were marked, the façades of many buildings were painted, and a regimen of general cleanliness was undertaken

On the fountain in front of the municipal (cabildo) offices:

In the glorious reign of Charles IV, being Viceroy the Most Excellent Juan Vicente de Güemes Pacheco de Padilla, Count of Revillagigedo, between 1790 and 1794 the principal streets of this city were paved: 545,039 square varas of paving were laid, 16,535 square varas of drainage canals, and 27,317 square varas of sidewalk with piping underneath;[59] and the plazas for markets were formed and arranged

The renovation of the Plaza Mayor represented on a grand scale what Revillagigedo and Castera attempted to accomplish throughout the city with their drainage and paving projects. Through the completion of drainage and paving projects, they transformed the city's main square from an uninhibited, poorly organized, and chaotic public space to one which embodied the Bourbon aesthetic: grand yet austere, symmetrical and organized, a true spatial representation of the order and efficiency that reformers strove for in all aspects of the colonial world. However, where they succeeded with the Plaza Mayor, they ultimately failed throughout the rest of the city.

Concluding Thoughts

An examination of the justification, organization, and implementation of drainage and paving projects leads us to a few key conclusions about the physical layout of the city and the relationships of groups within it. First, there was an important geographical element to the programs themselves. Edward Thornton Tayloe, an American who spent some time in Mexico City during the summer of 1825, best sums this up. About the city streets, he wrote:

In the central and most frequented parts of the city the streets are well paved and are kept clean; but removed from these they are amazingly dirty—the drains passing through the centre of them being open, offensive both to the sight and smell.[60]

While articulated as important to the overall health, comfort, and security of city residents, in the end urban renovations affected only specific districts of the city. Most repairs and renovation both to the drainage system as well as to street paving favored the city center, in particular wealthier streets, and those devoted to economic activity. To an extent, this should not be surprising. The economic stability and livelihood of the capital were extremely important, not only for the wealth it generated, but also for the daily necessities of life it provided. The wealthy, as a social group, benefited the most directly from improved city services, primarily because they lived in the city center—easily the most expensive part of the capital. Those farther removed from the center essentially saw little to no change in the drainage and paving situations in their neighborhoods. They lacked both the economic and the social power to become a priority in the eyes of the state. In effect, the spaces where elites and the poor coexisted side by side became the focus for the most aggressive changes in urban structure, as those spaces illuminated the root of elite anxieties regarding the physical and cultural disorder that emanated from the popular classes. The spaces beyond elite comprehension, the neighborhoods on the exterior fringes of the traza, faded from the scope of the projects themselves.

Besides the economic and geographic elements to the improvements advocated, there also existed the issue of safety, security, and stability that these renovations represented. This is especially true of the changes made to the Plaza Mayor and the establishment of the Volador market. The disorder and chaos that reigned in the Plaza Mayor, both physically, in the unstructured market, the presence of garbage, the irregularity of existing paving, as well as socially, in the presence of a large body of vagrants and the unemployed, who harassed residents and represented the most vile and immoral of colonial society, stood as a direct challenge to the order, productivity, and efficiency Bourbon inspired leaders strove for. What resulted was a plaza more in line with the Bourbon and elite aesthetic, and a main market that allowed freedom of commerce for some while severely controlling and restricting the activities of others.

The type of labor utilized in these projects also points to the concerns city leaders had regarding the place of the lower class within colonial society, as well as the use of public works projects to try to mold citizens into the Bourbon ideal. Most who worked on drainage and paving projects were overwhelmingly from the lower strata of society and were predominantly of casta and indigenous backgrounds. Those who came to the projects voluntarily performed heavy physical labor for little monetary return, while having to deal with stereotypes that they were lazy workers as well as drunkards. The perceived "rehabilitative" nature of physical labor encouraged the use of penal labor on these projects as well. It was one of the tools colonial officials used in their attempts to turn criminals into trustworthy, disciplined, and hardworking members of colonial society.

Finally, the role of Ignacio Castera in organizing drainage and paving projects helps to explain partially the ultimate failure of the projects as a whole. During the eighteenth century, engineers were increasingly favored over architects in the realm of urban planning because of their scientifically based training, as well as their focus on ways to solve urban problems through function. By favoring Castera, who prioritized form over function, Revillagigedo doomed the projects from the start. The way in which Castera perceived Mexico City's problems, in terms of irregularity rather than a lack of adequate services, emphasizes this fact. His pursuit of beauty and order through architectural and urban form, despite all the good design and brilliant architecture it produced—an austere and grand Plaza Mayor, the Volador Market, neatly constructed drainage canals, sidewalks, and paved streets in the city center—failed to provide the measure of order and reason in urban affairs that was his self-appointed mission. In the end, for the majority of residents in the viceregal capital, Bourbon changes were more an issue of form over substance. While there was some demonstrated concern for the health, safety, and well-being of all residents, most did not experience the benefits promised to them.

CHAPTER SEVEN

Concluding Thoughts

In the end, did the state and colonial elites gain the measure of order, efficiency, beauty, and control that they were after? Were they successful in bringing the Bourbon Reforms to the streets and the residents of Mexico City? By the 1820s, it seemed clear that the physical environment had improved. Foreign travelers such as G.F. Lyons and Edward Thornton Tayloe described the city as remarkably clean, especially in comparison to European capitals such as London and Paris. They commented on the wide, well-lit, and neatly paved streets, massive public structures, and spacious plazas. Although they criticized some aspects of life in the city, especially the large vagrant population, and the common practices of public nudity and defecation, overall they were impressed with what they found.

Certainly, during the latter part of the eighteenth century, and especially during the tenure of Viceroy Revillagigedo, the state introduced programs aimed at making Mexico City healthier. There was a clear acknowledgment by city leaders of the urban problems that residents of the capital faced, and these problems were critical enough to warrant an official response. City streets, littered with garbage and decomposing matter, often flooded after rainstorms. The popular practice of dumping household waste, including human excrement, added to this problem. Many residents did not have regular or affordable access to potable water. All of these things contributed to the constant presence of endemic disease in the capital city, as well as frequent epidemic outbreaks of smallpox, measles, and typhus. City officials argued that the introduction of new sanitation regulations and programs would improve the living conditions of urban residents, especially in terms of their health. There was also an aesthetic element to the public works projects that state leaders introduced. Bourbon rulers strove to make their colonial possessions more organized, efficient, and productive in the economic and political realm. These attributes were also reflected in the spatial realm as well. In the case of Mexico City, the "recolonization" of the New World extended into reshaping and ordering urban space. Improved sanitation schemes, new drainage systems and paving of city streets, the expansion of the public water supply, the establishment of new markets, and new bathhouse regulations and reform would make Mexico City the ultimate physical symbol of Bourbon reform and modernity, and progress.

However, along with the health and aesthetic improvements connected with urban reform, elites understood these improvements as a way to gain leverage over the plebeian classes. City officials, leaders of the church, urban planners, and the wealthy all viewed the urban poor as the root of many of the environmental problems the viceregal capital faced, and considered common practices among the popular classes, such as the indiscriminate dumping of garbage and waste, defecating and urinating in public, loitering, washing clothes and other personal items in public fountains, and public nudity as a threat to civic order and safety. In the eyes of both the state and elites, these behaviors marked the urban masses as uncivilized and unmodern. Elites also feared the danger that these activities represented, in challenging both the cultural norms upon which they based their social superiority, as well as the potential of these behaviors to transgress established boundaries. This was especially true with the issue of public defecation and urination. If the poor could not control their bodily functions, and did not have the moral decency to tend to themselves in private, they had the potential to lack control in other situations, which promised to digress into other types of public disorder, especially criminal activity.

This element of social control inherent in the justification and implementation of city projects is perhaps best reflected in the types of penalties that city officials established in conjunction with new programs and regulations. Racial and class elements were infused in the types of punishments carried out, and certain transgressions were associated with different social groups. The worst activity, punishable by monetary fines, that upper- and middle-class groups were accused of was the illegal dumping of garbage. Lower-class groups, however, were responsible for more serious and physical infractions, such as urinating and defecating in public. This lack of physical control demanded physical punishments, such as a series of lashes or time in the city's stocks, done to both humiliate and shame the offender into changing his or her

Concluding Thoughts

ways. The way in which these punishments were carried out, in public for all of colonial society to witness, was to make an example out of the individual and encourage others in colonial society to refrain from repeating his or her mistake. The use of convict labor on public works projects offered similar rehabilitative benefits.

These punishments were not an effective deterrent, and enforcement of sanitation laws in general was not terribly successful. The state in essence criminalized sanitation practices by making enforcement of regulations part of the responsibility of the Junta de Policía. This colonial police force was overextended, poorly paid, and did not have much legitimacy in the eyes of many colonial residents. On the one hand, as state agents, it was their responsibility to uphold unpopular mandates that aimed to control people's activities. On the other hand, they themselves were members of the communities and neighborhoods in which they worked. If they were too vigilant in their job, their fellow residents treated them with contempt. If they were too lax, problems continued. The establishment in the 1820s of a *Junta de Sanidad*, devoted specifically to the problems of sanitation and public health, began to alleviate some of these problems.

Limited funding, as well as conflicting levels of power and authority, also hampered the implementation of the projects. City planners and colonial leaders, even Viceroy Revillagigedo, struggled constantly to fund their projects in the face of other compelling needs in their budgets. The offices of the viceroy and municipal council were separate institutional structures, each with their own constituencies and their own economic and political interests, and so were often at odds over both the scope and the implementation of these reforms. Finally, there was no formal department of public works, which made the logistics for planning and executing larger projects even more complex and costly.

Despite the best intentions of city officials, there were a number of inherent problems with the solutions they offered. First, the scope of state responses to urban disorder and decay was limited primarily to the historical traza at the expense of the poorer outlying barrios surrounding the city center. Consequently, racial and class differences that existed in colonial society were reinforced within the structure of public services, as significant differences existed between wealthy and poor neighborhoods in terms of the urban environment. In the case of sanitation services, the poorer outskirts, such as the Indian barrio of Santiago Tlatelolco, as well as poorer mixed race neighborhoods to the east and the south of the traza, were not included in any significant way. Rather, they were the areas of the city where garbage dumps were established to contain waste. The same is true of large-scale drainage projects, expansion of paving of city streets, and improvements made to the public water supply. Instead of seeing significant change in their streets and plazas, neighborhoods dominated by the urban poor continued to withstand the worst of Mexico City's sanitation and public services deficiencies. In the end, the urban changes that elites sought to bring Mexico City into the modern era bypassed large segments of the urban population. Beauty and convenience in the urban center took precedence over any substantial material change in the poorer outlying neighborhoods. While the historical traza boundaries no longer functioned in maintaining racial and class separation between Spaniards and Indians, it did serve as the de facto boundary when it came to sanitation and public services.

Indeed, the role of poverty, in the context of both sanitation problems and urban disease, did not factor into the solutions put forth by city officials. The state favored environmental approaches to sanitation controls, disease containment, and eradication. Although it is clear that the consequences of poverty perpetuated disease, political leaders in the viceregal capital seemingly refused to acknowledge this, placing the blame on the poor themselves. They argued that disease was primarily the product of dirt and decomposing matter, and that once these problems were rectified, a more healthful environment would result. Some of the most extensive sanitation plans developed in Mexico City during the colonial period took place during the tenure of Viceroy Revillagigedo (1789–1794), between major epidemics in 1784–1787 and 1797. When it came to containing and eradicating disease, public matters, such as garbage collection, sewage systems, drainage, paving, and potable water were considered important, and worthy of state priority and funds. They considered factors such as overcrowded housing, poor diets, and frequent unemployment beyond their responsibility, and thus inappropriate objects for state action. Environmental responses were also more appealing to elites in that they took the victims of disease and the urban environment—the urban poor—out of the equation all together. The state could argue that they were focusing time and energy on programs that cleaned up public spaces, thus benefiting all colonial residents.

Although city officials ultimately failed in bringing about significant material change for a large segment of the urban population, it is possible to draw some wider conclusions about the nature of urban planning in general, as well as the functioning of colonialism in the final years before Independence. First, the central role that Viceroy Revillagigedo played in the development, organization, and implementation of city improvements in the 1790s points to the power that certain imperial political leaders still had, even at a time when dependents in the New World were increasingly questioning the validity of the colonial system and calling for the end of colonial rule. His focus on improving the material lives of colonial residents, providing urban order and security by criminalizing certain popular practices of the plebeian classes, and reordering urban space illustrate his unique commitment to the Bourbon agenda. While Bourbon policy makers focused their attention on political and economic issues, Revillagigedo's emphasis on urban planning demonstrates one of the ways in which the Bourbon Reforms created change on a material, social, and cultural level.

Revillagigedo's reliance on architects such as Ignacio Castera, as well as military engineers, is also indicative of the emergence and development of more professional and organized cadre of urban planners. Even though the viceroy's initiatives failed in part because of a lack of funding and commitment from city leaders, what limited progress was made was due to professionals who were given the opportunity to craft more cohesive planning policies. This partially explains why the tenure of Revillagigedo saw more material changes to the urban environment in Mexico City than any leader before or after him.

In her work on the religious origins of modernity in Mexico, historian Pamela Voekel argues that toward the end of the eighteenth century and into the nineteenth century, religious identity shifted from an outward, corporate, Catholic piety to that of a more inward, self-disciplined, and moderated sense of spiritualism and connections to God. Within the context of religion, urban elites called on the ideals of the Enlightenment and the intellectual undercurrents of the Bourbon Reforms, especially that of reason, to shape a new and modern Mexican citizen. Self-control was best expressed in a heightened sense of control over the body, and the ideals of secular reason and rationality pushed this transformation along.[1] In similar ways, I find Voekel's arguments helpful in understanding the broader significance of late colonial attempts to transform Mexico City from a dirty, chaotic, and unrestrained urban space, to a representation of rationality, order, and control. Although colonial officials and urban elites in Mexico City may have failed to implement the material and social change they were after, they were ahead of contemporaries elsewhere in Latin America and Europe when it came to connecting the issues of public health, urban planning, and social control to incipient ideas about modernity in a postcolonial world. Environmental factors contributing to disease, such as polluted water, dirt, and decomposing material, were a significant part of the public health, and consequently, urban planning debates in eighteenth-century Mexico City. In the case of Europe, the "ultra-sanitarian" movement in Great Britain, which made the same types of connections, did not emerge until the 1840s. More significant considerations of the links between public health, urban planning, and social control in Latin America did not develop again until the latter part of the nineteenth century, as urban populations began to explode and elites, in turn, attempted to cling to their positions of power.[2] While the programs that leaders in colonial Mexico City advocated were limited, they anticipated an emerging period of change in the ways in which public health, urban planning, and social control were perceived, and set the stage for subsequent change in the nineteenth and twentieth centuries.

This subsequent urban transformation from imperial to modern, anticipated by urban elites in the waning decades of the colonial, did not come quickly. The Wars of Independence, which engulfed Mexico from 1810 to 1824, created an immediate legacy of economic and political chaos. Within this context, Mexico City fell into decline. Lots and structures were abandoned, garbage and trash reclaimed the streets, and waves of the urban poor searched desperately for food and shelter. Even elites were not spared from the creeping decay and uncertainty. Revillagigedo's successes were long forgotten, as urban residents struggled to find a place within the chaotic world of mid-nineteenth-century Mexico.[3]

Stability reemerged with the reformist government of Benito Juarez, whose policies concerning the Catholic Church and their property holdings transformed the urban landscape. As elite families shifted to emerging neighborhoods west of the Zocalo (the Plaza Mayor of the colonial period), new developments revived the urban construction industry and compelled a new generation of urban planners to consider what a modern Mexico City should look like. Porfirio Diaz, leader of Mexico from 1876 to 1910, argued that one way to demonstrate the development and success of the modern Mexican state was through the organization of its cities; that in a sense, one could construct modernity. Modern cities, he argued, were to look a certain way, modeled after the great urban centers of Europe and the United States. Urban planning became important again, as Diaz undertook projects to alleviate flooding, improve sanitation, expand potable water systems, pave and widen streets and public plazas, electrify urban spaces, develop new transportation systems, and construct new suburbs.[4] The context, however, had changed in the interceding century. Unlike Revillagigedo, Diaz operated in a more singular and centralized political structure. He was not hampered by the divisions between imperial and local power that Revillagigedo was forced to negotiate. Diaz also enjoyed massive foreign aid and investment, which provided him with the revenue to not only embark upon, but successfully complete numerous public works projects within Mexico City proper. In the case of the capital of modern Mexico, the "order" in Diaz's slogan Order and Progress would be expressed through a rationally constructed and organized urban space.

Urban residents were also to reflect new ideas about modernity through their actions. Much like his colonial counterparts, Diaz expressed concerns about the behaviors of the urban masses—many of the behaviors of the late colonial period that so disgusted elites continued unabated—and so in this way, modernity could also be constructed through personal actions, an extension of culture. In a sense, the ideas about restoring order out of chaos that shaped Revillagigedo's approach to urban sanitation came full circle in the goals of Diaz, thus reinforcing the connections between the colonial and the modern in the physical structure of Mexico City.

NOTES

One Shaping the Colonial City

1. According to Charles Gibson, the rainy season was delayed, with a corresponding drought in May of that year. Almost all the maize was destroyed by severe frost. Shortages began in September, with a corresponding sharp increase in the price of corn in the last months of the year, into 1786. See Charles Gibson, *The Aztecs Under Spanish Rule: A History of the Indians of the Valley of Mexico, 1519–1810* (Stanford: Stanford University Press, 1964), 457–458. Between 1784 and 1787, in response to the drought, 40,000 people migrated into the city in search of work. See Silvia Marina Arrom, *The Women of Mexico City, 1790–1857* (Stanford: Stanford University Press, 1985), 6.
2. Although this process began to develop sooner in many regions of New Spain (i.e., Chiapas), one of the consequences of the Bourbon Reforms was to turn payment of Indian tribute from kind into cash, thus forcing many Indians into the fledgling cash economy of the cities.
3. John Kicza, "Migration to Major Metropoles in Colonial Mexico," in *Migration in Colonial Spanish America*, ed. David J. Robinson (Cambridge: Cambridge University Press, 1990), 193–211.
4. Ibid., 207.
5. Along with drought and famine, the other large-scale catastrophe that the population of New Spain faced in the eighteenth century was disease. Smallpox epidemics were constant during this time; Mexico City in particular faced crises in 1736–1739, 1779–1780, 1798, and 1804. The city also faced epidemics of measles in 1727–1728, and 1768–1769. Various diseases, fevers, and maladies were part of everyday life for the inhabitants of the Spanish colonies, especially in the cities; see Gibson, *The Aztecs*, 448–449.
6. Mexico City was not alone in this experience. In Paris, for example, there were connections made between the rise in urban populations and the general decline of health and cleanliness in the city. City leaders believed that migrants brought problems to the city, and they demonized the homeless in particular because of their inability to secure gainful employment. In return, they had to rely on begging and stealing to survive and were forced to live on the streets. All of their actions and behaviors, especially the "ones which pollute," were on public display, and thus easy targets. See Louis Chevalier, *Laboring Classes and Dangerous Classes in Paris During the First Half of the Nineteenth Century* (Princeton, NJ: Princeton University Press, 1973), 148. The same attitudes prevailed in Mexico City in regard to increasing problems with public sanitation. In their attempts to organize new sanitation programs, city officials perceived the daily activities of lower-class groups, such as public defecation and urination, and the indiscriminate dumping of garbage, as the main cause of urban pollution and the spread of disease.

7. Recent scholarship has done an excellent job at examining the role of crime in Mexico City for the late colonial and early independence periods. See Michael C. Scardaville, *Crime and the Urban Poor: Mexico City in the Late Colonial Period*. (Ph.D. Dissertation, University of Florida, 1977); and Gabriel Haslip-Viera, *Crime and Punishment in Late Colonial Mexico City, 1692–1810* (Albuquerque: University of New Mexico Press, 1999).
8. Archivo Histórico de la Ciudad de México (hereafter AHCM), Clausura de Callejónes, Vol. 443, Exp. 24.
9. AHCM, Clausura de Callejónes, Vol. 443, Exp. 25.
10. *Pulque* is an alcoholic beverage made from fermented agave cactus. It was extremely popular among the lower classes during the colonial period.
11. Linda Curcio-Nagy, "Giants and Gypsies: Corpus Christi in Colonial Mexico City," in *Rituals of Rule, Rituals of Resistance: Public Celebrations and Popular Culture in Mexico*, ed. William H. Beezley, Cheryl English Martin, and William E. French (Wilmington: Scholarly Resources, 1994), 1–24; Susan Deans-Smith, "The Working Poor and the Eighteenth-Century Colonial State: Gender, Public Order, and Work Discipline," in *Rituals of Rule, Rituals of Resistance*, 47–76; Cheryl English Martin, "Public Celebrations, Popular Culture, and Labor Discipline in Eighteenth-Century Chihuahua," in *Rituals of Rule, Rituals of Resistance*, 95–126; Haslip-Viera, *Crime and Punishment*; Michael Scardaville, "(Hapsburg) Law and (Bourbon) Order: State Authority, Popular Unrest, and the Criminal Justice System in Bourbon Mexico City," *The Americas* 50, 4 (April 1994): 501–525; and "Alcohol Abuse and Tavern Reform in Late Colonial Mexico City," *Hispanic American Historical Review* 60, 4 (November 1980): 643–671; Pamela Voekel, "Peeing on the Palace: Bodily Resistance to Bourbon Reforms in Mexico City," *Journal of Historical Sociology* 5, 2 (1992): 183–208; and *Alone before God: The Religious Origins of Modernity in Mexico* (Durham, NC: Duke University Press, 2002); Juan Pedro Viquera Albán, *Propriety and Permissiveness in Bourbon Mexico*, trans. Sonya Lipsett-Rivera and Sergio Rivera Ayala (Wilmington: Scholarly Resources, 1999); Silvia Marina Arrom, *Containing the Poor: The Mexico City Poor House, 1774–1871* (Durham, NC: Duke University Press, 2000). Mexico City was not the only city that was concerned with "unruly" classes. European cities, such as London and Paris, also suffered from the consequences of urbanization and the desire to alter the behavior of the lower classes. See M. Dorothy George, *London Life in the Eighteenth Century* (New York: Harper and Row, 1926); A.L. Beier and Roger Finlay, eds. *The Making of the Metropolis: London, 1500–1700* (London: Longman Press, 1985); Jeffrey Kaplow, *The Names of Kings: The Parisian Laboring Poor in the Eighteenth Century* (New York: Basic Books, 1972); Robert Woods and John Woodward, *Urban Disease and Mortality in Nineteenth-Century England* (New York: St. Martin's Press, 1984); Chevalier, *Laboring Classes*.
12. James Scott argues that the ordinary weapons of powerless groups, such as foot-dragging, false compliance, and feigned ignorance, what he terms "everyday forms of resistance," are just as effective as more overt, openly organized and violent uprisings. Everyday resistance is important in its implicit disavowal of elite goals, yet at the same time, the state often does not want to publicize the insubordination, for fear of admitting its policy is unpopular and a challenge to their authority. While Scott's arguments are based on the peasant experience in Malaysia, his ideas are certainly applicable to colonial Mexico City. See James Scott, *Weapons of the Weak: Everyday Forms of Peasant Resistance* (New Haven, CT: Yale University Press, 1985).
13. Arrom, *Containing the Poor*, 17.
14. Ibid., 32–38.
15. Pedro Fraile, *La otra ciudad del Rey: ciencia de policía y organizacion urbana en España* (Madrid: Celeste Ediciones, 1997).
16. Josef W. Konvitz, *The Urban Millennium: The City-Building Process from the Early Middle Ages to the Present* (Carbondale: Southern Illinois University Press, 1985), 46.

17. In the case of Mexico City and Lima, the Viceroy's palace would take up space along one side of the Plaza Mayor along with the residence of the Archbishop.
18. Christopher Lutz, *Santiago de Guatemala, 1541–1773: City, Caste, and the Colonial Experience* (Norman: University of Oklahoma Press, 1994), 45–49.
19. Ibid., 47.
20. This can certainly be seen in examining the developing sophistication and accuracy of maps of Mexico City. The maps of the early colonial period, especially through the sixteenth and into the seventeenth centuries, tend to be more illustrative in nature, depicting Mexico City as a landscape, and are generally inaccurate in size and scale. By the late seventeenth century, and into the eighteenth, mapmakers become much more accurate, as they master principles of mathematics and geometry and translate that knowledge into maps more accurate in scale. For examples of the development of maps of Mexico City, see Sonia Lombardo de Ruíz, *Atlas Histórico de la Ciudad de México* (México: Smurfit Cartón y Papel de México, 1997).
21. There are a number of excellent anthologies and monographs that deal in part with the history of Mexico City during the colonial period. They include the following: Carlos Illades y Ariel Rodríguez, compilers, *Ciudad de México: instituciones, actores sociales, y conflicto político, 1774–1931* (México: El Colegio del Michoacán y la Universidad Autónoma Metropolitana, 1996); Regina Hernández Franyuti, ed., *La Ciudad de México en la primera mitad del Siglo XIX*, 2 volumes (México: Instituto de Investigaciones Dr. José Mariá Luis Mora, 1994); R. Douglas Cope, *The Limits of Racial Domination: Plebeian Society in Colonial Mexico City, 1660–1720* (Madison: University of Wisconsin Press, 1994); Timothy Anna, *The Fall of the Royal Government in Mexico City* (Lincoln: University of Nebraska Press, 1994); John E. Kicza, *Colonial Entrepreneurs: Families and Business in Bourbon Mexico City* (Albuquerque: University of New Mexico Press, 1983); Linda Arnold, *Bureaucracy and Bureaucrats in Mexico City, 1742–1835* (Tucson: University of Arizona Press, 1988); Juan Javier Pescador, *De bautizos a fieles difuntos: Familia y mentalidades en una parroquia urbana: Santa Catarina de México, 1568–1820* (México: El Colegio de México, 1992). See also Arrom, *The Women of Mexico City*, the chapter on Indians in the city in Gibson, *The Aztecs*, and Haslip-Viera, *Crime and Punishment*.
22. Throughout the colonial period in Mexico City, issues surrounding water, from drainage and flooding, to access to potable water, presented constant struggles for the city's inhabitants. An excellent examination of one of the worst floods the city faced is found in Louisa Schell Hoberman, *City Planning in Spanish Colonial Government: The Response of Mexico City to the Problem of Floods, 1607–1637* (Ph.D. Dissertation, Columbia University, 1972).
23. AHCM, Aguas: Fuentes Públicas, Vol. 58, Exp. 25.
24. AHCM, Aguas: Cañerías, Vol. 21, Exp. 107.
25. This term is used as a collective reference to people of lower class, common, status. It is juxtaposed against *gente decente*, or the "decent" people, who represented those within colonial society of high social and economic standing.
26. As mentioned earlier, see the following: Scardaville, "(Habsburg) Law and (Bourbon) Order" and "Alcohol Abuse and Tavern Reform"; Voekel, "Peeing on the Palace"; Deans-Smith, "The Working Poor and the Eighteenth-Century Colonial State." An excellent examination of the State's attempt to alter popular cultural activities, such as the celebrations of Corpus Christi, Carnival, *El Dia de los Muertos*, and other popular diversions like dancing, theater, and drinking, can be found in Albán, *Propriety and Permissiveness*.
27. Anne Staples discusses the issue of public space as an extension of private space in her article "Police and *Buen Gobierno*: Municipal Efforts to Regulate Public Behavior, 1821–1857," in *Rituals of Rule, Rituals of Resistance*, 115–126. I believe this same kind of blurring between public and private space was even more prevalent for the colonial period. Juan Pedro Viquera Albán also discusses the importance of the street in the population's social life, arguing that in reality vicregal authorities believed the public nature of everyday life actually made

it easier for the state to monitor the activities of the lower classes. Privacy was seen as an "obstacle to the power of the state and thus an enemy of social peace." See Albán, *Propriety and Permissiveness*, 101.
28. Archivo del Tribunal Superior de Justicia del Distrito Federal (hereafter ATJ), Civil, Vol. 112, No. 9.
29. It is not clear whether Don Leandro lived in the same building as Matheana, but it was a common practice for property owners to rent the lower floors to poorer tenants, while they and their families would occupy the more desirable upper floors. If they did indeed live in the same building, this might explain why Don Leandro was so concerned about her activities, since it would be well known that they shared the same address.
30. James Riley, *The Eighteenth-Century Campaign to Avoid Disease* (London: Macmillan Press, 1987). While the state ultimately implemented these policies on a limited basis in the colonies, it illustrates that the state's new role in public health and cleanliness, along with an environmental approach to disease, were important factors in the subsequent drive to control disease.

Two Splendor and Misery in the Viceregal Capital: The Physical, Material, and Political Environment of Bourbon Mexico City

1. Hipólito Villarroel, *Enfermedades polílicas que padece la capital de esta Nueva España en casi todos los cuerpos de que se compone y remedios que se le deban aplicar para su curación si se quiere que sea útil al Rey y al público* (México: Grupo Editorial Miguel Angel Porrúa, 1999), 175. The discourse over the place of the poor in the urban environment was also common in Europe at this time, most notable in Paris. Discussions regarding the condition of the city in the late eighteenth century included issues regarding race and class as well as the material situation. See Chevalier, *Laboring Classes*.
2. *Historia Urbana de Iberoamerica, Tomo II: La Ciudad Barroca 1573–1750* (Madrid: Consejo Superior de los Colegios de Arquitectos de España, 1990), 163–168.
3. G.F. Lyons, *Journal of the Residence and Tour in the Republic of Mexico in the year 1826 with some account of the mines of that country* (London: Albemarie Street, 1828), 105–106.
4. *Historia Urbana*, 163–168.
5. According to the 1790 census commissioned by Viceroy Revillagigedo, the poor, defined as "unemployed vagrants, semi-skilled and factory workers, and artisans," constituted 88.1 percent of the total population. Voekel, "Peeing on the Palace," 185. Getting accurate population numbers, however, was exceedingly difficult during this time. Individuals with no fixed residence were often not counted in census records. In addition, it was common for Indians to move in and out of the city regularly, especially when employment needs dictated. While the city at times may have seemed crowded, it is difficult to know how many people were regular residents of the capital.
6. Other cities in the world, particularly in Europe, suffered some of the same problems as Mexico City. The air in London, for example, was heavily polluted due to the burning of coal and dominated by poorly constructed and crowded tenement housing. Sanitary conditions were also deplorable, with defective sewers and the dumping of garbage in the city streets a particular problem. See George, *London Life*, 63–107.
7. Gibson, *The Aztecs*, 368.
8. The Spaniards attempt to establish hegemony in the colonies was highly dependent on convincing Indians and other non-European groups to buy into this racial system. Colonial scholars, argue that the Spanish largely achieved this goal. See Patrick J. Carroll, *Blacks*

in Colonial Veracruz: Race, Ethnicity, and Regional Development (Austin: University of Texas Press, 1991), 32. At the same time, one should not assume that Indians blindly accepted this racial system. They found many ways to challenge Spanish authority and were able to maintain to an extent social and cultural autonomy. In many ways, ethnic identity was contested terrain in the relationship between conquerors and conquered. The division between Spaniards and Indians was further complicated in urban areas by the emergence of large casta, or mixed race populations, by the early seventeenth century. For elites, this group was particularly troublesome. They did not fit into the system of Spanish and Indian that justified colonialism and were often blamed for many of the problems, such as crime and disorder that were common features of the urban landscape. See Cope, *The Limits*, Introduction.

9. The numbers for 1811 are based on the census taken that year, with some increase due to groups fleeing emerging rural unrest due to the Hidalgo Revolt. The dramatic drop two years later is due to deaths (20,385) from a major epidemic that hit the city, as well as rural residents returning home after the suppression of the Hidalgo Revolt. See Anna, *The Fall*, 4. Getting accurate numbers was problematic due to the shifting nature of the city's population. Many homeless people were never accounted for, and thousands of Indians, primarily involved in petty trade and commerce, moved in and out of the city daily.
10. Anna, *The Fall*, 6.
11. Linda Newson, "Indian Population Patterns in Colonial Spanish America," *Latin American Research Review* 20 (1985): 41–74. Smallpox was one of the main culprits of indigenous decline, introduced to the mainland shortly before the arrival of Hernan Cortes in 1519. The encomienda, a grant of Indian labor initially given to the conquistadors as material reward for their participation in the conquest of Tenochtitlan, placed a heavy toll on Indians, primarily through abusive working conditions. These conditions often made Indians even more susceptible to illness.
12. Gibson, *The Aztecs*, 448–451. Although the general trend in population numbers among indigenous groups for the eighteenth century is upward, there were always instances that would allow for drops in population numbers. For example, epidemic outbreaks still managed to kill large numbers of Indians and would result in temporary drops in population numbers. Indians also were still predominantly rural, so outmigrations from rural villages toward larger urban centers would also mask as temporary population losses. In reality, it was merely a geographic shift in numbers; while some Indians retained their traditional lifestyles in the midst of urban resettlement, others did not, and chose to adopt more non-Indian cultural attributes, such as language, dress, religion, and material consumption patterns.
13. Ibid., 140–144.
14. David Brading, *Miners and Merchants in Bourbon Mexico, 1763–1810* (Cambridge: Cambridge University Press, 1971), 14. Other important studies that corroborate this upward trend in population include the following: Wolfgang Trautmann, *Las transformaciones en el paisaje cultural de Tlaxcala durante la época colonial* (Wiesbaden: Franz Steiner Verlag, 1981); José Miranda, "La población indígena de Ixmiquilpan y su distrito en la época colonial," *Estudios de Historia Novohispana* 1 (1966): 121–130; Delfina López Sarrelangue, "La población indígena de la Nueva Espana en el siglo XVIII," *Historia Mexicana* 12, 4 (April–June 1963): 515–530.
15. *Pueblos de Indios* were corporations built on the indigenous political bodies of the conquest period. According to Bernardo García Martínez, these corporations were "significant as political bodies with a territorial basis...a direct line linked the early colonial *pueblos de indios* with the Nahuatl *altepetl*...collective symbols and ceremonies could be traced back to pre-Hispanic ritual practices as well. They also possessed the necessary resources, organization, and experience to face internal and external demands. They were involved in the pursuit of common interest and the preservation of social structure through the performance

of a number of ritual functions and administrative tasks. Relations with the outside world, mainly tribute, labor, and matters of property and jurisdiction, were managed by each *pueblo* as a collective concern." Bernardo Garcia Martinez, "*Pueblos de Indies, Pueblos de Castes*; New Settlements and Traditional Corporate Organization in Eighteenth-Century New Spain," in *The Indian Community of Colonial Mexico*, ed. Aril Owned and Simon Miller (Amsterdam: CEDLA Latin American Studies), 105. Benefits for indigenous members of *pueblos* included access to Indian communal landholdings and the defense/legitimization of land claims, collective welfare, and participation in religious rituals.

16. Ibid., 116.
17. Guy P.C. Thompson, *Puebla de los Angeles: Industry and Society in a Mexican City, 1700–1850* (Boulder, CO: Westview Press, 1989), 155–167.
18. Some cities in the New World suffered population declines not directly connected to out-migration. Lima, for example, lost close to one-tenth of its population in the earthquake of 1746 and barely recovered those numbers by the end of the colonial period. See Susan M. Socolow, "Introduction," in *Cities and Society in Colonial Latin America*, ed. Louisa Schell Hoberman and Susan Migden Socolow (Albuquerque: University of New Mexico Press, 1986), 6.
19. Arij Ouweneel, "Growth, Stagnation, and Migration in Anáhuac, 1720–1800," *Hispanic American Historical Review* 71, 3 (August 1991): 531–577.
20. Casta refers to those of mixed race ancestry that did not fit into the mestizo or mulatto categories. Recent scholarship has shown that as early as the sixteenth century, black slaves founded one pueblo de indio in Guadalajara. William Taylor argues that by the eighteenth century, Indians in Guadalajara "allowed mestizos, mulattos, and Spaniards to register as Indian members, live within the village, and share in the lands assigned to Indian families" in an attempt to increase revenues for village fiestas and other expenses. This presumably was an attractive way for non-Indians to gain access to land during a time when increased population pressures made land scarcer. Conversely, this trend also encouraged Indians to migrate elsewhere when they themselves were pushed off land by non-Indians. See William Taylor, "Indian *pueblos* of Central Jalisco on the Eve of Independence," in *Iberian Colonies, New World Societies: Essays in Memory of Charles Gibson*, ed. Richard L. Garner and William B. Taylor (S.I; s.n., 1985), 166.
21. Ouweneel, "Growth," 537.
22. Anna, *The Fall*, 5.
23. Population numbers (for 1815) are as follows (all approximations): London 1,250,000; Paris 500,000; Naples 500,000; Istanbul 500,000; Moscow 250,000; St. Petersburg 250,000; Vienna 250,000. Within Spain, the largest cities were Madrid, Seville, Cadiz, and Valencia, all with populations ranging from 80,000 to 120,000. See Colin McEvedy, *The Penguin Atlas of Modern History (to 1815)* (Harmondsworth: Penguin Books, 1972).
24. Scardaville, *Crime and the Urban Poor*, 53–54. Alejandra Morneo Toscano and Carlos Aguirre Anaya, in their study of the 1811 census in Mexico City, reiterate Scardaville's conclusions. See Alejandra Moreno Toscano and Carlos Aguirre Anaya, "Migrations to Mexico City in the Nineteenth Century: Research Approaches," *Journal of Interamerican Studies and World Affairs* 17 (1975): 27–42. This increase due to migration was also the case for the other major urban center in the region, Guadalajara. See Rodney D. Anderson, *Guadalajara a la consumación de la Independencia: estudio de su población según los padrones de 1821–1822* (Guadalajara: Unidad Editorial, 1983).
25. Thompson, *Puebla de los Angeles*, 155–167.
26. Ouweneel, "Growth," 562.
27. Kicza, "Migration," 193–211. It should be noted that the sex ratio for Mexico City in 1790 was approximately 79 men for every 100 women. Silvia Arrom attributes this imbalance to the fact that men could often migrate to other haciendas and mines in search of work. They did not necessarily have to move on to the city. Women, on the other hand, were limited

NOTES

in the types of employment they could seek, often within the context of domestic activities, and so the city was generally their only option. See Arrom, *The Women*, 106. Another examination of the reality of Indian women who migrated to Mexico City to seek employment can be found in Juan Javier Pescador, "Vanishing Women: Female Migration and Ethnic Identity in Late-Colonial Mexico City," *Ethnohistory* 42, 4 (Fall 1995): 617–626.

28. Kicza, "Migration," 210. This information is culled from the 1811 census of Mexico City, which listed people's occupations. *Atole* is a popular drink made out of corn and served hot, usually with breakfast.
29. Ibid., 208.
30. Kicza, "Migration," 198.
31. Ibid., 201.
32. Manuel Carrera Stampa, *Planos de la Ciudad de México (desde 1521 hasta nuestros dias)* (México: Sociedad Mexicana de Geografía y Estadistica, 1949), 275.
33. Mons. D'Auteroche Chappe, *A Voyage to California to Observe the Transit of Venus* (London: Edward and Charles Dilly, 1778), 39–45.
34. Kicza, "Migration," 205.
35. Albán, *Propriety and Permissiveness*, 27.
36. The Spanish destroyed the Mexica imperial capital of Tenochtitlan in 1521 and replaced with the Spanish capital of Mexico City. Hernan Cortes and his men went so far as to use the rubble from the Mexica temples and other religious structures to partially build the Cathedral and government buildings. These actions certainly sent the message to the Indian population that Spanish control and domination was here to stay. It also represents the important convergence of worldly and spiritual power within the structure of colonial Spanish American cities.
37. Part of the attraction to the New World for Spanish settlers was the promise of ample land and free labor to exploit, supporting a gentry's lifestyle that they sought after.
38. It has been estimated that throughout the colonial period, anywhere from 75 to 90 percent of the total population of Spanish and Portuguese America lived in rural areas. See Susan Migden Socolow, "Introduction to the Rural Past," in *The Countryside in Colonial Latin America*, ed. Louisa Schell Doberman and Susan Migden Socolow (Albuquerque: University of New Mexico Press, 1996), 3.
39. In English the "Ordinances of Discovery and Population." These ordinances postdate the founding of most of the major cities in the New World (e.g., Mexico City), but they were still important in organizing subsequent growth and development. See Socolow, "Introduction," 4.
40. Ibid.
41. Salvador de Madariaga, *The Rise of the Spanish American Empire* (New York: Hollis and Carter, 1947), 191.
42. Gibson, *The Aztecs*, 370.
43. The map grid is from Haslip-Viera, *Crime and Punishment*, 14, and it is based on an original map drawn in 1789 by José Antonio de Alzate y Ramiréz titled "Map of Tenochtitlan, Court of the Mexican Emperors." The original is held in National Library of Paris and reproduced in Lombardo de Ruíz, *Atlas Histórico*, 335. The *traza* boundaries are from Marcela Dávalos, *Basura e ilustración: la limpieza de la Ciudad de México a fines del Siglo XVIII* (México: Instituto Nacional de Antropología e Historia, 1997), 149. The dotted line is the division between the barrios of Santiago Tlatelolco and San Juan. This division was later broken down into smaller barrios, as indicated on map 2.1.
44. The project of physical separation between colonizer and colonized can also be seen in British colonialism during the nineteenth century in Africa. Dane Kennedy's work on colonial Kenya and Southern Rhodesia examines the European struggle between the need for social segregation and economic integration. While the British feared close contact with the African population, they were heavily dependent on their labor. In the end, British

colonialists established outright regulations controlling the residence, labor, and mobility of African populations. They also depended on "symbolic" segregation, such as separate public facilities, establishment of dominance in the household, differences in language, and emphasis on biological differences to illustrate their separateness and superiority in the face of daily contact with their African counterparts. See Dane Kennedy, *Islands of White: Settler Society and Culture in Kenya and Southern Rhodesia* (Durham, NC: Duke University Press, 1987), 148–166. For a similar discussion on British colonial Sierra Leone, see Leo Spitzer, *The Creoles of Sierra Leone: Responses to Colonialism, 1870–1945* (Madison: University of Wisconsin Press, 1974). In the case of colonial Mexico City, even though there were attempts to separate physically the Spanish and Indian populations, the Spanish were also heavily dependent on Indian labor, so their presence in the traza was constant from the very beginning of Spanish colonization.
45. Gibson, *The Aztecs*, 373.
46. Another term commonly used during the colonial period for city council, besides cabildo is *ayuntamiento*. I use these terms interchangeably in this study.
47. Ibid., 376. This breakdown of the traza was not exclusive to Mexico City. Santiago de Guatemala, the colonial capital of Guatemala, suffered the same type of breakdown. Initial divisions between Spaniards and Indians fell apart as casta populations began to take over predominantly Indian barrios, and Spaniards began to encroach upon Indian space by buying up lots in indigenous neighborhoods. Unlike the case in Manila, where the laws supporting divisions between the Spanish and the Chinese were stringently upheld, in Santiago cabildo officers were "largely indifferent" to the collapse of separate spaces for Spaniards and Indians. See Lutz, *Santiago*, 45–49.
48. For a detailed examination of this riot, and the implications it had for urban order and security, see Cope, *The Limits*, 125–160.
49. Gibson, *The Aztecs*, 377.
50. These new district divisions are represented in a map that was drawn up by Manuel Villavicencio under the orders of Viceroy Don Martín de Mayorga. Archivo General de la Nación (hereafter AGN), Núm. Cat. 4246, Neg. 978.2104, Ramo de Bandos, Vol. 12, fc. 124.
51. This information, as well as the divisions placed on the corresponding map (map 2.1), come from a 1793 map drawn by chief architect for Mexico City, Ignacio Castera. Castera used this map to explain where sanitation services (namely city dumps) would be located. The original map is in the Archivo General de las Indias, Seville, Spain, *Planos de México* (México 2.773), TL. 444. I consulted a photograph of the original for this project in Lombardo de Ruíz, *Atlas Histórico*, 343.
52. Gibson, *The Aztecs*, 385. A Spanish *vara* is approximately thirty-three inches.
53. Haslip-Viera, *Crime and Punishment*, 8.
54. Carrera Stampa, *Planos*, 275.
55. Gibson, *The Aztecs*, 385–386.
56. Haslip-Viera, *Crime and Punishment*, 8.
57. Ibid., 10.
58. Ibid. The Parián, a market especially favored by elites, remained a fixture of the Plaza Mayor, until 1828, when fire destroyed it in an ensuing riot. See Silvia Marina Arrom, "Popular Politics in Mexico City: The Parián Riot, 1828," in *Riots in the Cities: Popular Politics and the Urban Poor in Latin America, 1765–1910* ed. Silvia M. Arrom and Servando Ortoll (Wilmington: Scholarly Resources, 1996), 71–96.
59. Gibson, *The Aztecs*, 395.
60. Carrera Stampa, *Planos*, 305.
61. Lyons, *Journal of the Residence*, 130.
62. Gibson, *The Aztecs*, 395.

NOTES

63. Carrera Stampa, *Planos*, 310. This practice of selling certain items in particular areas of the city was typical in preindustrial towns and is still common in Mexico City today.
64. Villarroel, *Enfermedades*, 142–143.
65. Ibid.
66. Bucareli was viceroy from 1771 to 1779, and Revillagigedo from 1789 to 1794.
67. Priests, both secular and regular, heavily favored establishing themselves in urban areas over rural ones. Educated clerics perceived cities as being able to provide a cultured and sophisticated lifestyle that they were after, while they shunned rural areas because of the isolation and difficult lifestyles that these appointments entailed. Throughout the colonial period, the church had a difficult time staffing their rural parishes. This preference for urban locals also followed patterns that were common in Spain at this time. See Paul Ganster, "Churchmen," in Hoberman and Socolow, *Cities and Society*, 139.
68. Ibid., 137.
69. Haslip-Viera, *Crime and Punishment*, 11. Society understood that social services throughout the colonial period, such as caring for the physically and mentally ill, were the responsibility of the church.
70. Ibid.
71. Besides the western neighborhoods, the other areas popular with the church included areas directly off the Plaza Mayor, and the southeast quadrant of the city. Almost all other convents were housed in these areas, along with monasteries, the remaining city hospitals (Hospital General de San Andrés, Hospital de Terceros, Hospital La Cuña, La S.Sma. Trinidad, and Hospital de Jesús), and the Casa de Locas Misericordia (an insane asylum for women). Interestingly, these were the districts in the city that had the best access to water, and many of these structures had their own private fountains, wells, and sewage systems, something very rare for the rest of the city. The exception to this was the Hospital de San Lázaro, and insane asylum that was located on the eastern fringes of the city. This information comes from a city map commissioned by Viceroy Revillagigedo and drawn up by Diego García Conde. The original is located in the Museo de la Ciudad de México, with a copy at the British Library. Considered one of the most detailed maps of the city, cartographers made numerous reproductions well into the nineteenth century.
72. Deans-Smith, "The Working Poor," 50. A more detailed examination of the tobacco economy in Mexico City is in Susan Deans-Smith, *Bureaucrats, Planters, and Workers: The Making of the Tobacco Monopoly in Bourbon Mexico* (Austin: University of Texas Press, 1992).
73. Haslip-Viera, *Crime and Punishment*, 23.
74. Ibid., 24.
75. Ibid., 24–25.
76. Ibid.
77. Edward Thornton Tayloe, *Mexico, 1825–1828: The Journal and Correspondence of Edward Thornton Tayloe*, edited by C. Harvey Gardiner (Chapel Hill: University of North Carolina Press, 1959), 53–54. While Tayloe wrote his account shortly after Independence, it corroborates other descriptions of Mexico City for the late colonial period.
78. Anna, *The Fall*, 22. These numbers were probably not that significantly different during the last half of the eighteenth century.
79. Ibid., 16. These streets also housed some of the most exclusive shops at the time, focusing on such goods as jewelry and imported goods from Europe and Asia.
80. Ibid.
81. A particular Baroque style of architecture, named after Spanish architect José Chirriguera (1650–1723). It was popular in Spain and its Latin American colonies during the sixteenth and seventeenth centuries. This style is characterized by elaborate, ornate, and extravagant decorations and details.

82. Haslip-Viera, *Crime and Punishment*, 11.
83. *Historia Urbana*, 360–363.
84. Albán, *Propriety and Permissiveness*, 42.
85. Villarroel, *Enfermedades*, 171–174.
86. Haslip-Viera, *Crime and Punishment*, 12. These types of residences were common in Mexico City throughout the colonial period. See Cope, *The Limits*, 30.
87. Ibid.
88. Anna, *The Fall*, 21–22.
89. Ibid.
90. Ibid., 310.
91. Anna, *The Fall*, 24.
92. Haslip-Viera, *Crime and Punishment*, 31. Even though 100 years separate the two groups, the working poor in 1900 London suffered the same fate as the urban poor in Mexico City when paying for the basic necessities of life. Most earned between 18 and 26 shillings a week, which was to cover rent, burial insurance, coal and light, cleaning materials, clothing, and food. Rent was by far the largest expenditure, which could consume approximately one-third of the weekly income (compared to the wealthy at one-eighth, and the middle class at one-sixth). Properties for the poor were often very small, dark, with very little ventilation. After rent and other necessities, little remained for food, which was the one part of the weekly budget that families slashed. By far the most important staple for the poor was bread (much like tortillas for those in Mexico City), and other items would be sacrificed before it if there were shortfalls in the budget. The other foodstuff that was often discarded was milk. Despite its known importance in the diet of children, it was simply too expensive for working-class families. See Mande Pember Reeves, *Round about a Pound A Week* (London: G. Bell and Sons, 1913), 22–24, 95–99.
93. The equivalent of a *fanega* is approximately 1.5 bushels. Throughout the colonial period, corn continued to be the main staple in the diet in New Spain. It was common for the working poor to consume a majority of their daily calories in corn (e.g., tortillas). In theory, the state was supposed to monitor both the cost and supply of corn in order to meet the basic needs of urban residents, but this did not always happen. Large landowners often manipulated the price and supply of corn to maximize profits. See Enrique Florescano, *Precios de maíz y crisis agrícolas en México, 1708–1810* (México: El Colegio de México, 1969).
94. Haslip-Viera, *Crime and Punishment*, 32.
95. AHCM, Hacienda: Rentas de Ciudad, Vol. 2242.
96. Haslip-Viera, *Crime and Punishment*, 33
97. AJT, Civil, Leg.8, No. 22.
98. An excellent examination of the role of pawning in colonial Mexico City can be found in Marie Francois, *A Culture of Everyday Credit: Housekeeping, Pawnbroking, and Governance in Mexico City, 1750–1920* (Lincoln: University of Nebraska Press, 2006).
99. Haslip-Viera, *Crime and Punishment*, 34.
100. Ibid.
101. Chappe, *A Voyage*, 34–36.
102. Haslip-Viera, *Crime and Punishment*, 34.
103. Albán, *Propriety and Permissiveness*, 120
104. Ibid., 101.
105. Ibid., 129–163.
106. Ibid., 163; 183–203.
107. Villarroel, *Enfermedades*, 142–143.
108. Refer to the narrative in chapter one on rich historiography that addresses the social and cultural implications of the Bourbon Reforms.

Three In Sickness and Health: Disease, Healing, and the Urban Population

1. While the Spanish colonies in the New World were impacted by the outbreak of such diseases as smallpox, measles, and typhus, other areas in the Americas also suffered greatly from epidemic forms of the above. Smallpox, for example, was common throughout the British colonies during the eighteenth century; Boston itself suffered seven major outbreaks between 1721 and 1792. Typhus was also common, primarily in coastal (or near coastal) cities such as Philadelphia, Baltimore, New York, Boston, and Portsmouth. Three diseases that seemed to affect the British holdings to a greater extent than their Spanish counterparts were yellow fever, dysentery, and malaria; all tropical-oriented illnesses. This probably has to do with the location of major centers of population in North America in low-lying coastal regions, as opposed to Spanish America, where major cities tended to be located away from tropical regions. For example, Charleston, South Carolina was hardest hit by yellow fever in colonial British North America, with epidemic outbreaks in 1706, 1728, 1732, 1745, 1758, 1790–1792, 1795, and 1798–1799. New York and Philadelphia also suffered through regular outbreaks of the disease. Mexico City, on the other hand, never faced a major outbreak of yellow fever during the entire colonial period. See Geoffrey Marks and William K. Beatty, *Epidemics* (New York: Charles Scribner's Sons, 1976), especially Chapter 11, "The Fruits of Exploration and Colonization," 148–190.
2. I gleaned data for this table from Gibson, *The Aztecs*, 450–451. There is much debate as to classifying the epidemic that broke out in the capital in 1813. Existing documents are unclear, referring to the outbreak as "pestilential fevers." While some contemporaries at the time believed it to be yellow fever, this is highly unlikely, as yellow fever was a predominantly tropical disease, very rarely seen in the highlands of Central Mexico. More likely, it was an outbreak of typhus. For a detailed discussion of this debate, see Donald Cooper, *Epidemic Disease in Mexico City, 1761–1813: An Administrative, Social and Medical Study* (Austin: University of Texas Press, 1965), 157–158.
3. Ibid.
4. Gibson, *the Aztecs*, 456–459. As mentioned in chapter one, 1786 was known as *"el año de hambre,"* or the year of hunger.
5. Smallpox was initially brought to the mainland of Mexico in 1520 by a black slave accompanying the expedition of Pánfilo de Narváez. For a discussion of the role of disease in cross-cultural exploration, see Alfred Crosby, *The Columbian Exchange: Biological and Cultural Consequences of 1492* (Westport, CT: Greenwood Press, 1972).
6. In her article on Indian population patterns in colonial Spanish America, Linda Newson argues that the actual decline of indigenous numbers due to disease varied between regions. She accounts for three different case scenarios. The first scenario includes areas where Indian groups after contact became extinct within one to two generations. This covers the islands of the Caribbean and its mainland fringe. The second scenario includes Indian populations that after European contact slowly decline in numbers throughout the colonial period, never to recover. Areas of Argentina, Chile, parts of the Andes, and Central America fall into this category. The last scenario focuses on areas where Indians experienced a sharp decline followed by a period of slow and gradual recovery, often punctuated by epidemics that forced short-term population losses. This covers central and southern Mexico, the highlands of Central America, and the Andean region of the Incan empire (Peru, Bolivia, and Ecuador). It is this last scenario that Mexico City falls under. Newson, "Indian Population Patterns."
7. Gibson, *The Aztecs*, 448–451.
8. Although there is some discrepancy regarding the total number of deaths from the epidemic in 1779, the most reliable source is that of senior Audiencia judge Cosme de Mier de

Trespalacios, who, based on records kept during the epidemic, estimated a death toll of approximately 18,000. Cooper, *Epidemic Disease*, 68. In the case of the epidemic of 1797, a well-organized and funded charity effort helped to keep the death toll down comparatively. In this case, the most reliable sources are the parish death reports, which were submitted to the Archbishop on a weekly basis between September 9, 1797 and January 26, 1798. These reports set the death toll for the 1797 epidemic at 7,147. Cooper, *Epidemic Disease*, 153.

9. Noble David Cook and W. George Lovell, "Unraveling the Web of Disease," in *Secret Judgments of God: Old World Diseases in Colonial Spanish America*, ed. Noble David Cook and W. George Lovell (Norman: University of Oklahoma Press, 1991), 217–218.
10. The disfiguring nature of smallpox, especially scarring, had other psychological affects on its survivors. For example, among North American Eastern Woodland males whose pride was in their personal appearance, it was customary to spend hours plucking out unseemly facial and body hair. Thus, pox marked survivors were unable to grow beards to cover their scars. Even though surviving the outbreak rendered them immune to further outbreaks, this was unknown to them, and the scarring was mistakenly interpreted as disease. James Adair, in his writings on an outbreak in 1738 among the Cherokee, observed that scores of survivors, in seeing their pockmarked faces in mirrors brought by European traders, and in "being naturally proud," committed suicide. It is possible in both cases that men who were disfigured or rendered blind by smallpox (which was a sometimes consequence of the disease) were rejected by women as suitable sexual and marriage partners. See James Axtell, *Beyond 1492: Encounters in Colonial North America* (Oxford: Oxford University Press, 1992), 145.
11. Cooper, *Epidemic Disease*, 111.
12. While colonial medical practitioners did not consider measles as dangerous as smallpox, it was a serious disease for children under three. Cook and Lovell, "Unraveling the Web," 220.
13. Ibid.
14. Ibid., 225. The elderly were most severely stricken, while mortality rates for children were less than 5 percent.
15. AHCM, Policía: Matanza de Perros, Vol. 3662, Exp. 2, 5, 6, 8.
16. *Gazeta de México, compendio de noticias de Nueva España, de los años de 1790*. Por Don Manuel Antonio Valdes (México: Imprenta de Don Mariano de Zúñiga y Ontiveros). Vol. 12, December 20, 1805.
17. Cook and Lovell, "Unraveling the Web," 238.
18. This held true for most of the city's convents and hospitals as well. See Carlos Flores Marini, *Casas virreinales de la Ciudad de México* (México: Fondo de Cultural Económica, 1970) and Ignacio Gonzalez Polo, *El palacio de los condes de Santiago de Calimaya* (México: Instituto de Investigaciones Estéticas Universidad Nacional Autónoma de México, 1973).
19. This is somewhat ironic as Orizaba was not spared from the regional outbreak of smallpox that accompanied the epidemic in the viceregal capital. By the time the epidemic was about half over, Orizaba had documented 1,727 cases with 277 deaths. Its overall percentage of death to the total population was slightly higher than in Mexico City. Cook, "The Smallpox Epidemic," Table II, 952.
20. Reproduced versions of all three texts were consulted for this project at the John Carter Brown Library, Brown University, Providence, Rhode Island.
21. This goddess has contemporary meaning to Mexicans as well and is evidence of the modern Mexican state's commitment to emphasizing its Indian heritage and legitimacy. She is the symbol of Mexico's National Public Health Congresses, and a likeness of her decorates the base of the statue of Hippocrates in the main entrance of the auditorium in Mexico

City's National Medical Center. Gordon Schendel, *Medicine in Mexico: From Aztec Herbs to Betatrons* (Austin: University of Texas Press, 1968), 27.
22. Ibid., 26–28.
23. Ibid., 29.
24. Bernard R. Ortiz de Montellano, *Aztec Medicine, Health, and Nutrition* (New Brunswick, NJ: Rutgers University Press, 1990), 121. In many ways, Mexica supernatural influences in medicine, along with the rationale of disease as a punishment for offenses committed against a particular deity, is not much different from European explanations, which explained widespread disease, such as epidemics, as God's punishment against a sinful society.
25. Ibid., 163.
26. Medical research was considered an important aspect of the profession in Mexica culture. An extensive botanical garden and zoo was established by Moctezuma I (grandfather of Moctezuma II, emperor at the time of the Spanish arrival in 1519) not only to encourage medical study, both in providing the raw materials for different healing concoctions, but also to allow for medical research and experimentation. Even Cortes and his men were impressed by the sophistication of Mexica medical research. Schendel, *Medicine in Mexico*, 37.
27. Unfortunately, very few of the medicinal plants in the Americas made it into widespread use in Europe. They were often difficult to grow in the colder and drier climates of the continent, and those that shipped across the Atlantic lost their potency before they reached their final destination. Outlandish claims made by some doctors over the potential of these new drugs failed to materialize, and more conservative doctors tended to shun medicines from the New World as somehow being inferior to those indigenous to Europe. Some New World medicines were misclassified; humoral theory still dominated in Europe, and medicines from the New World were often classified in terms of heat, dryness, cold, and moisture. This led to many failed attempts to force New World drugs into Old World classification, which in the end led to the distortion of their use and effectiveness. Guenter B. Risse, "Transcending Cultural Barriers: The European Reception of Medicinal Plants from the Americas," in *Botanical Drugs of the Americas in the Old and New Worlds* (Stuttgart: Wissenschaftliche Verlagsgesellschaft MBH, 1984), 32; Jonathan Sauer, "Changing Perception and Exploitation of New World Plants in Europe, 1492–1800," in *First Images of America*, ed. Fredi Chiapelli (Berkeley: University of California Press, 1976), 819; Charles H. Talbot, "America and the Drug Trade," in *First Images of America*, 836–837.
28. While curanderos were predominantly Indian in the early years of Spanish colonialism, Africans, mulattos, and mestizos increasingly joined their ranks. A more detailed discussion of curanderos, including the racial and gendered components of their practices, follows later in this chapter.
29. Risse, "Transcending Cultural Barriers," 36.
30. In this sense, the use of religious beliefs to explain the cause of various ailments was not much different from the Mexica use of gods to justify why certain people suffered from illness while others did not.
31. Sheldon J. Watts, *Epidemics and History: Disease, Power, and Imperialism* (New Haven, CT: Yale University Press, 1997), 13.
32. Luz María Hernández-Sáenz, *Learning to Heal: The Medical Profession in Colonial Mexico, 1767–1831* (New York: Peter Lang, 1997), 57–59.
33. The medical college at the University of Edinburgh was well known for its progressive and innovative approach to its medical curriculum, especially clinical medicine, and training of doctors, not only from the United Kingdom, but from other parts of Europe as well. The program emphasized the importance of firsthand observation of symptoms over the complaints expressed by the patient. Guenter Risse, *Hospital Life in Enlightenment Scotland: Care*

and *Teaching in the Royal Infirmary of Edinburgh* (Cambridge: Cambridge University Press, 1986), 240–255. Physicians from the college were among the first in Europe to advocate inoculation as a method of controlling smallpox, as early as 1765 (inoculation had been used fairly successfully in the Middle East—Istanbul, for example—long before its acceptance by Europeans). Watts, *Epidemics and History,* 114. Critics of the program, however, pointed to the continued use of Hippocrates as an important part of the curriculum; as with most physicians at this time, even though progress was being made in the understanding of the workings of disease, there continued to be heavy reliance on the classics. The other program considered of high quality at this time was the University of Paris, but a lack of experienced instructors and cadavers for anatomy courses plagued the program. It was also severely affected by the French Revolution, when the Revolutionary National Assembly, in an effort to erase past injustices, targeted all privileged academies and corporations for destruction, and in March 1791 abolished the masters' degree and the examination requirements. Toby Gelfand, *Professionalizing Modern Medicine: Paris Surgeons and Medical Science and Institutions in the 18th Century* (Westport, CT: Greenwood Press, 1980), 145. For a detailed examination of medicine in revolutionary France, see Matthew Ramsey, *Professional and Popular Medicine in France, 1770–1830: The Social World of Medical Practice* (Cambridge: Cambridge University Press, 1988).

34. For an excellent examination of the education and training of doctors in Spain at this time, which included many who emigrated to the New World, see Hernández-Sáenz, *Learning to Heal,* Chapter 1, "Practicing Medicine: Colonial Physicians in New Spain," 23–119. By 1770, the medical curriculum at Salamanca included logic, metaphysics, arithmetic, algebra, geometry, and experimental physics. The University of Seville surpassed Salamanca's reforms, with a five-year curriculum that included natural sciences, anatomy, physiology, therapy, pharmacy, and practice, and combined traditional and modern sources. In 1786, the University of Valencia became the first Spanish university to initiate clinical training. The reforms were so far reaching that even Englishman Joseph Townsend, in his travels through Spain in 1786, admitted the program at Valencia to be superior to that of Edinburgh. Ibid., 60–61.

35. Ibid., 69.

36. Watts, *Epidemics in History,* 13. We will see that the belief that bad air was the key contributor to poor health drove many of the sanitation programs suggested by city leaders. Initiatives designed to make air healthier to breathe were justified by the positive effects that clean air would have on the health of the residents of Mexico City.

37. Hernández-Sáenz, *Learning to Heal,* 395. In comparison, the ratio for Paris was 3.7 doctors per 10,000 inhabitants; London 2.29 doctors per 10,000 inhabitants.

38. During the eighteenth century, Scottish doctors were considered the best trained and most innovative in the world when it came to advances in medicine. In the case of smallpox, they were the group that early on advocated the use of inoculation to control the spread of the disease, as early as 1765. On the continent, even thirty years later, most physicians were still clinging to Greco-Hellenistic humoral theories, which focused on treating the patient, rather than the practice of preventive medicine. Doctors in colonial Mexico City fall into this camp. Hernández-Sáenz, *Learning to Heal,* 114–115.

39. Francisco Guerra, *El hospital en Hispanoamérica y Filipinos, 1492–1898* (Madrid: Ministerio de Sanidad y Consumo, 1994), 213–312.

40. Ibid. An ironic twist to this discussion is that the Hospital Real de los Naturales also acted as the center of practical study for medical students in Mexico City. It was the only hospital where physicians regularly conducted autopsies to teach students the finer points of anatomy and diagnosis.

41. There existed in total 1,275 beds among the city's various hospitals. Guerra, *El hospital en Hispanoamérica,* 213–312.

42. Guenter Risse, "Medicine in New Spain," in *Medicine in the New World: New Spain, New France, and New England*, ed. Ronald Numbers (Knoxville: University of Tennessee Press, 1987), 33.
43. Guerra, *El hospital en Hispanoamérica*, 302–305.
44. See Voekel, *Alone before God* for an excellent examination of the role of Catholicism in the development of modern Mexican identity.
45. AGN, Epidemias, Vol. 16, Exp.7, fs. 264–267.
46. AGN, Epidemias, Vol. 16, Exp. 7, f. 3v.
47. For a more detailed discussion of Branciforte's arguments in favor of private donations to fight the epidemic, see Cooper, *Epidemic Disease*, 119–120.
48. AGN, Epidemias, Vol. 1, Exp. 5, f. 445. In total, close to 128,000 pesos were spent during the epidemic of 1797 caring for those infected, so the 90,000 pesos donated constituted a significant amount. AGN, Epidemias, Vol. 6, Exp. 8, f. 586.
49. Ibid.
50. These organizations had also been established during the smallpox epidemic of 1779 and were such a great success that Branciforte decided to bring them back.
51. Although clothing and medical care (medicines, visits by doctors and bleeders) accounted for part of the money spent, a much larger portion of the resources went to providing food for the sick. This is probably a reflection of the important role that certain types of food played in remedies. It is also indicative of the fact that many of the city's poor lacked sufficient resources to maintain adequate diets. AGN, Epidemias, Vol. 6, Exp. 8, fs. 599–607.
52. Ibid. These had also been established, and functioned successfully, during the smallpox epidemic of 1779. In 1797, there were in total 181 committees offering poor relief in the city. AGN, Epidemias, Vol. 6, Exp. 8, f. 568.
53. Guerra, *El hospital en Hispanoamérica*, 213–312.
54. Ibid.
55. AGN, Epidemias, Vol. 16, Exp. 7, f. 267.
56. AGN, Epidemias, Vol. 6, Exp. 1, fs. 7–9.
57. Ibid.
58. Guerra, *El hospital en Hispanoamérica*, 312.
59. *Gazeta de México*, Vol. 4, April 27, 1790; Vol. 12, February 29, 1804.
60. Ibid., Vol. 1, March 24, 1784.
61. Ibid., Vol. 1, October 20, 1784.
62. Ibid., Vol. 12, December 20, 1805.
63. Ibid., Vol. 4, January 19, 1790.
64. Ibid., Vol. 7, September 18, 1795. Generally, the term "fever" described a whole host of ailments, especially when the symptoms were not clearly indicative of a specific disease.
65. Ibid.
66. Juan Manuel Venegas, *Compendio de la Medicina, ó Medicina Practica* (México: D. Felipe de Zúñiga de Ontiveros, 1788).
67. AHCM, Hospitales: San Juan de Dios, Vol. 2304, Exp. 9.
68. This most likely refers to traditional herbal remedies from curanderos. The idea that residents of the capital would turn to "traditional" (and thus backward) forms of health care, rather than the enlightened and modern Western medicine, was troubling to many members of the formal medical community. AHCM, Policía: Salubridad-Epidemias, Vol. 3674, Exp. 4, f. 22.
69. Centro de Estudios de Historia de México (hereafter CONDUMEX), "Instrucciones del Revillagigedo a Branciforte," Fondo XCI; AGN, Bandos, Vol. 6, Exp. 2, fs. 21–37.
70. Brian Pullan, "Plagues and Perceptions of the Poor in Early Modern Italy," in *Epidemics and Ideas: Essays on the Historical Perception of Pestilence*, ed. Terence Ranger and Paul Stack (Cambridge: Cambridge University Press, 1992), 109.

Four A Basic Necessity: Water and the Urban Environment

1. Legislation passed in 1790, which specifically forbade the washing of horses in public fountains and canals. For those who broke the law, city government levied a fine of nine pesos, which applied to the fund to pay for public works. AHCM, Baños y Lavaderos, Vol. 3621, Exp. 2.
2. *Puente* translates to bridge in English. Carrera Stampa, *Planos*, 287. The contemporary route of the colonial aqueduct runs down Avenida Melchor Ocampo, San Cosme, Puente de Alvarado, and Avenida Hidalgo, and terminates at the intersection of Aquilés Serdán, Avenida Hidalgo, and Calle de Tacuba.
3. Carrera Stampa, *Planos*, 288. For this aqueduct, the contemporary route skirts the southern boundaries of Chapultepec Park, runs along the center of Avenida Chapultepec, and continues onto Avenida Arcos de Belén, ending at the colonial fountain of Salto de Agua. Unlike the northern aqueduct, sections of the southern aqueduct are still standing today, as is the Salto de Agua fountain.
4. Carrera Stampa, *Planos*, 288.
5. Haslip-Viera, *Crime and Punishment*, 13.
6. AHCM, Aguas: Cañerías, Vol. 19, Exp. 29.
7. A vara is equal to approximately 33 inches. The Puente de Mariscala, along with its branch lines, provided 202,000 feet of water lines to the northern districts and neighborhoods of the city. The fuente at Salto de Agua, along with its branch lines, provided 162,000 feet of water lines to the southern districts and neighborhoods of the city.
8. Ibid.
9. Carrera Stampa, *Planos*, 288.
10. AHCM, Aguas: Cañerías, Vol. 19, Exp. 28.
11. AHCM, Aguas: Cañerías, Vol. 19, Exp. 37.
12. AHCM, Aguas: Fuentes Públicas, Vol. 58, Exp. 20.
13. AHCM, Aguas: Fuentes Públicas, Vol. 58, Exp. 23.
14. AHCM, Aguas: Fuentes Públicas, Vol. 58, Exp. 13.
15. AHCM, Aguas: Fuentes Públicas, Vol. 58, Exp. 36.
16. Refer to table 4.3.
17. AHCM, Aguas: Cañerías, Vol. 19, Exp. 52.
18. A more detailed discussion of this issue follows later in the chapter.
19. This discussion of the water situation in Santiago Tlateloco was part of larger concerns of the viceroy and city council over the general state of the public water system, and in particular the lack of access to water for residents outside the city center. On August 5, 1788, Viceroy Manuel Antonio Flores published a statement in the *Gazeta de México*, which listed the general problems that the city faced regarding water. Certainly, these discussions and concern set the stage for Revillagigedo's plans. *Gazeta de México*, Vol. 3, August 5, 1788.
20. The cabildo named the fountain Nuestra Señora de Guadalupe, in honor of the Virgin of Guadalupe, who by this time had become the preeminent "protector" of Mexico City, displacing the once popular Virgin de Remedios.
21. AHCM, Aguas: Fuentes Públicas, Vol. 58, Exp. 25.
22. Ramiréz estimated the total population at approximately 200,000. Census information for 1790 placed the city population at 112,926, while in 1792 that number had jumped to 120,602, both well below Ramiréz's estimates.
23. AHCM, Aguas: Cañerías, Vol. 19, Exp. 52.
24. Ibid.

Notes

25. A photographed copy of map used to place, spatially, cañerías and fuentes públicas in Tables 4.4 and 4.5 is in Lombardo de Ruíz, *Atlas Histórico*, 353.
26. AHCM, Aguas: Cañerías, Vol. 21, Exp. 107
27. AHCM, Aguas: Fuentes Públicas, Vol. 58, Exp. 44.
28. AHCM, Aguas: Cañerías, Vol. 21, Exp.107.
29. There is no specific addressee in the petition. It is simply addressed to the *Juez de Cañerías*.
30. AHCM, Aguas: Fuentes Públicas, Vol. 58, Exp. 46.
31. AHCM, Aguas: Cañerías, Vol. 21, Exp. 125.
32. AHCM, Aguas: Fuentes Públicas, Vol. 58, Exp. 47.
33. Ibid.
34. Refer to table 4.3 provided earlier in this chapter.
35. AHCM, Aguas: Fuentes Públicas, Vol. 58, Exp. 41. The cases of San Sebastían and La Palma illustrate the important role that parish priests played in protesting against the inconsistent nature of city policy regarding public services. They were intimately involved in the day-to-day functioning of their parishes, knew local residents very well, and in the case of poorer neighborhoods, often represented illiterate residents. Their positions as priests also gave them social status and power that their parishioners did not enjoy. It is also possible that priests chose openly to criticize the state in an era where the power and status of the church in colonial Latin America was declining vis-à-vis increasing calls for the end of colonialism in the New World.
36. AHCM, Aguas: Cañerías, Vol. 21, Exp. 107. While de León holds no official title in the document, I assume he was a member of the cabildo at this time, since this document is part of the city council records, and does not appear to come from some other source (e.g., parish priest, private individual, or other government official).
37. Ibid.
38. Anthony Pagden, *European Encounters with the New World: From Renaissance to Romanticism* (New Haven, CT: Yale University Press, 1993), 186. Pagden also recounts the belief that Queen Isabella, monarch of Spain at the time of the Spanish conquest of the New World, was bathed on only three occasions: once just after her birth, once on the night before she married Ferdinand, and once after she had died and was being prepared for burial.
39. Georges Vigarello, *Concepts of Cleanliness: Changing Attitudes in France since the Middle Ages*, trans. Jean Birrell (Cambridge: Cambridge University Press, 1988).
40. This was true of other Indian populations elsewhere in New Spain. For example, residents of Tepoztlán routinely bathed twice a day, while those of Ocopetlayuca took baths at midnight (these were both indigenous communities located south of Mexico City). The Spanish viewed these practices as a ritualistic element of devil worship, rather than differing cultural attitudes toward personal hygiene. Serge Gruzinski, *The Conquest of Mexico: The Incorporation of Indian Societies into the Western World, 16th–18th Centuries*, trans. Eileen Corrigan (Cambridge, MA: Polity Press, 1993), 84.
41. Schendel, *Medicine in Mexico*, 41.
42. Ibid.
43. Ibid., 39.
44. Ibid., 42.
45. Ibid., 43. The original recipe for Mexica body deodorant is located in the Badianus Manuscript, written in 1552 by Martín de la Cruz.
46. Gruzinski, *The Conquest of Mexico*, 84.
47. AHCM, Baños y Lavaderos, Vol. 3621, Exp. 5.
48. Ibid.
49. AGN, Bandos, Vol. 17, fs. 186–188.
50. Ibid.; AHCM, Baños y Lavaderos, Vol. 3621, Exp. 21.

180   *Notes*

Five Restoring Order Out of Chaos: Garbage Collection in Theory and Practice

1. AHCM, Cloacas, Vol. 515, Exp. 20.
2. As discussed earlier, the high cost of living in Mexico City proved a challenge even to those who did have a job and could rely on a steady income. For most members of the lower class, the bulk of their income was spent on food and housing, with very little disposable income left over. See Haslip-Viera, *Crime and Punishment*, 31.
3. For a discussion on similar events in Paris, see Chevailer, *Laboring Classes*, 202–205.
4. A more detailed discussion of the idea of civilization as a specific transformation of human behavior is in Norbert Elias, *The Civilizing Process*, trans. Edmund Jephcott (Oxford: Blackwell, 1994).
5. Tracing the evolution of sanitation legislation for Mexico City during the colonial period is difficult because documentation regarding this issue before the eighteenth century is relatively scant. While sixteenth-century notables, such as Fray Toribio de Benavente, wrote in glowing terms about the cleanliness of the Mexica capital of Tenochtitlan, Spanish habits and customs in both city planning and personal hygiene soon introduced numerous sanitation problems. These problems, while constant throughout the colonial period, escalated during the eighteenth century, as rising population levels for the city stressed an already overwhelmed urban environment. For a more detailed discussion of the history of sanitation legislation for Mexico City before the eighteenth century, see Cooper, *Epidemic Disease*, 17–23.
6. I assume that this was a directive aimed particularly at the issue of flooding during the rainy season.
7. AHCM, Licencias para limpieza de la Ciudad, Vol. 3240, Exp. 13.
8. AHCM, Licencias para limpieza de la Ciudad, Vol. 3240, Exp. 15.
9. Ibid.
10. AGN, Bandos, Vol. 7, Exp. 173. The viceroy's connection between polluted air and bodily imbalance is reflective of continued acceptance in the New World of explaining disease through the humoral theory. The general belief at this time was that breathing in bad air was the primary cause of infection and the spread of diseases, especially during epidemic periods, and that the best way to contain disease was through improved sanitation.
11. AGN, Bandos, Vol. 7, Exp. 173. Some of the most serious offenders, according to de Croix, were butchers, members of different trades, such as blacksmiths, silversmiths, and carpenters, and food vendors.
12. AGN, Bandos, Vol. 7, Exp. 173, fs. 178–179.
13. AGN, Bandos, Vol. 8, Exp. 2.
14. AHCM, Licencias para limpieza de la Ciudad, Vol. 3240, Exp. 20. Cleaning cars were actually horse drawn carts.
15. Cooper, *Epidemic Disease*, 20–21. Galvez's arguments in favor of Indian labor for sanitation projects is also a refection of their position in society vis-à-vis other racial groups. Since the collection of garbage and human waste was considered one of the most disgusting and demoralizing jobs that one could have during colonial times, it seemed obvious to elites that Indians, who fell to the bottom of the social hierarchy, fit the bill.
16. AHCM, Licencias para limpieza de la Ciudad, Vol. 3240, Exp. 20.
17. This information is cited from Cooper, *Epidemics*, 21; the document from which it appears is in AGN, Ayuntamientos, Vol. 58, Exp. 1, fs. 1, 5–6.
18. Ibid.
19. Written by Dr. Jose Ignacio Bartolache, *An Instruction Which Can Serve the Cure the Sufferers of Epidemic Smallpox* provided prescriptions for treating the disease, as well as a condemnation of the more popular remedies used by *curanderos*, or traditional healers in the wake of

the epidemic. *Instrucción que puede servir para que se cure a los enfermos de las viruelas epidémicas, que ahora se padecen en México, desde fines del Estío, en el ano corriente de 1779, extendida y presentada a la Nobilísima Ciudad por el Dr. D. José Ignacio Bartolache, Profesor que ha sido de Medicina Y Matemáticas en esta Real Universidad, y ahora Apartador general de Oro y Plata de todo el Reyno* (Mexico City, 1779). A microfilm copy of this document was consulted at the John Carter Brown Library, Brown University, Providence, R.I.
20. AHCM, Licencias para limpieza de la Ciudad, Vol. 3240, Exp. 24.
21. AHCM, Licencias para limpieza de la Ciudad, Vol. 3240, Exp. 26.
22. The exception to this, as demonstrated later in this chapter, is during epidemic outbreaks, when the urgency of containing the spread of disease calls for stepping up the scope of city sanitation services.
23. AHCM, Licencias para limpieza de la Ciudad, Vol. 3240, Exp. 26.
24. AHCM, Licencias para limpieza de la Ciudad, Vol. 3241, Exp. 39; AGN, Bandos, Vol. 15, fs. 208–210.
25. Marcela Dávalos, *Basura e ilustración*, 29. In its place was a series of smaller dumps, located in the various neighborhoods that ringed the central district, or *traza*. I discuss the issue of using the city suburbs as dumping grounds later in this chapter.
26. AHCM, Licencias para limpieza de la Ciudad, Vol. 3241, Exp. 39.
27. AHCM, Policía: Matanza de Perros, Vol. 3662, Exp. 2. While Revillagigedo generally called for the containment of dogs by their owners, earlier debates advocated the outright extermination of dogs left to run wild. In 1779, it was argued that cities in Europe, such as Cadiz, Spain, routinely killed wild dogs. The consequence was that these cities were much quieter, especially at night, allowing people to rest in peace. In the context of public health, cities that exterminated unclaimed dogs also had fewer problems with rabies. Public regulations advocating the termination of wild dogs appear again in 1797, 1799, and 1809.
28. AHCM, Licencias para la limpieza de la Ciudad, Vol. 3241, Exp. 42; Policía: Salubridad—Zahurdas, Vol. 3687, Exp. 19.
29. Apparently, this was particularly a problem with pigs, which roamed freely the streets throughout the city, as well as invade the various markets. As the situation with dogs mentioned earlier, pigs were seen as a public nuisance as well as a physical blight on the city landscape.
30. AHCM, Policía: Salubridad-Zahurdas, Vol. 3678, Exp. 12; AGN, Bandos, Vol. 16, f. 115. To put into perspective, the yearly wage for someone of the working class was roughly 60–300 pesos per year. Even though butchers, as business owners, had more economic stability than their employees did, a fifty peso fine would be significant.
31. Elias, *The Civilizing Process*, 47.
32. AHCM, Licencias para limpieza de la Ciudad, Vol. 3241, Exp. 39.
33. AHCM, Pulquerías, Vol. 3719, Exp. 8.
34. Twenty-four hours for the first offense, forty-eight hours for the second and third offenses. AHCM, Licencias para limpieza de la Ciudad, Vol. 3241, Exp. 39.
35. AHCM, Licencia para limpieza de la Ciudad, Vol. 3241, Exp. 42.
36. AHCM, Cloacas, Vol. 515, Exp. 11.
37. Ibid.
38. Ibid. In 1782, Mexico City was divided into eight *quarteles mayores*, or districts. These districts were then subdivided into four smaller units, or *quarteles menores*, for a total of thirty-two districts in the city. The decision on where common sites were to be located fell to the *maestro del quartel*, individuals of high standing in colonial society who were responsible for the tranquility and security of their particular district.
39. Apparently, the reissue of the 1790 bando in late 1792 did little to encourage property owners to get behind Revillagigedo's ideas regarding the construction of latrines, and so on. He once again published the bando, this time in March 1793, in yet another attempt to execute this part of his sanitation program. He argued that he felt compelled to because of "the in

observance of measures that were in the best interest of the cleanliness and dignity of the vice regal capital, as well as the health of its inhabitants." AGN, Bandos, Vol. 17, f. 77.

40. Pulquerías were similar to taverns, whose business focused specifically on the sale of pulque, an alcohol fermented from the agave cactus. Extremely popular with the lower classes, pulque accounted for a large percentage of colonial revenue through both production and taxes.
41. AHCM, Cloacas, Vol. 515, Exp. 18.
42. See Scardaville, "Alcohol Abuse and Tavern Reform," 658. A number of different viceroys specifically targeted pulquerías for reform. Revillagigedo's, however, were the most extensive. The numbers of taverns operating in the city, their physical structure, interior design, and operating hours were all regulated. The main underlying goal of these reforms was to discourage patrons from hanging around these establishments for hours on end, disrupting the peace, and so on; rather, they were to consumer their alcohol quickly, and then go on their way.
43. Ibid. Given the precarious socioeconomic condition of many city residents, alcohol functioned as an escape, and excessive drinking was common. City and church officials considered alcoholism a serious problem during the late colonial period, and this abuse was often cited as the cause of the corruption and excess of the urban population. For a more detailed examination of the role of pulquerías in colonial Mexico City, see Scardaville, "Alcohol Abuse and Tavern Reform," and Albán's chapter on pulquerías in *Propriety and Permissiveness*.
44. AHCM, Licencias para limpieza de la Ciudad, Vol. 3241, Exp. 64.
45. Ibid.
46. AHCM, Clausura de Callejónes, Vol. 443.
47. AHCM, Clausura de Callejónes, Vol. 443, Exp. 11, Petition from Don Clemente Flores and Don Jacinto Delgadillo, owners of property near the Conventa de la Concepcíon, who request that the alleyway named Dolores be closed because it has become a site where people dump garbage and *inmundicias* (filth; generally understood as human and animal waste), as well as a site of crime (1772); Exp. 12, Petition from Don Juan Jossef Monted de Oca, who owns a home near the Convento de San Lorenzo, requesting that an alleyway that runs behind the convent be closed off since it has become a dumping site for filth (1772); Exp. 14, Petition from Don Ignacio de Barzenas y Castro, requesting that the alleyway named Organo (in the Barrio de Santa Catarina Mártir) be closed as it has become a dumping ground for the neighborhood's garbage (1773); Exp. 20, Petition from Don Joaquin Jose Pardo, resident of the Barrio de Santa Catarina Mártir, asking that an alley adjacent to the neighborhood's main plaza be closed because it has become a site to dump garbage and waste, as well as other activities deemed offensive to God (1781); Exp. 28, Petition from Don Francisco Barron, resident and businessman of the city, who lives near the Plazuela de San Pablo, requesting that the alleyway named el Mono be closed, as it is a popular place to dump garbage and waste and has also become a high crime area (1798).
48. This is yet another example of the continued use of traditional dumping sites in the face of the state's establishment of communal sites for garbage and other waste. Again, because they were not part of the state sanctioned system, collection was intermittent to nonexistent.
49. AHCM, Clausura de Callejónes, Vol. 443, Exp. 24.
50. AHCM, Clausura de Callejónes, Vol. 443, Exp. 25.
51. AHCM, Calles: Apertura de, Vol. 451, Exp 1, 2. The original ordinance requesting the naming of streets and numbering of homes justified the project by stating that it would help the police keep public order and tranquility, as well as providing a sense of uniformity to the city. AHCM, Calles: Nomenclature en general, Vol. 484, Exp. 1.
52. Original map is located in the Archivo General de las Indias, Seville, Spain, *Planos de México* (Mexico 2.773), TL. 444. I consulted photographed copies from Lombardo de Ruiz, *Atlas Histórico*, 343, and Dávalos, *Basura e ilustración*, to construct the map 5.1.

NOTES

53. Dávalos, *Basura e ilustracíon*, 91.
54. The sewage system itself in the traza was generally limited to major thoroughfares and plazas, and often were in disrepair as well. As with his waste collection and disposal programs, Revillagigedo also attempted to repair and expand the city's sewage system, for many of the same reasons.
55. Dávalos, *Basura e ilustracíon*, 99. Revillagigedo himself viewed the barrios as places that were filthy and unhealthy, offending God.
56. Ibid., 85.
57. AHCM, Licencias para limpieza de al Ciudad, Vol. 3241, Exp. 62. Despite his claims that the health of the residents of the viceregal capital had been improved, a mere three years later, in 1797, the city experienced a large-scale smallpox epidemic. Debate surrounding the role of public sanitation in the perpetuation of the epidemic increased again, emphasizing the notion that Revillagigedo's perceived success was most likely short lived.
58. AHCM, Licencias para limpieza de la Ciudad, Vol. 3241, Exp. 47. Letter from Viceroy Revillagigedo to the city council asking that Ignacio Castera be allotted 11, 500 pesos for citywide cleaning. The petition was eventually granted.
59. AHCM, Licencias para limpieza de la Ciudad, Vol. 3241, Exp. 64. The fact that bodies were included among other garbage is probably indicative of the fact that garbage collection in these neighborhoods was extremely infrequent at best. The particular emphasis on the bodies of infants may be reflective of higher rates of infant mortality in poorer neighborhoods, as well as the practice of infanticide as a form of birth control.
60. Ibid.
61. AHCM, Licencias para limpieza de la Ciudad, Vol. 3241, Exp. 64.
62. AHCM, Licencias para limpieza de la Ciudad, Vol. 3241, Exp. 62.
63. CONDUMEX, *Instrucciones del VR Revillagigedo*, fondo XCI, par. 239, 241
64. Ibid., par. 246.
65. Ibid., par. 248–253. Public nudity was another theme that elites used to separate themselves from the lower classes. Elites in colonial Mexico City modeled their norm of appropriate behavior on European elites, who argued that the only parts of the body that should be exposed were the head and hands; everything else should be covered. The fact that Revillagigedo expressed concern about public nudity illustrates that like public defecation, public nudity challenged elite cultural norms and sensibilities, and represented the uncivilized, and hence dangerous, nature of the urban masses. See Elias, *The Civilizing Process*, 109.
66. C.H. Haring, *The Spanish Empire in America* (Oxford: Oxford University Press, 1947), 129.
67. Next to the Conde de Regla, the Conde de Santiago de Calimaya was one of the wealthiest men in the colonial Americas, with vast rural landed holdings and a wide variety of urban economic enterprises. The Museum of Mexico City now occupies that former palace of the Conde de Santiago. It is located on Calle Piño Suarez, which feeds south out of the central plaza. For a discussion on the design and building of the palace, see Ignacio Gonzalez Polo, *El palacio de los condes de Santiago de Calimaya* (México: Instituto de Investigaciones Estéticas Universidad Nacional Autónoma de México, 1973).
68. AHCM, Licencias para limpieza de la Ciudad, Vol. 3242, Exp. 69.
69. AHCM, Licencias para limpieza de la Ciudad, Vol. 3242, Exp. 81. The system of fines for public dumping of garbage had not changed significantly since the 1790 regulations put in place by Revillagigedo.
70. AHCM, Licencias para limpieza de la Ciudad, Vol. 3242, Exp. 100. This same evaluation found that many of the streets south of the hospital were overflowing with garbage, as well as the Plazuela de Santo Tomas and the Plazuela de los Pelos. The other hospital in the city that consistently suffered under the same kinds of conditions was the Hospital de San Lázaro, a leper's hospital on the eastern edge of the city.
71. Like many other place descriptions in this study, this information is from a city map originally commissioned by Viceroy Revillagigedo, in 1793. Considered one of the most

accurate spatial representations of the city to date, cartographers reproduced it numerous times into the nineteenth century. I have used one of these reproductions, done by Diego García Conde in 1824, to locate most of the places discussed in this study. It is housed at the Centro de Estudios de Historía de México (CONDUMEX), located in Mexico City.
72. AHCM, Licencias para limpieza de la Ciudad, Vol. 3242, Exp. 103.
73. As discussed earlier, city officials advanced corporal punishment as a solution before, but obviously it was ineffective as a deterrent, as the problems existed. Why city leaders continued to advocate its use is unclear.
74. AHCM, Licencias para limpieza de la Ciudad, Vol. 3242, Exp. 78.
75. There is debate regarding the diseases that were at play during the epidemic outbreak in 1813. Contemporaries described the illnesses merely as "pestilential fevers," while others attributed the symptoms to yellow fever. A tropical disease, yellow fever was rare in the temperate highlands of New Spain, so it is unlikely that this caused the epidemic. Later observers, reviewing documents from the epidemic, argue that it was probably typhus that most people suffered from. See Cooper, *Epidemic Disease*, 157–158.
76. Interestingly, it was brought up by members of the city council that since the economy was in good shape during the 1779 epidemic, the public need was not as dire, and people were more willing to contribute to poor relief. By 1797, the economy of New Spain was stagnating, which increased the number of people in the city who needed aid, and depressed charitable contributions. Cooper, *Epidemic Disease*, 130.
77. Cooper, *Epidemic Disease*, 99–102. Inoculation was one of the few medical responses to the epidemic that the state funded without hesitation, even though the viceroy himself favored quarantine over inoculation in attempts to halt the spread of the virus. Inoculation, however, was limited in its scope primarily due to negative perceptions by both plebeian classes and the church. While elite families generally were willing to and did participate in inoculation programs, the poorer classes, and Indians in particular, strongly resisted. This resistance probably came from misunderstanding about the procedure, as well as the fact that state leaders and elites were heavily pushing it. Garcia Jove, the president of the Protomedicato, made it his goal to convince these groups that they should be inoculated. He even suggested to Archbishop Nuñez de Haro prepare a public statement "so that the people...incapable of understanding the advantages of inoculation would accept its benefits." Ibid., 123. As the epidemic expanded, rumors and innuendoes stating that inoculation was dangerous and even fatal flew throughout the city, with the chief judge of the Audiencia, Cosme de Mier y Trespalacios accusing parish priests of perpetuating these rumors. Part of this resistance was probably due in part to perceived state intrusion into the realm of medicine and healing, which up until this time had been almost exclusively the domain of the church. The connections between inoculation and the scientific advances of the Enlightenment also made it a threatening activity. Ibid., 130.
78. It is important to note here the valuable work done by Linda Curcio-Nagy on the Catholic Church and the function of public rituals in colonial Mexico City. In particular, she emphasizes the shift in the nature of these rituals from the seventeenth century into the eighteenth century, as they come to model more of the ideal of Bourbon structure and order. See Curcio-Nagy, *The Great Festivals of Colonial Mexico City: Performing Power and Identity* (Albuquerque: University of New Mexico Press, 2004).
79. AGN, Epidemias, Vol. 16, Exp. 7, fs. 264–267.
80. AGN, Epidemias, Vol. 16, Exp. 7, f. 3v
81. Ibid.
82. AHCM, Licencias para limpieza de la Ciudad, Vol. 3242, Exp. 79.
83. Ibid.
84. AGN, Epidemias, Vol. 9, Exp. 16, fs. 11–12.
85. AHCM, Licencias para limpieza de la Ciudad, Vol. 3242, Exp. 111.
86. AHCM, Licencias para limpieza de la Ciudad, Vol. 3242, Exp. 110.

NOTES 185

87. Cooper, *Epidemic Disease*, 170.
88. AHCM, Licencias para limpieza de la Ciudad, Vol. 3242, Exp. 115.
89. Ibid.
90. AHCM, Licencias para limpieza de la Ciudad, Vol. 3242, Exp. 100, 117, 122. In 1815, Licenciado Estevan Perez Rivas, who took over from Prieto as manager of the city's sanitation programs, argued that the system devised by Revillagigedo should remain as the foundation, since the city was cleaner than either before or after his tenure.
91. Once the epidemic crisis of 1813 was over, the importance of keeping barrios outside the city center clean lost priority as normality returned to the capital. This is illustrated in the division and allocation of cleaning carts. By 1819, twenty-three of the thirty-three carts funded by the *ayuntamiento* covered the traza area, while the remaining eight were expected to cover the rest of the urban area. AHCM, Licencias para limpieza de la Ciudad, Vol. 3242, Exp. 117.
92. Ibid.
93. For a more detailed discussion of the role of the police in late colonial Mexico City, see Jorge Nacif Mina, " Policía y seguridad pública en la Ciudad de México, 1770–1848," in *La Ciudad de México en al primera mitad del Siglo XIX*, ed. Regina Hernández Franyuti (México: Instituto de Investigaciones Dr. José Maria Luis Mora, 1994), 9–50.
94. See Scardaville, "Alcohol Abuse and Tavern Reform" for a more detailed discussion of the conflict of interest that elites and the state faced in dealing with issues and outcomes of alcohol reform during the late colonial period.
95. For an excellent discussion on the changing roles of race in Mexico City, see Cope, *The Limits*.
96. AHCM, Licencias para limpieza de la Ciudad, Vol. 3240, Exp. 20.

Six   Mastery over the Streets: Drainage, Street Paving, and Renovation of Urban Space

1. Lyons, *Journal of the Residence*, 126.
2. Ibid., 106, 112, 129–130.
3. Michael C. Meyer, William L. Sherman, and Susan M. Deeds, *The Course of Mexican History*, Sixth Edition (Oxford: Oxford University Press, 1999), 84–85.
4. Enrique Espinosa López, *Ciudad de México: compenido cronologico de su desarrollo urbano, 1521–1980* (México: Private Press, 1991), 4–5.
5. Ibid., 27. The flooding was a consequence of a major storm beginning on September 17, and lasting four days. The flooding was so bad that residents could only get around via canoe.
6. López, *Ciudad de México*, 42. For a discussion of bureaucratic responses to this urban catastrophe, see Louisa Hoberman, "Bureaucracy and Disaster: Mexico City and the Flood of 1629," *Journal of Latin American Studies* 6 (1974): 211–230.
7. Dávalos, *Basura e ilustración*, 33–36.
8. AGN, Empedrados, Tomo 15, f. 181.
9. This title implies that Castera held the highest position within the architectural community in Mexico City and was consider to be by both his peers and the state as one of the most thoroughly trained in his craft. The title also takes into account a certain level of experience in both architectural design as well as city planning.
10. Costanzo's official title was *Teniente Coronel de Ingenieros*, or Lieutenant Coronel of Engineers.
11. Konvitz, *The Urban Millennium*, 46.
12. Ibid., 53.

13. Mardith K. Schuetz, *Architectural Practice in Mexico City: A Manual for Journeyman Architects of the Eighteenth Century* (Tucson: University of Arizona Press, 1987), 6.
14. Ibid.
15. AGN, Obras Públicas, Vol.2, Exp. 1, f. 4.
16. I was unable to locate documents for these decades within other volumes either at the AHCM or at the AGN. This is not to say, however, that these documents do not exist. At this point it is unclear what has happened to them.
17. I used a French reproduction of the original city map, commissioned by Viceroy Revillagigedo in 1793, to place spatially the drainage projects listed in table 6.1. A photograph of the original, used for the map above, is in Lombardo de Ruíz, *Atlas Histórico*, 353.
18. AHCM, Licencias: Atarjeas (limpia), Vol. 3238, Exp. 44. This is based on the approximate length of a *vara* at thirty-three inches.
19. Gibson, *The Aztecs*, 14.
20. AHCM, Licencias: Atarjeas (limpia), Vol. 3238, Exp. 44. A more detailed discussion of the street paving projects undertaken by Revillagigedo and Castera follows later in this chapter.
21. AHCM, Licencias: Atarjeas (limpia), Vol. 3238, Exp. 16.
22. Corpus Christi was one of the major holidays on the church calendar and generally celebrated in a grand fashion.
23. This project was also to repave the streets and to provide permanent sidewalks.
24. AHCM, Licencias: Atarjeas (limpia), Vol. 3238, Exp. 23.
25. A much more detailed discussion of the disjuncture between elite perceptions of social disorder and the socioeconomic reasons behind it is in Haslip-Viera, *Crime and Punishment*, Chapter Three.
26. AGN, Obras Públicas, Vol. 2, Exp. 4, f. 259. The *Junta de Policía* the body responsible for public order, cleanliness, and safety, was primarily responsible for the continued functioning and adherence to the new sanitation laws and ordinances set up by Revillagigedo. The *fondo de Desagüe* was a large account set up by the state to fund the massive project of draining Lake Texcoco; in 1794, it had a balance of 297,622 pesos.
27. AHCM, Licencias: Atarjeas (limpias), Vol. 3238, Exp. 18. Don José Damían Ortiz is the same man who assisted Ignacio Castera with many of the public works projects during this time. It is unclear, however, what amount of the total cost of the project these donations covered.
28. AHCM, Licencias: Atarjeas (limpia), Vol. 3238, Exp. 15.
29. AHCM, Licencias: Atarjeas (limpia), Vol. 3238, Exp. 22.
30. AHCM, Licencias: Atarjeas (limpia), Vol. 3238, Exp. 33.
31. AHCM, Licencias: Atarjeas (limpia), Vol. 3238, Exp. 46.
32. AHCM, Licencias: Atarjeas (limpia), Vol. 3238, Exp. 47, 50, 55, 59, 63–65, 67, 73, 78.
33. AHCM, Historia: Inundaciones, Vol. 2272, Exp. 30.
34. Of these streets, Calles de San Francisco, Coliseo, Estampa de Regina, and la Palma underwent significant grading and paving improvements, also to help with the drainage of water. Refer to table 6.2.
35. Refer to table 6.1 for the corresponding listing of drainage projects completed during the tenure of Revillagigedo.
36. An arroba is the equivalent of approximately 11.5 kilograms. Twenty arrobas of sugar would equal approximately 230 kilograms, or roughly 506 pounds.
37. AHCM, Desagüe, Vol. 740, Exp. 40.
38. Villaroel, *Enfermedades*, 188–198. No legislation of any kind supporting Villaroel's ideas ever passed.
39. This list represents a sampling of paved streets in the city center; it is not an exhaustive listing, however.

40. It is interesting that the excessive use of carriages by elites was not mentioned as one of the causes.
41. AHCM, Empedrados, Vol. 881, Exp. 74.
42. AHCM, Empedrados, Vol. 881, Exp. 80.
43. AHCM, Empedrados, Vol. 881, Exp. 93. The *ramo de Pulque* was essentially the profits gained from the sale of pulque. These profits included the cost of the product along with the taxes included in its sale.
44. AHCM, Empedrados, Vol. 881, Exp. 106.
45. AGN, Bandos, Vol. 15, f. 247. A second bando, issued on April 21, 1792, confirmed the continuation of Castera's paving projects. AGN, Bandos, Vol. 16, f. 156.
46. Photographed copy of city map used to place paving projects is in Lombardo de Ruíz, *Atlas Histórico*, 353.
47. AGN, Bandos, Vol. 15, fs. 181–182. A special condition was placed on laborers connected to the paving projects. In the case of fire, they were to stop work on their respective projects and turn their attentions to fighting the fire. So in effect, they also served as informal firefighters. AHCM, Policía: Incendios, Vol. 3649, Exp. 6.
48. AGN, Bandos, Vol. 15, f. 247.
49. As mentioned in the discussion of drainage projects, the *fondo de Real Desagüe* was the official account set up to fund the ongoing drainage of Lake Texcoco.
50. AHCM, Empedrados, Vol. 882, Exp. 156.
51. Carrera Stampa, *Planos*, 303.
52. Ibid., 305.
53. AGN, Obras Públicas, Vol. 8, Exp. 5, f. 58.
54. AGN, Obras Públicas, Vol. 8, Exp. 5, fs. 59–60.
55. Carrera Stampa, *Planos*, 303.
56. AGN, Obras Públicas, Vol. 8, Exp. 5, fs. 60–61. The establishment of the Volador was part of a larger project of renovating markets throughout the city. Revillagigedo also cleaned and reorganized the market in the Plaza de Santa Catarina Mártir (1791) and built a new permanent market in the Plaza de la Cruz del Factor (1793). Carrera Stampa, *Planos*, 303.
57. The total cost of the construction of these fountains was 4,999 pesos. AHCM, Fuentes Públicas, Vol. 58, Exp. 28; AGN, Obras Públicas, Vol. 36, Exp. 18, fs. 414–415.
58. Translation from William B. Taylor, "Late Eighteenth-Century Inscriptions in Mexico City," in *Colonial Spanish America: A Documentary Reader*, ed. Kenneth Mills and William B. Taylor (Wilmington: Scholarly Resources, 1998), 332–333.
59. Equivalent measurements would be 1,635,117 square feet of paving; 49,605 square feet of drainage canals; 81,951 square feet of sidewalk.
60. Tayloe, *Mexico, 1825–1828*, 51.

Seven Concluding Thoughts

1. Voekel, *Alone before God*, 2–5.
2. Two of the better works that examine this process deal with the history of Brazil. See Gilberto Freyre, *Ordem e progresso; proceso de desintegracão das sociedades partiarcal e semipatriarcal no Brasil...e da monarqia para a república* (Rio de Janeiro: J. Olympio, 1959); Teresa Meade, *"Civilizing" Rio: Reform and Resistance in a Brazilian City, 1889–1930* (University Park: Pennsylvania State University Press, 1997).
3. For an excellent examination of the process of urban reconstruction and its links to modern Mexican identity, see Michael Johns, *The City of Mexico in the Age of Diaz* (Austin: University of Texas Press, 1997).

4. For more detailed discussions of the application of late nineteenth-century ideas about modernity to urban planning and development, see Johns, *The City of Mexico in the Age of Diaz* and Mark Overmyer-Velazquez, *Visions of the Emerald City: Modernity, Tradition, and the Formation of Porfirian Oaxaca* (Durham, NC: Duke University Press, 2006). These debates were not localized to Mexico; they represent a wider trend in late nineteenth-century urban development throughout Latin America. One of the best treatments of how urban reform is used to articulate modernity can be found in Teresa A. Meade, *"Civilizing" Rio.*

GLOSSARY

aguadores	water sellers
alcaldes de barrio	neighborhood representative to city government
arroba	unit of weight equal to 11.5 kilograms
bando	royal decree announcing new regulations, policies, rules
banqueta	sidewalks
barrio	neighborhood
cabildo	city council
cañería	piping used to distribute water throughout the city
casa de vecindad	roominghouse
casta	general term used for those of mixed race background
corregidor	city councilman
criollo/a	those of Spanish descent born in the New World
curandero/a	traditional healer of Indian, African, or *casta* background
fanega	unit of volume equal to 1.5 bushels
fuentes particulares	fountains within private residences connected to the public water supply
fuentes públicas	public fountains
Gazeta de México	city's only daily newspaper during the late colonial period
gente de bajo	popular term used to describe the lower class; literally "people below"
Juez de Cañería	Head of Mexico City's water projects
Junta de Policía	municipal police force
juntas de caridad	municipal charitable societies established to aid epidemic victims
léperos	pejorative term for poor underclass
mestizo/a	person of Spanish and Indian background
mulato/a	person of Spanish and African background
novena	special prayers and processions given during epidemic outbreaks and other natural disasters
peninsular	those of Spanish descent born on the Iberian Peninsula

peso	unit of currency equaling eight *reales*
Plaza Mayor	main plaza located in the center of Mexico City; housed the Cathedral, government offices, and viceroy's palace
pulpería	corner store
pulque	alcoholic beverage made from fermented agave cactus
pulquería	tavern selling *pulque*
quartel mayor	major city districts
quartel menor	minor city districts
real(es)	unit of currency equaling one-eighth of a *peso*
targea	open gutters running alongside the street or underneath sidewalks
traza	central district in Mexico City initially reserved for Spanish residence only
vara	unit of measurement equaling approximately thirty-three inches
vecinos	residents
Volador	Mexico City's major market, relocated from the Plaza Mayor in 1791; directly southeast of the Plaza Mayor

BIBLIOGRAPHY

Archives and Manuscript Collections

Archivo del Centro de Estudios de Historia de México (CONDUMEX), Mexico City.

Archivo General de la Nación (AGN), Mexico City.
    Ayuntamientos
    Bandos
    Epidemias
    Obras Públicas

Archivo Histórico de la Ciudad de México (AHCM), Mexico City.
    Aguas: Cañerías
    Aguas: Edificios Públicos
    Aguas: Fuentes Públicas
    Baños y Lavaderos
    Calles: Apertura de
    Calles: Nomenclature en general
    Clausura de Callejónes
    Cloacas
    Desagüe
    Empedrados

    Hacienda: Rentas de Ciudad
    Historia: Inundaciones
    Hospitales: San Juan de Dios
    Licencias: Atarjeas (limpia)
    Licencias para limpieza de la Ciudad
    Policía: Incendios
    Policía: Matanza de Perros
    Policía: Salubridad-Epidemias
    Policía: Salubridad-Zahurdas
    Pulquerías

Archivo del Tribunal Superior de Justicia del Distrito Federal (ATJ), Mexico City.
    Civil

The John Carter Brown Library (JCB), Brown University, Providence, Rhode Island.

Bibliography

Published Primary Sources

Periodicals

La Gazeta de México

Travel and Descriptive Literature

D'Auteroche Chappe, Mons. *A Voyage to California to Observe the Transit of Venus.* London: Edward and Charles Dilly, 1778.

Lyons, G.F. *Journal of the Residence and Tour of the Republic of Mexico in the year 1826 with some account of the mines of that country.* London: Albemarie Street, 1828.

Tayloe, Edward Thornton. *Mexico, 1825–1828: The Journal and Correspondence of Edward Thornton Tayloe,* edited by C. Harvey Gardiner. Chapel Hill: University of North Carolina Press, 1959.

Villaroel, Hipólito. *Enfermedades políticas que padece la capital de esta Nueva España en casi todos los cuerpos de que se compone y remedios que se le deban aplicar para su curación si se quiere que sea útil al Rey y al público.* Reprint. México: Grupo Editorial Miguel Angel Porrúa, 1999.

Medical Literature

Bartolache, Dr. Jose Ignacio. *Instrucción que puede servir para que se cure a los enfermos de las viruelas epidémicas, que ahora se padecen en México, desde fines del Estío, en el ano corriente de 1779, extendida y presentada a la Nobilísima Ciudad por el Dr. D. José Ignacio Bartolache, Profesor que ha sido de Medicina Y Matemáticas en esta Real Universidad, y ahora Apartador general de Oro y Plata de todo el Reyno.* México, 1779.

Venegas, Juan Manuel. *Compendio de la Medicina, ó Medicina Practica.* México: D. Felipe de Zuniga de Ontiveros, 1788.

Secondary Works

Historia Urbana de Iberoamerica, Tomo II: La Ciudad Barroca 1573–1750. Madrid: Consejo Superior de los Colegios de Arquitectos de España, 1990.

Aguirre Beltran, Gonzalo. *Medicina y magica: el proceso de aculturación en la estructura colonial.* México: Instituto Nacional Indigenista, 1963.

Alchon, Suzanne Austin. *Native Society and Disease in Colonial Ecuador.* Cambridge: Cambridge University Press, 1991.

Anderson, Rodney. *Guadalajara a la consumación de la Independencia: estudio de su población según los padrones de 1821–1822.* Guadalajara: Unidad Editorial, 1983.

Anna, Timothy. *The Fall of the Royal Government in Mexico City.* Lincoln: University of Nebraska Press, 1994.

Arnold, Linda. *Bureaucracy and Bureaucrats in Mexico City, 1742–1835.* Tucson: University of Arizona Press, 1988.

Arrom, Silvia Marina. *The Women of Mexico City, 1790–1857.* Stanford: Stanford University Press, 1985.

———. "Popular Politics in Mexico City: The Parián Riot, 1828." In *Riots in the Cities: Popular Politics and the Urban Poor in Latin America, 1765–1910*, edited by Silvia M. Arrom and Servando Ortoll, pp. 71–96. Wilmington: Scholarly Resources, 1996.

———. *Containing the Poor: The Mexico City Poor House, 1774–1871*. Durham: Duke University Press, 2000.

Ashburn, Percy. *The Ranks of Death: A Medical History of the Conquest of America*. New York: Howard-McCann, 1947.

Axtell, James. *Beyond 1492: Encounters in Colonial North America*. Oxford: Oxford University Press, 1992.

Beier, A.L. and Roger Finlay, eds. *The Making of the Metropolis: London, 1500–1700*. London: Longman Press, 1985.

Brading, David. *Miners and Merchants in Bourbon Mexico, 1763–1810*. Cambridge: Cambridge University Press, 1971.

Cahill, David. "Financing Health Care in the Viceroyalty of Peru: The Hospitals of Lima in the Late Colonial Period." *The Americas* 52, 2 (October 1995): 123–154.

Carrera Stampa, Manuel. *Planos de la Ciudad de México (desde 1521 hasta nuestros días)*. México: Sociedad Mexicana de Geografía y Estadística, 1949.

Carroll, Patrick J. *Blacks in Colonial Veracruz: Race, Ethnicity, and Regional Development*. Austin: University of Texas Press, 1991.

Chevalier, Louis. *Laboring Classes and Dangerous Classes in Paris During the First Half of the Nineteenth Century*. Princeton, NJ: Princeton University Press, 1973.

Cook, Noble David. *Demographic Collapse: Indian Peru, 1520–1620*. Cambridge: Cambridge University Press, 1981.

Cook, Noble David and W. George Lovell, eds. *Secret Judgments of God: Old World Diseases in Colonial Spanish America*. Norman: University of Oklahoma Press, 1991.

Cook, Sherburne F. "The Smallpox Epidemic of 1797 in Mexico." *Bulletin of the History of Medicine* 7 (1939): 937–969.

Cooper, Donald. *Epidemic Disease in Mexico City, 1761–1813: An Administrative, Social and Medical Study*. Austin: University of Texas Press, 1965.

Cope, R. Douglas. *The Limits of Racial Domination: Plebeian Society in Colonial Mexico City, 1660–1720*. Madison: University of Wisconsin Press, 1994.

Crosby, Alfred. *The Columbian Exchange: Biological and Cultural Consequences of 1492*. Westport, CT: Greenwood Press, 1972.

Curcio-Nagy, Linda. "Giants and Gypsies: Corpus Christi in Colonial Mexico City." In *Rituals of Rule, Rituals of Resistance: Public Celebrations and Popular Culture in Mexico*, edited by William H. Beezley, Cheryl English Martin, and William E. French, pp. 1–24. Wilmington, DE: Scholarly Resources, 1994.

———. *The Great Festivals of Colonial Mexico City: Performing Power and Identity*. Albuquerque: University of New Mexico Press, 2004.

Dávalos, Marcela. *Basura e ilustración: la limpieza de la Ciudad de México a fines del Siglo XVIII*. México: Instituto Nacional de Antropología e Historia, 1997.

Deans-Smith, Susan. *Bureaucrats, Planters, and Workers: The Making of the Tobacco Monopoly in Bourbon Mexico*. Austin: University of Texas Press, 1992.

———. "The Working Poor and the Eighteenth-Century Colonial State: Gender, Public Order, and Work Discipline." In *Rituals of Rule, Rituals of Resistance: Public Celebrations and Popular Culture in Mexico*, edited by William H. Beezley, Cheryl English Martin, and William E. French, pp. 47–76. Wilmington, DE: Scholarly Resources, 1994.

Elias, Norbert. *The Civilizing Process*. Translated by Edmund Jephcott. Oxford: Blackwell, 1994.

Espinosa López, Enrique. *Ciudad de México: compenido cronologico de su desarrollo urbano, 1521–1980.* México: Private Press, 1991.
Flores Marini, Carlos. *Casas virreinales de las Ciudad de México.* México: Fondo de Cultural Económica, 1970.
Florescano, Enrique. *Precios de maíz y crisis agrícolas en México, 1708–1810.* México: El Colegio de México, 1969.
Foucault, Michel. *The History of Sexuality: An Introduction, Volume I.* Translated by Robert Hurley. New York: Random House, 1990.
Fraile, Pedro. *La otra ciudad del Rey: ciencia de policia y organizacion urbana en España.* Madrid: Celeste Ediciones, 1997.
Francois, Marie. "When Pawnshops Talk: Popular Credit and Material Culture in Mexico City, 1775–1916." Ph.D. dissertation, University of Arizona, 1998.
———. *A Culture of Everyday Credit: Housekeeping, Pawnbroking, and Governance in Mexico City, 1750–1920.* Lincoln: University of Nebraska Press, 2005.
Freyre, Gilberto. *Ordem e progresso; proceso de desintegracão das sociedades patriarcal no Brasil. . . e da monarqia para a república.* Rio de Janeiro: J. Olympio, 1959.
Ganster, Paul. "Churchmen." In *Cities and Society in Colonial Latin America,* edited by Louisa Schell Hoberman and Susan Migden Socolow, pp. 137–164. Albuquerque: University of New Mexico Press, 1986.
García Martínez, Bernardo. "*Pueblos de Indios, Pueblos de Castas*: New Settlements and Traditional Corporate Organization in Eighteenth-Century New Spain." In *The Indian Community of Colonial Mexico,* edited by Arij Ouweneel and Simon Miller, pp. 99–115. Amsterdam: CEDLA Latin American Studies.
Gelfand, Toby. *Professionalizing Modern Medicine: Paris Surgeons and Medical Science and Institutions in the 18th Century.* Westport, CT: Greenwood Press, 1980.
George, M. Dorothy. *London Life in the Eighteenth Century.* New York: Harper and Row, 1926.
Gibson, Charles. *The Aztecs under Spanish Rule: A History of the Indians of the Valley of Mexico, 1519–1810.* Stanford: Stanford University Press, 1964.
Gonzalez Polo, Ignacio. *El palacio de los condes de Santiago de Calimaya.* México: Instituto de Investigaciones Estéticas Universidad Nacional Autónoma de México, 1973.
Gruzinski, Serge. *The Conquest of Mexico: The Incorporation of Indian Societies into the Western World, 16th–18th Centuries.* Translated by Eileen Corrigan. Cambridge, MA: Polity Press, 1993.
Guerra, Francisco. *El hospital en Hispanoamérica y Filipinos, 1492–1898.* Madrid: Ministerio de Sanidad y Consumo, 1994.
Haring, C.H. *The Spanish Empire in America.* Oxford: Oxford University Press, 1947.
Haslip-Viera, Gabriel. *Crime and Punishment in Late Colonial Mexico City, 1692–1810.* Albuquerque: University of New Mexico Press, 1999.
Hernández Franyuti, Regina, ed. *La Ciudad de México en la primera mitad del Siglo XIX.* 2 volumes. México: Instituto de Investigaciones Dr. José María Mora, 1994.
Hernández-Sáenz, Luz María. *Learning to Heal: The Medical Profession in Colonial Mexico, 1767–1831.* New York: Peter Lang, 1997.
Hoberman, Louisa Schell. "City Planning in Spanish Colonial Government: The Response of Mexico City to the Problem of Floods, 1607–1637." Ph.D. dissertation, Columbia University, 1972.
———. "Bureaucracy and Disaster: Mexico City and the Flood of 1629." *Journal of Latin American Studies* 6 (1974): 211–230.
Illades, Carlos and Ariel Rodríguez, compilers. *Ciudad de México: instituciones, actores sociales, y conflicto político, 1774–1931.* México: El Colegio de Michoacán y el Universidad Autónoma Metropolitana, 1996.

Bibliography

Johns, Michael. *The City of Mexico in the Age of Diaz*. Austin: University of Texas Press, 1997.
Kaplow, Jeffrey. *The Names of Kings: The Parisian Laboring Poor in the Eighteenth Century*. New York: Basic Books, 1972.
Kennedy, Dane. *Islands of White: Settler Society and Culture in Kenya and Southern Rhodesia*. Durham, NC: Duke University Press, 1987.
Kicza, John E. *Colonial Entrepreneurs: Families and Business in Bourbon Mexico City*. Albuquerque: University of New Mexico Press, 1983.
———. "Migration to Major Metropoles in Colonial Mexico." In *Migration in Colonial Spanish America*, edited by David J. Robinson, pp. 193–211. Cambridge: Cambridge University Press, 1990.
Konvitz, Josef W. *The Urban Millennium: The City-Building Process from the Early Middle Ages to the Present*. Carbondale: Southern Illinois University Press, 1985.
Lanning, John Tate. *The Royal Protomedicato: The Regulation of the Medical Profession in the Spanish Empire*, edited by John Jay TePaske. Durham: Duke University Press, 1985.
Lombardo de Ruiz, Sonia. *Atlas Histórico de la Ciudad de México*. México: Smurfit Cartón y Papel de México, 1997.
López Sarrelangue, Delfina. "La población indígena de la Nueva España en el siglo XVIII." *Historia Mexicana* 12, 4 (April–June 1963): 515–530.
Lutz, Christopher. *Santiago de Guatemala, 1541–1773: City, Caste, and the Colonial Experience*. Norman: University of Oklahoma Press, 1994.
Madariaga, Salvador de. *The Rise of the Spanish American Empire*. New York: Hollis and Carter, 1947.
Marks, Geoffrey and William K. Beatty. *Epidemics*. New York: Charles Scribner's Sons, 1976.
Martin, Cheryl English. "Public Celebrations, Popular Culture, and Labor Discipline in Eighteenth-Century Chihuahua." In *Rituals of Rule, Rituals of Resistance: Public Celebrations and Popular Culture in Mexico*, edited by William H. Beezley, Cheryl English Martin, and William E. French, pp. 95–126. Wilmington: Scholarly Resources, 1994.
McEvedy, Colin. *The Penguin Atlas of Modern History (to 1815)*. Harmondsworth: Penguin Books, 1972.
Meade, Teresa. *"Civilizing" Rio: Reform and Resistance in a Brazilian City, 1889–1930*. University Park: Pennsylvania State University Press, 1997.
Meyer, Michael C., William L. Sherman, and Susan M. Deeds. *The Course of Mexican History*. Sixth Edition. Oxford: Oxford University Press, 1999.
Miranda, José. "La población indígena de Ixmiquilpan y su distrito en la época colonial." *Estudios de Historia Novohispana* 1 (1966): 121–130.
Moreno Toscano, Alejandra and Carlos Aguirre Anaya. "Migrations to Mexico City in the Nineteenth Century: Research Approaches." *Journal of Interamerican Studies and World Affairs* 17 (1975): 27–42.
Nacif Mina, Jorge. "Policía y seguridad pública en la Ciudad de México, 1770–1848." In *La Ciudad de México en la primera mitad del Siglo XIX*, edited by Regina Hernández Franyuti, pp. 9–50. México: Instituto de Investigaciones Dr. José Maria Luis Mora, 1994.
Newson, Linda. "Indian Population Patterns in Colonial Spanish America." *Latin American Research Review* 20 (1985): 41–74.
Ortiz de Montellano, Bernard R. *Aztec Medicine, Health, and Nutrition*. New Brunswick, NJ: Rutgers University Press, 1990.
Ouweneel, Arij. "Growth, Stagnation, and Migration in Anáhuac, 1720–1800." *Hispanic American Historical Review* 71, 3 (August 1991): 531–577.

Overmyer-Velazquez, Mark. *Visions of the Emerald City: Modernity, Tradition, and the Formation of Porfirian Oaxaca.* Durham, NC: Duke University Press, 2006.

Pagden, Anthony. *European Encounters with the New World: From Renaissance to Romanticism.* New Haven, CT: Yale University Press, 1993.

Pember Reeves, Mande. *Round about a Pound a Week.* London: G.Bell and Sons, 1913.

Pescador, Juan Javier. *De bautizos a fieles difuntos: Familia y mentalidades en una parroquia urbana: Santa Catarina de México, 1568–1820.* México: El Colegio de México, 1992.

———. "Vanishing Women: Female Migration and Ethnic Identity in Late-Colonial Mexico City." *Ethnohistory* 42, 4 (Fall 1995): 617–626.

Pickstone, John. "Dearth, Dirt, and Fever Epidemics: Rewriting the History of British 'Public Health', 1780–1850." In *Epidemics and Ideas: Essays on the Historical Perception of Pestilence*, edited by Terence Ranger and Paul Stack, pp. 125–148. Cambridge: Cambridge University Press, 1992.

Pullan, Brian. "Plagues and Perceptions of the Poor in Early Modern Italy." In *Epidemics and Ideas: Essays on the Historical Perception of Pestilence*, edited by Terence Ranger and Paul Stack, pp. 101–124. Cambridge: Cambridge University Press, 1992.

Ramsey, Matthew. *Professional and Popular Medicine in France, 1770–1830: The Social World of Medical Practice.* Cambridge: Cambridge University Press, 1988.

Riley, James. *The Eighteenth-Century Campaign to Avoid Disease.* London: Macmillian Press, 1987.

Risse, Guenter B. "Transcending Cultural Barriers: The European Reception of Medicinal Plants from the Americas." In *Botanical Drugs of the Americas in the Old and New Worlds*, pp. 28–40. Stuttgart: Wissenschaftliche Verlagsgesellschaft MBH, 1984.

———. "Medicine in New Spain." In *Medicine in the New World: New Spain, New France, and New England*, edited by Ronald Numbers, pp. 30–48. Knoxville: University of Tennessee Press, 1987.

———. *Hospital Life in Enlightenment Scotland: Care and Teaching in the Royal Infirmary of Edinburgh.* Cambridge: Cambridge University Press, 1986.

Sauer, Jonathan. "Changing Perception and Exploitation of New World Plans in Europe, 1492–1800." In *First Images of America*, edited by Fredi Chiapelli, pp. 815–832. Berkeley: University of California Press, 1976.

Scardaville, Michael. "Crime and the Urban Poor: Mexico City in the Late Colonial Period." Ph.D. dissertation, University of Florida, 1977.

———. "Alcohol Abuse and Tavern Reform in Late Colonial Mexico City." *Hispanic American Historical Review* 60, 4 (November 1980): 643–671.

———. "(Hapsburg) Law and (Bourbon) Order: State Authority, Popular Unrest, and the Criminal Justice System in Bourbon Mexico City." *The Americas* 50, 4 (April 1994): 501–525.

Schendel, Gordon. *Medicine in Mexico: From Aztec Herbs to Betatrons.* Austin: University of Texas Press, 1968.

Schuetz, Mardith K. *Architectural Practice in Mexico City: A Manual for Journeyman Architects of the Eighteenth Century.* Tucson: University of Arizona Press, 1987.

Scott, James. *Weapons of the Weak: Everyday Forms of Peasant Resistance.* New Haven, CT: Yale University Press, 1985.

Socolow, Susan M. "Introduction." In *Cities and Society in Colonial Latin America*, edited by Louisa Schell Hoberman and Susan Migden Socolow, pp. 3–18. Albuquerque: University of New Mexico Press, 1986.

———. "Introduction to the Rural Past." In *The Countryside in Colonial Latin America*, edited by Louisa Schell Hoberman and Susan Migden Socolow, pp. 3–18. Albuquerque: University of New Mexico Press, 1996.

Bibliography

Spitzer, Leo. *The Creoles of Sierra Leone: Responses to Colonialism, 1870–1945*. Madison: University of Wisconsin Press, 1974.

Staples, Anne. "Police and *Buen Gobierno*: Municple Efforts to Regulate Public Behavior, 1821–1857." In *Rituals of Rule, Rituals of Resistance: Public Celebrations ad Popular Culture in Mexico*, edited by William H. Beezley, Cheryl English Martin, and William E. French, pp. 115–126. Wilmington: Scholarly Resources, 1994.

Talbot, Charles H. "America and the Drug Trade." In *First Images of America*, edited by Fredi Chiapelli, pp. 835–848. Berkeley: University of California Press, 1976.

Taylor, William B. "Indian *pueblos* of Central Jalisco on the Eve of Independence." In *Iberian Colonies, New World Societies: Essays in Memory of Charles Gibson*, edited by Richard L. Garner and William B. Taylor, pp. 160–172. S.l: s.n., 1985.

———. "Late Eighteenth-Century Inscriptions in Mexico City." In *Colonial America: A Documentary Reader*, edited by Kenneth Mills and William B. Taylor, pp. 332–333. Wilmington: Scholarly Resources, 1998.

Thompson, Guy P.C. *Puebla de los Angeles: Industry and Society in a Mexican City, 1700–1850*. Boulder, CO: Westview Press, 1989.

Trautmann, Wolfgang. *Las tranformaciones en el paisaje cultural de Tlaxcala durante la época colonial*. Weisbaden: Franz Steiner Verlag, 1981.

Vigarello, Georges. *Concepts of Cleanliness: Changing Attitudes in France Since the Middle Ages*. Translated by Jean Birrell. Cambridge: Cambridge University Press, 1988.

Viquera Albán, Juan Pedro. *Propriety and Permissiveness in Bourbon Mexico*. Translated by Sonya Lipsett-Rivera and Sergio Rivera Ayala. Wilmington: Scholarly Resources, 1999.

Voekel, Pamela. "Peeing on the Palace: Bodily Resistance to Bourbon Reforms in Mexico City." *Journal of Historical Sociology* 5, 2 (1992): 183–208.

———. *Alone before God: The Religious Origins of Modernity in Mexico*. Durham, NC: Duke University Press, 2002.

Watts, Sheldon J. *Epidemics and History: Disease, Power, and Imperialism*. New Haven, CT: Yale University Press, 1997.

Woods, Robert and John Woodward. *Urban Disease and Mortality in Nineteenth-Century England*. New York: St. Martin's Press, 1984.

INDEX

Acequia (calle), 39
aguadores (water carriers), 77, 82, 84–85
Alameda, 4, 10, 28, 33, 38, 44
alcaldes de barrios, 120
Alzate Ramirez, Jose Antonio de, 84–86
Apartado, marqués de, 37
aqueducts, as part of public water system, 77–79, 85, 91
Arrom, Silvia, 6–7
Audiencia, 45

Badiano, Juan, 56
Badianus Manuscript, 56
banquetas (sidewalks), 131–132, 134–135, 138, 140, 154
Belén y Campo de Florida (barrio), 28
Borda, José de, 37
Bourbon economic and design ideas, 87, 90, 127, 133–134
Bourbon Reforms, influences on bodily propriety and public health, 97–100, 103–106, 108, 113, 118, 122–126, 128, 131, 132, 147, 149, 152–156, 158–159, 161; influences on urban planning, 5–6, 9–10, 13–16, 38, 43; relation to political structures, 45–46, 69, 74–75, 78, 93
Brading, David, 21
Branciforte, marques de (viceroy), instructions regarding sanitation, 116–117; to reaction smallpox epidemic of 1797, 56, 67–68, 72, 74; suspension of public works, 120
A Brief Treatise on Medicine, 57
Bucareli y Ursúa, Antonio María de (viceroy), 79

cabildo (Mexico City), complains regarding flooding, 137, 140–141; complaints regarding inoperable fountains, 83, 89–90; complaints regarding vagrants, 4; donations for 1797 epidemic relief, 67–68; enforcement of sanitation controls (1813), 120; indifference regarding comingling of Spaniards and Indians, 8; place within political hierarchy, 45; private sanitation plans, 104; review of sanitation conditions, 101–102
Calleja del Rey, Félix María (viceroy), 120–121
Caneda (calle), 30, 37, 118–119, 140–141, 143, 148
cañerías (water pipes), distribution of water, 79–86, 89, 94, 98, 110, 111, 115, 128, 135, 137–138
Canoa (calle), 104
Capuchinas (calle), 30, 37, 118, 141, 143, 148
casa de vecindad, 39, 41. See also urban planning; housing
Castera, Ignacio, as master architect, 84, 86; investigation of public fountain in

Castera—*Continued*
  Plazuela de San Sebastían, 89;
  overseeing sanitation projects, 132–134;
  overseeing Corpus Christi project, 137,
  140–142, 148, 152, 154, 159; tearing
  down abandoned buildings, 112, 120
Chapultepec, 79, 85, 128
city dumps, location of, 99; focus on
  lower class neighborhoods, 115, 121,
  124, 131, 141, 157, 158; reforms and
  regulations about, 101–106
Colegio de las Niñas, 39
Coliseo (calle), 141
colonial urban planning, 8
Contanzo, Miguel, 132
Corpus Christi (calle), 30
Cruz, Martín de la, 56, 58
curanderos, 50, 56, 59–60, 63–65, 71–72
Curcio-Nagy, Linda, 6

d'Arignon, Villiet, 18, 26
Deans-Smith, Susan, 6
demographic development, 20–24, 26
Diaz, Porfirio, 160–161
drainage, 9–10, 12, 16, 19, 25, 40, 45, 47,
  84, 103, 115, 119; details of
  renovations, 133–135, 144, 152–154,
  156, 158; public health issues, 128–131

Empadradillo (calle), 33
endemic disease, cultural attitudes,
  12–14, 47, 49; factors shaping
  presence, 53–55, 62, 65, 68, 71, 73–74
Enlightenment, influences on urban
  planning, 8–9; ideas regarding
  personal hygiene, 99–100
epidemic disease, cultural attitudes,
  12–14, 21, 47, 51, 55, 60; elite
  responses, 66–69, 73, 75
Espíritu Santo (calle), 141

Farfán, Fray Augustín, 57–58
flooding, 4, 9, 12, 19, 32, 39, 47, 55,
  116; history of, 127–130, 132, 137,
  141–143, 149, 160

Francisco de Croix, Carlos (viceroy), 102
Fuente de Salto de Agua, 79
fuentes particulares (private fountains), 77,
  79, 81–82, 95

Gage, Thomas, 18
Gálvez, Bernardo de, 39
Gálvez, Jose de (viceroy), 102–103
Gálvez, Matías de (viceroy), 143
García Jove, Dr. José Ignacio, 72, 109
García Martínez, Bernardo, 21
Gazeta de México, 69–71
Gibson, Charles, 21
Guevara, Balthasar Ladrones de, 10

Haslip-Viera, Gabriel, 138
healing 50, 57–61; critiques of Indian
  practices, 59; Mexica systems of,
  56–60, 62, 65, 70–71; Spanish/
  European practices of, 54–55
Hernández, Dr. Francisco, 57–58
History of the Plants of New Spain, 57
Hospicio de Pobres, 34
Hospital de Espíritu Santo, 64, 68
Hospital de Jesus, 64, 68
Hospital de San Andres, 64, 68–69, 118
Hospital de San Antonio Abad, 64, 68
Hospital de San Juan de Dios, 64, 68
Hospital de San Lazaro, 81
Hospital Real de los Naturales, 34, 64, 68

Imperial College of Santa Cruz de
  Tlateloco, 56
Indians (social disorder), migrating to
  cities, 3; avoidance of tribute
  payments, 85–86; in bathhouses,
  91–92; dumping of garbage, 101–103,
  109; irregularity of Indian markets,
  32; physical separation, 26; poverty,
  36; *República de los indios* 8; riot of
  1692, 28; as subjects of elite anxiety,
  115; as subjects of penal labor, 139;
  regulations in markets, 145, 147, 149,
  151, 153
Inquisition, 30

INDEX

Jala, conde de, 37
Jaral, marqués de, 24, 37, 55
Juarez, Benito, 160
juez de cañerías, 89
Junta de Policía, concerns over urban sanitation, 101; defense of public works projects during epidemics, 104–105, 120; protests against lack of progress with reforms, 109, 116; collection of fines, 118–123, 139; 1780 regulations regarding street paving, 143, 157
Junta de Sanidad, 157
juntas de caridad, 67

La Alameda (barrio), 2
Lagunilla, de la (barrio), 28
Lake Texcoco, 12, 129, 134
La Palma (barrio), 90
Lyons, G.F., 18, 32, 127–128, 155

Madriaga, Salvador de, 25
markets, 10, 30, 32, 34, 40. *See also* Volador, Plaza Mayor, Parián
Martin, Cheryl English, 6
material conditions, 18, 23–24, 33; of elites, 37–39; of plebeians, 39–40; 42–43
measles, 13, 21, 47, 49, 51–54
Mecateros (calle), 33
Meleros, de (calle), 32
Mendoza, Francisco de, 56
Mexica deities related to healing, 57–58
Mexica sanitation, bathing, 81, 91–92; health care, 50, 78, 81, 85, 90–91, 95, 108; garbage collection, 82, 83, 97, 101–102, 104, 109, 111, 129; potable water, 82, 129
Monseque, Jean de, 18, 26
Monte de Piedad, 142

novenas, 60

Ordenanzas de Descubrimiento y Poblacion, 25
Ortiz, Joseph Damian, 132

Ouweneel, Arij, 21

Palma (calle), 141
Parián (market), 30, 40–41
Paseo de Bucareli, 33, 38
Paseo de Revillagigedo, 33, 38, 115
paving, 4, 10, 16, 19, 39, 47, 83–84, 101, 103, 128, 130–134, 137–138, 140–144, 147, 149, 152–154, 156, 158
penal labor, on public works projects, 138–139; on paving projects, 144; as social reform, 139
physical organization, *traza*, 7–8, 14, 24–35
Plateros (calle), 30, 32, 41
Plaza de Santiago Tlateloco, 32
Plaza de Santo Domingo, 11, 30
Plaza de Volador, 30, 118
Plaza Mayor, in urban organization, 8, 16, 24, 26, 30, 32–33; site of regulation of public space, 10; as elite space, 37–40; problems with public fountains, 90; as site of social disorder, 95; drainage renovations, 128; paving renovations, 132, 143, 148–154, 160
Plazuela de San Sebastían, 89
Plazuela de Santísima Trinidad y Santa Cruz, 89–90
Poinsett, Joel, 37
political structures, 45–46. *See also Audiencia, cabildo*
potable water, 77–79, 85, 87, 95, 103, 134, 155, 160
Protomedicato, 50, 62, 72, 121
public baths, 78; regulations and controls, 91–94
public fountains, 3, 9–11, 40, 47; as part of public water system, 77–79; state of disrepair, 82–87, 89–90, 92, 95–96, 100, 102–103, 118, 151
public sanitation, lack of, 3, 9, 78, 84, 97–105, 107–108, 111, 113, 116, 119, 127, 129–131, 137, 155
public space, attitudes regarding use, 11, 98, 113; dumping of garbage in, 110–112; as sites of illicit activities, 112

public urination and defecation, 4, 8, 32, 55, 82, 93, 97–99; elite concerns, 108–110, 117–118, 122–124, 127, 149, 155–156; punishments against, 101–102
Puente de Mariscala (barrio), 79
Puente de Mariscala (calle), 79
Puente de Merced (calle), 118
pulquerias, 11, 12, 41; culture of drinking, 44, 78; issues with public sanitation, 111
punishments, 93–94, 97–107, 109, 117–124, 156–157

Rabago, conde de, 35
Regla, conde de, 24, 35, 55
regulations (bandos), concerning potable water, 78, 93–94, 97–98; about garbage collection and sanitation, 100–104, 106–107, 109–111, 113, 115, 117, 122, 124
Revillagigedo, Juan Vicente de Güemes Pacheco y Padilla, segundo conde de (viceroy), 5, 15, 33; attitudes regarding polluting behavior of the masses, 97–100; bathhouse reforms, 93–95; class and race dimensions of reforms, 123–125; concerns over access to potable water, 82–83; design of public water system, 86–87; details of drainage and paving projects, 131– 134; evaluation of sanitation programs, 115–117; ideas about renovation of city water system, 77–78; impact of drainage initiatives, 139–143; influence of his reforms, 120–121; institutional power, 45–46, 61–62; legacies, 154–155, 157–158, 160–161; paving renovations, 144; public perceptions of, 9; renovations to Plaza Mayor and Volador, 147–152; response to 1797 epidemic, 72–75; sanitation programs and regulations, 105–113; scope of drainage and paving projects, 128

Royal Mint, 30
Royal Tobacco Factory, 34; access to water, 81

Salto de Agua (barrio), 28
San Andrés (barrio), 79
San Andrés (calle), 30, 79; as site of potable water project, 87
San Bernardo (calle), 30, 42, 118, 140–141, 143, 148
San Carmen (barrio), 28, 141
San Cosme (barrio), 34
San Francisco (calle), 30, 37; as site of paving, 143, 148; as site of potable water project, 87; sanitation during 1797 epidemic, 104, 134, garbage overwhelming sanitation system, 140–141
San Jose de Real (calle), 33
San Juan (barrio), 26–28, 64, 102; as location of city dumps, 115; lack of paving, 148
San Mateo de Valparaiso, conde de, 55
San Pablo (barrio), 28, 141
San Sebastián (barrio), 28, 89, 95, 141
San Sebastián (calle), 84
Santa Anna (barrio), 28
Santa Clara (calle), 30; as site of potable water project, 87, 137, 140, 143
Santa Cruz (barrio), 28, 89, 141
Santa Cruz (calle), 84
Santa Isabel (barrio), 79
Santa Isabel (calle), 79
Santa María (barrio), 28
Santiago de Calimaya, conde de, 24, 35, 55, 117–118
Santiago Tlateloco (barrio), lack of potable water, 9, 40, 77, 83–87, 95; lack of sanitation, 99; lack of sanitation reforms, 128, 138, 141, 148, 157; as location of city dumps, 115–116; residents as street cleaners, 102; in urban organization, 26–28, 30
Santo Domingo (calle), 30
Santo Tomas (barrio), 28, 141

Index

Scardaville, Michael, 6, 123
smallpox, 13, 21, 47, 49; definitions, 51–58; 66–69, 72, 74, 91–92, 102, 104, 119–120, 155
social classes, ecclesiastical orders 3; 5; hierarchies 35–36, 40; *República de los indios vs. República de los españoles* 8, 21, 26, 28
Spanish connections between disease and public sanitation, 4, 12–13, 50, 53–54, 61–62; between poverty and disease, 13, 15, 49–50, 55, 66, 72–74

Tacuba (calle), 30; as site of potable water project 87, 137; problems with flooding, 141, 143, 148
targeas (gutters), 128, 134, 137, 140
temascaleros, 92
temazcal, 91
Templo Mayor, 38
Tenochtitlan, public sanitation, 12, 32; urban development, 19, 38, 58, 91, 129, 137
Thorton Tayloe, Edward, 36
Tlapaleros, de (calle), 32
Tolsa, Manuel, 37
typhus, 21, 47, 49, 51, 53–54, 65, 70

urban culture, 11–12, 23–24, 38–39; Semana Santa, 43; street diversions, 44
urban employment, 3, 22–24, 34, 42, 47

urban housing, 26–29, 39; rents, 41–42. See also *casa de vecindad*
urban sanitation programs, racial and class dimensions, 77–79, 82–83, 87, 89–90, 92–93, 95–102, 104–105, 107– 110, 113, 118–119, 121–125, 128–131, 133, 138–139, 142–144, 147, 153–159, 161

vagrants, illicit public activity, 4, 11; disorder in bathhouses, 95; illicit sex in public, 83; *léperos*, 36; occupation of public spaces, 78; social welfare institutions, 34; as subjects of elite anxiety, 100, 105, 107, 112; as subjects of elite charity, 67, 120; as subjects of market regulations, 149–150; as subjects of penal labor, 138–139; as viewed by foreigners, 18, 32, 155; violence against young girls, 89–90
Valle de Orizaba, conde de, 24, 55
Verarga (calle), 137, 141
Villarroel, Hipolto, 17–19, 26, 33, 36, 39, 44
Viquera Alban, Juan Pedro, 6
Voekel, Pamela, 6, 15
Volador, 16, 30, 118; as site of renovations and regulations, 149–151

Zuleta (calle), 118, 137, 1417

GPSR Compliance

The European Union's (EU) General Product Safety Regulation (GPSR) is a set of rules that requires consumer products to be safe and our obligations to ensure this.

If you have any concerns about our products, you can contact us on

ProductSafety@springernature.com

In case Publisher is established outside the EU, the EU authorized representative is:

Springer Nature Customer Service Center GmbH
Europaplatz 3
69115 Heidelberg, Germany

www.ingramcontent.com/pod-product-compliance
Lightning Source LLC
LaVergne TN
LVHW051912060526
838200LV00004B/111